Local history research
and writing

DAVID IREDALE

Local history research and writing

A manual for local history writers

THE ELMFIELD PRESS

THE ELMFIELD PRESS
Elmfield Road, Morley, Leeds, U.K.

Copyright © 1974 by David Iredale
ISBN 0 7057 0041 0
Library of Congress Catalog Card Number: 74-83354

Printed by Maund & Irvine Ltd., Brook Street, Tring, Herts.

DAVID IREDALE

Local history research and writing

A manual for local history writers

THE ELMFIELD PRESS

THE ELMFIELD PRESS
Elmfield Road, Morley, Leeds, U.K.

Copyright © 1974 by David Iredale
ISBN 0 7057 0041 0
Library of Congress Catalog Card Number: 74-83354

Printed by Maund & Irvine Ltd., Brook Street, Tring, Herts.

CONTENTS

Illustrations referred to in the text are between pages 42 and 43.

CHAPTER 1

Local history

'AND if you wish to learn anything about town history go and see old Mrs Bell. She must be eighty if she's a day. She's lived in that cottage of hers all her life, and her parents before her.' My neighbour smiled as he kindly welcomed me to the new home.

'As a matter of fact,' I answered, 'I was puzzled by the mound I noticed from the railway carriage window as I neared the station.'

'Oh, Mrs Bell can tell you about that. We were discussing it only last month. It's an old castle, something to do with Oliver Cromwell or Julius Caesar or somebody.'

I was indeed to discover the town castle but this lay on the other side of the settlement near the river. The station mound had almost certainly been created when men removed tons of earth from above the railway tunnel in order to lighten the burden on the sagging roof.

'It's a pity Mrs Bell doesn't write down what she knows', I continued to my neighbour.

'No book could hold what Mrs Bell knows, though I do agree with you. When she goes there will be no way of finding out about history. No, there's no book. I went into Barnes the bookshop and they said there is nothing, and they should know. Mind you there's nothing special about this place. What's the point of writing the history? It takes all our energy and time to live today and tomorrow. The past cannot help us earn and save.'

'I would not agree. Why, only the other day I was able to tell a farmer that an upland meadow of his called Forgesfield was the site of the manorial forches or gallows and indeed to point out the probable spot at the junction of two drove roads. He was so surprised that he gave me a dozen eggs and a bottle of fresh cream.'

This book is for people wanting to write a local history. Every community has a history. Even if there seems to be nothing in print and not a single document accessible, there is at least the evidence of the place-name, the sites of houses and fields, archæological digs and traces of men's work in past ages. The following chapters thus stress the importance of fieldwork, of walks in the locality with eyes and mind open to notice features that require explaining or that explain those queries about the past already raised through conversations with other intelligent observers. The present work of course points also to the treasury of books and other printed matter, such as maps, that reveal local history. It delves into the great heritage of documents available in British borough, county and private archive centres.

I myself have written several local studies. Once I described the origin in 1775 and growth till 1845 of a canal settlement community. I concentrated on economic conditions: how people earned money, which types of job men could seek, on what articles families spent their wages; but I also dealt with political organisation and religious or educational societies. What follows is based on the method of research which I adopted at that time.

Because local historians are in the main intelligent but part-time researchers this book relies on material readily accessible to most of us. It does not concern itself with the royal archive at Windsor or with priceless original Anglo-Saxon charters at the British Museum. Chapters do not stress monuments like Stonehenge or even the typical ancient parish church because reasonably adequate printed reports by experts already exist for such features, and the local historian will wish to spend his time on village cottages, colliery railed-way or town field boundary hedge. I include in the term historian the teacher on vacation reading inventories in order to gain a picture of everyday life in Stuart times for her next month's class on that subject; the retired postman tracing the history of his house; the housewife looking up her family tree; the surveyor using a tithe map to find an estate boundary. These historians can contribute valuable chapters to a local history though they may not themselves be researching on a sufficiently broad front to produce a full local history. Granted that local history is in general a part-time interest and even as a lifetime's hobby is not normally a means of earning daily bread, its study none the less is worthwhile and educational. It teaches about the past in terms of our own locality and is thus meaningful to each of us. It shows how our ancestors lived and what problems they confronted, opens our eyes to the infinitely varied pattern of the landscape and attempts to explain how the present pattern emerged. Local history traces the origin of political and religious institutions. It is indeed an intellectual discipline in so far as the researcher learns how to interpret documents, to read old handwriting, some in Latin and French, to plan a study of his town and to carry the task to completion.

The local historian's work contributes to a general history of this country. His researches on the open fields, houses and landownership in Puddlecombe will be placed with the studies of other people so that from many particular cases a general statement might be hazarded by the lecturer or writer of British history. When the university historian speaks of the growing prosperity of thirteenth-century boroughs he bases his idea on specific studies carried out by local and academic workers in Exeter, Norwich, Yarmouth and elsewhere. Of course local histories are often important in themselves because most places have longer histories than the kingdoms of England and Scotland. Some projects yield information that differs from the ordinary pattern or unearth early examples of, say, paternal co-operative communities or the first use of a rotative steam engine or the country's earliest iron bridge. If none of this is of interest the researcher may still enjoy discovering his own community's past just for the sake and joy of investigating a place he knows and loves. The houses he sketches are inhabited by his neighbours. People in the history still have descendants walking village streets. The church he attends once echoed to the tramp of Cromwell's soldiers.

The local historian tells how over the years men and women have tamed the primeval waste or woodland, built towns and churches and castles, laid out and planted gardens, orchards and cornfields creating today's landscape that reflects at every view the work of people's hands and minds. The researcher explains the process by which prosperous city grocer has replaced Norman baron or Tudor squire in county affairs. He states as precisely as need be why and when the market was founded and where exactly the deserted village site lies. He usually begins with some community (manor, township, borough or whatever) that now has or once had an existence of its own apart from (or perhaps against and in spite of) all others. Isolation by distance is not implied here, merely a community feeling that 'we are Newtonians while they across the stream are mere Newfordians'. The local historian narrates and explains (to follow the definition of Professor H. P. R. Finberg) his community's origin, growth, periods of stability and depression, decline and fall. Obviously the whole chronological story need not, alas all too often cannot, be told. It is frequently impossible to know the origin and early growth of the place, and there is probably little sign of decay, though opinions especially of old people will vary about this. Certainly there is no sign of a fall unless the place is a deserted village. Since there is no need to be too pedantic about what is and is not local history our local historian is not confined to villages or towns but may choose a whole county or economic region, a monastic institution, business enterprise or scattered manor because these are all in certain respects local communities.

The local historian defines as exactly as is possible the physical bounds of his chosen district. Ordinarily he takes the township, parish or borough. Not only are the boundaries marked clearly on maps but these communities have had for some generations at least and usually for several centuries an existence in some respects independent of all other places. Men have felt themselves members of a body different from if not superior to an adjoining community. To write the history of such a gathering of people gives satisfaction because the place and inhabitants gain a personality through years of communal life, of pulling together, of shared institutions. Creating an artificial unit like south Derbyshire or Pilkington Street, Puddlecombe, provides a defined area for study and is acceptable as local history but leads to overlapping of research since documents are produced by political and religious units such as the parish and county rather than the street and semi-county. I have written the story of a settlement that was only a small part of a township. Though the people felt themselves to be a separate community nearly all my documents referred to the wider political organisation. Consequently information had to be sifted to see what applied to the settlement and this led to difficulties. To take yet a smaller unit—a house or family—is not local history. Of course if that house itself has been the only habitation in a township then the story of house and land may prove a very interesting local history because, when trying to explain the survival of the single dwelling, the researcher could come across a deserted village, Georgian imparking or something more remarkable.

Some units of local organisation should at the outset be defined. A township is in origin a fortified enclosure where men settled in the midst of forest, moor or plain. Most were already in existence at the end of the Anglo-Saxon period and figure in Domesday. They are the main unit of local government from Tudor to Victorian times, governed by a town or vestry meeting of ratepayers and appointing officers such as overseer of the poor and supervisor of the highways. The English ecclesiastical parish is a district in the pastoral care of a single priest to whom accrue ecclesiastical dues, such as tithes. Parishes date from Saxon times but at that date were vast in area. Some 9,500 parishes had been created, however, by the fourteenth century so that in populous counties every township built its parish church and paid its priest. Here therefore parish and township boundaries often coincide whereas in the less populous districts one parish might contain a number of townships. Large towns like York were divided into several parishes. Parish boundaries altered little between about 1350 and 1800. New churches did appear of course but usually as chapels of ease to the mother church, their districts being chapelries. The parish has always tended to undertake secular duties. During the Tudor period it was given responsibility for poor-relief affairs, law and order and the highways. The vestry meeting acts either in place of a town meeting where town and parish coincide or as supervisor of individual town meetings where the parish contains several townships.

A town ordinarily grew up round a market in medieval times and some, as at Mountsorrel in Leicestershire, lie astride parish boundaries. Its built-up area rarely takes note of township boundaries either. A borough is a place that has gained a royal or local seigneurial charter of privileges normally granting markets and fairs. For many purposes a borough lives independent of the county and supports several parishes. The county or shire was the district in the care of a steward or reeve responsible to the king for taxes and justice. Manorial organisation was superimposed prior to 1066 on a countryside already divided into estates of varying size. A manor is an estate possibly forming only part of a township, embracing several townships in a block or containing bits and pieces of property over a wide area. A hundred is a group of townships having in medieval times some semblance of government and judicial organisation. It is obviously of importance to decide what unit to study remembering that there are also tithings, frankpledges, honors, palatinates, sokes, archdeaconries and bishoprics not to mention peculiars.

It is wise to base the choice of district on subjects that are of interest. The specialist on medieval social life, farming and customs normally chooses a manor rather than a parish, a hundred or an honor because medieval manorial documents are concerned with the economic and social arrangement of the community. Poor-law administration in Georgian days is based on the parish or township or borough not the manor or family estate. The historian therefore defines his topic as narrowly as he may before he begins. Some students choose to study most aspects of a community's life or as many aspects as documents will reveal, though it would be a brave researcher who would try to discover in relation to his fourteenth-century village, what inhabitants did or thought about birth control, sanitation, meals, medicine or art. Something is known about these matters for the country as a whole and for certain places whose records survive but the local historian is writing a history of Puddlecombe and cannot suppose that his village is like Newford or Newton whose history is known. He may go round the problem of ignorance by carefully stating 'if Puddlecombe's history resembles that of Newton and Newford, then it is possible to assert . . .'.

Then again the wise man chooses a topic within his capabilities and with regard to the time available. To write a history of Oxfordshire from stone age to today or about the English settlement of a county or describing everyday life in neolithic times demands in the first case much time and energy, in the second a knowledge of Anglo-Saxon and Scandinavian languages and place-names as well as topographical intelligence and in the third archaeological training and acumen. I well recall a student coming into the record office intending to write about social life in his village in the middle ages.

'I have just what you need', I replied. 'These manorial court rolls and custumals date from 1394 to 1615 and there are four boxes of miscellaneous deeds, surrenders and admittances accompanying them.'

'But I cannot read this handwriting', said the student as he examined the first roll.

'You will soon learn after a little practice. You know Latin of course?'

'No I don't read Latin and I'm afraid I have limited time for the project. The thesis should be in next month. The typist in fact is waiting for the manuscript now.'

'What you really need then is either the printed translation of manor court rolls of some other village or a general work such as H. S. Bennett's *Life on the English Manor.*'

The researcher decided to make notes from the latter. He had chosen as I recommended some lines ago a subject that interested him but had forgotten to consider his academic limitations.

Just as the local historian uses a microscope to study every square inch of his territory so he produces a digging stick mentally to penetrate deep beneath the surface of town life. He analyses the community in order to discover the whys and wherefores of its structuring. In one project he dissects a yeoman's house to know the stages by which portions were erected. Similarly he considers different aspects, land-scape, population and landownership and examines these in depth. Thus he investigates the pattern of landholding in all centuries, explaining changes as far as possible. He examines each social, political and economic group in the population and asks how and why these people influenced local life and were in turn affected by community decisions. Thus too he finds it essential to prove the interaction of different features of local life. Economic conditions obviously govern the style of house people could afford to build, the sanitary arrange-ments, the health and standard of living, political institutions and religious organisation. Religious and educational changes affect the type and range of occupations locally available. In several cases nonconformity's dislike of the liquor trade cut down the number of breweries, inns and publicans but this caused men to turn to chocolate manufacturing, social welfare, making model villages and political activity. Longer schooling changed men from labourers to foremen and clerks. The type of job held by people affects growth of popula-tion. In one community well-paid industrial work replaced farm labouring in the period 1780-1840, and people began to produce twice as many children, probably partly as a result of the larger wage packet. Their grandchildren, however, taking work as clerks, accountants and suchlike and getting even higher wages, reduced the size of families but spent more on food, clothing and schooling for each child. There are of course many factors at work here, some originating from out-side the settlement, which are all to be considered. The lie of the land whether marsh, high moor or rich wheatland bears upon a community's economic life and health. A remote moorland village has survived only in short periods when pressure of population in richer areas has forced families up into the hills. Such a settlement's houses are rough and ready, its school and church tiny and un-decorated. Religion and politics interact. Catholic farming areas of Lancashire have been conservative in politics for centuries. Trading communities have tended to be radical in politics and religion as long as such beliefs have boosted commerce. It is obviously too simple to say that aspect *a* affected *b* and caused *c*. There is nearly always interaction, so that causes of change or indeed of stagnation are usually complicated. None the less it is the researcher's task not merely to chronicle events but to explain cause and effect.

Such an approach by Professor A. Everitt in *The Pattern of Rural Dissent* (1972) suggests the relationship between nineteenth-century dissent and certain types of rural community. In the four counties chosen for study the writer finds nonconformity most flourishing wherever self-employed craftsmen, shopkeepers or modest freeholders predominated in a village, usually also where the community was situated some distance from the parish church and the landowner's seat. Such places include industrial, canal or railway settlements, townships whose land was subdivided among resident freeholders, decayed market towns, communities lying across parish boundaries, outlying hamlets of extensive parishes as well as villages with large populations in intensive arable farming districts. Dissenters seem to be numerous in townships settled either very early in Saxon times or late in modern centuries. The former, growing from folk or tribal communities, were usually large in area and population, local meeting and market places, rarely controlled by one landowner, centres of worship long before the days of manorial chapels and probably independently inclined while showing an interest in affairs beyond the parish bounds. Later settlements were similarly free of control by local lord and often neglected by the established church. Townships founded in the period 1000-1500 by way of contrast are generally seen to be small places in the hands of one family that endowed the church and later frowned on nonconformity among the villagers. Dissent in the seventeenth and eighteenth centuries tends to prevail in forest and pasture parishes whose areas are large and whose population is scattered so that neither squire nor parson could oversee every hamlet. Methodist and later dissenters were strong where old dissenters had never taken root, in chalk, limestone and lias regions corresponding perhaps coincidentally with the area of the ancient Danelaw. It is this interesting and possibly significant relationship of Danelaw, freeholders' parish, craftsmen, ancient tribal centre, soil and dissent that the historian investigates in his own locality for there may possibly be some aspects of the social and economic arrangement of certain villages that makes them peculiarly prone to religious nonconformity.

The historian attempts to set chronological bounds to his topic. The reader finds it convenient to know whether the thirteenth century is going to be discussed or not, and the researcher needs a limited field or he will never finish his task. 'Puddlecombe from the beginning to today' usually means in effect from 1066 to 1955 (or whenever the worker gave up research). It is advisable to say 1066-1955. A local historian proposed to study his township from 1837 to 1901 with particular reference to the cotton industry. But what sort of relevance have such dates? What importance had the accession of a new queen for a cotton town and did her death in 1901 cause any economic changes? It would be far wiser to choose a starting date to coincide with the building of the first mill or (if the study is to be purely nineteenth century) when the first steam-driven machinery was installed. Perhaps 1861, the year when cotton famine began to be felt and the beginning of the end of English supremacy in manufacturing, would be an alternative date to commence research. A closing date might lie further into the twentieth century possibly coinciding with the abandonment of free trade. The year 1688, to take another example, is a textbook date very meaningful in British history. But for a history of cottage industry in Puddlecombe it is probably neither an opening nor a closing date of any significance. Admittedly it is going to be difficult to find significant covering dates for such a general subject and many people would research by the century : 'Cottage industries in Puddlecombe in the seventeenth century.' Here the period, subject and community are exactly defined. This is by reason of its limited subject matter just a contribution towards a local history. Chronological bounds are acceptably relevant to research on cottage industry but the historian of Puddlecombe would doubtless choose different dates for a study of the whole community.

When considering the period for research it is well to recall that prior to the twelfth century any history will have to be built on archaeological and place-name evidence, and that much of the work will not have been completed already by previous historians. For medieval studies the handwriting, verbiage and Latin of documents may be considerable drawbacks. Modern histories could be snowed down under the weight of documentary evidence especially for Victorian topics. But for a study of the present-day, archival material will not even be released. It is hardly likely that local political parties are going to allow the researcher to consult minute books recording quarrels and machinations of only five years ago.

The local historian sees his locality, period and subject in its proper context. He has some knowledge of cotton or cottage industries in the country as a whole though he does not try to mould his local facts to the shape of national patterns. He need be no expert on national history but realises enough not to overestimate the importance of his own locality. His township is unlikely to have been first to produce cotton cloth or to have manufactured more than a tiny percentage of all English cotton wares. It would have made few decisions about style, colour or markets but was often shaken by national decisions concerning hours of employment, export duties and war. The historian is not surprised to discover that a visit was made in 1535 by royal commissioners eager to survey the local monastery. The same men had already called in at neighbouring places and were to cover the whole country. Similarly when tithe payments in kind were commuted into cash payments in 1839 he stresses the advantages for local farmers and parson but does not treat the affair as of more than local importance. Most other villages had also commuted tithes in kind as a result of an act of Parliament in 1836. It can of course be argued that there are advantages in knowing almost nothing of general history because then (to use the words of Professor W. G. Hoskins) everything about local history 'comes fresh, bright-polished, and newly-minted to the eager eye'. Such a man does not rack his brains and almost invent three open fields in his village simply because textbooks say this is the normal pattern in midland England. On the other hand I think of a friend of mine whose researches had revealed the sudden appearance in 1831-5 of seven new alehouses in his small industrial township, a sevenfold increase. As a civil engineer he had little time to study national history and looked round his village for reasons for the new buildings. He suggested a falling standard of living, a split in the local Methodist society and the decline of the old poor law as encouragement to men to drink more. One wonders if the 1830 act of Parliament altering old licensing regulations might be more significant. The implications of this paragraph are enormous in the sense that the historian of one place is expected to acquire very wide interests and skills. If he writes about the 1530s in Puddlecombe he still must know something about Wolsey, Cromwell, Henry VIII and Anne Boleyn, about medieval catholicism and Luther, about England's opposition to foreign ecclesiastical control, about depopulation, wage rates, inflation and devaluation, land law and local government, about the literature of the period, international trade routes and parliamentary activity.

Differences therefore rather than similarities help to make local history worth writing and publishing. It is obviously of local interest that one-quarter of all villagers claimed poor relief in the years 1808-14 and that the rate burden intolerably weakened the old system. But most places in Britain experienced difficulties at this unhappy period. What would be worth stressing is the history of a township that could find no paupers at that time. An enclosed village in the midst of open-field agriculture in the thirteenth century cries out for investigation as does a brick house of the early sixteenth century, a church without a village, a trackway that goes nowhere. Of course it is probable that Puddlecombe is in most respects an average settlement, and similarities will have to be accepted and stated as such. Here is one reason why the wise student keeps his eye on neighbouring places to save exaggerated claims of uniqueness that come naturally to the local patriot. But an ordinary history of this type cannot expect to sell beyond the bounds of the village, and publication (rather than cheaper duplication) would be financially crippling.

The local historian continually comes across material that ought not to be taken unquestioningly. I recall visiting the former home of a local worthy. Its stone-faced walls, large windows, twenty rooms and solid furnishings led me to assume that the man was wealthy. But not so because the house was built on borrowed money and on the credit of a respected name, was always mortgaged and had passed to creditors before the original owner died. The 1834 report of the poor-law commissioners presents evidence that generally favours their opinion about the iniquity of the old law. The local squire does not necessarily ask to be taken literally when he writes that his woods are full of poachers. That letter is written to impress Home Office civil servants with the importance of maintaining the severe game laws. The squire knows, his brother magistrates know and we should know that countryside affairs are not all that desperate. Statistics must be studied carefully, even or perhaps most of all in the nineteenth century. In fact no evidence can be believed implicitly. When royal commissioners organised a local jury to provide facts for the medieval inquisition *post mortem* they presented the evidence as if it had come from the lips of this group of local men. But in most cases it is almost certain that the information was provided by the family steward of the dead man. The steward would have every fact at his fingertips but might well keep the commissioners in the dark about some of his lord's affairs. There is an entry in Northallerton parish register about the baptism of George, son of Matthew Flower and Mary his wife. Can we ever be sure that George was son of his parents and not son of just one, or even a foundling? In fact George was probably not Matthew's son because Mary had been returned to her husband some time before by magistrate's removal order being 'now with Child of a bastard Child'. Of course the words of the order might have been a legal formality in order to remove Mary swiftly whether the child was bastard or not. An affectionate letter can mean as little as our own 'dear sir'. The ruined hilltop tower is as likely to be a Georgian folly as a medieval castle.

The historian himself is biased in the sense that he is a modern man, perhaps a retired factory foreman once active in trade union affairs. With what feelings does he read documents about the eighteenth-century working labourer? How can he understand and sympathise with an employer in the period of the industrial revolution? Can or should he write local history dispassionately? There is really no need to produce an account so scientific and finely balanced that it is colourless, featureless and boring. Local history is for the use, enjoyment and education of this present generation, not necessarily for the future. Children will eventually write their own histories. Provided that the historian's bias or personal interests are stated clearly, a little care and sympathy, even some passion, should be acceptable. This is not to invite the writer to use his book as a vehicle for stating his hatred of the pope or of socialists, of Cromwell or the French. Bitter and usually irrelevant asides about personal likes and dislikes have no place in a history and set the reader's teeth on edge. There is the world of difference between the writing of a life-long political radical fully in control of his passions but naturally in sympathy with reformers and the outbursts of a thoughtless local historian. The latter is continually tempted to use parenthesis as a political and religious platform, believing he has a captive and spellbound audience. In the same way this historian's obvious joy in Georgian architecture of church and hall blinds him to the merits of all other styles, and causes him to survey manor house and church to the exclusion of nonconformist chapels and ordinary village houses. One section of the population tends to hold the stage, too, while other, usually poorer and less documented, people are relegated to the wings.

QUESTIONS

The historian asking the right questions unquestionably writes the most worthwhile account of his community. He cannot merely read relevant documents, take notes and turn out undigested information.

Nowadays the researcher is expected to interpret his material and to explain as carefully as possible why men and women adopted certain attitudes, beliefs and policies while rejecting others; why his township bears a particular shape and character and not another; why specific industries flourished; why the death rate rose so high; why churches were founded rather than schools. The historian decides clearly prior to commencing work what kind of questions he wants answered and reads his material with these points in mind. Questions that the worker should be considering are fluently set out in a book prepared by Dr A. Rogers to accompany BBC broadcasts on local history in 1972. *This was their World* (1972) concentrates mainly on nineteenth-century topics, these being most familiar and real to the present generation.

The researcher should first deal with the size of the community at various relevant dates, explaining if the place was expanding or declining at those times. The reasons for any increase or decrease are important; why people are attracted to or repelled from the place, why they bear more or fewer children, or die sooner or later than their ancestors, or become more often diseased than their fathers' generation. If the pattern differs in any respects from the normal for the county or region an inquiry is initiated. The student digs deeper to lay out the structure of the community: to show how and why the birth, marriage and death rates altered; to learn whether there were more parents in the locality or more children for each family; fewer old people; a lower death rate among young and middle-aged persons because of the availability of good food, medicine, hospitals, comfortable homes, doctors and pensions; more deaths through war, disease, famine or wretched living conditions. The community structure alters as old people live longer, folk marry later or children stay at school till fourteen, leaving a larger group of non-productive men and women to the care of a smaller working population. Elsewhere there may on the other hand live many more marriageable women and fewer possible husbands. Marriage ages can vary from century to century as a result of such shifts in the balance of the sexes. The historian seeks to relate the size of each family to its occupational and social status, the level of income, type of house and availability of domestic help. He estimates from registers how soon after marriage the first child arrives and what length in months separates the birth of each subsequent child. A family bearing five children in seven years boosts the population more swiftly than one with five children in twelve years. Fertility has been assessed in a number of ways not merely by the crude birth rate related to the number of women aged fifteen to forty-five but also by the number of girls who survive childhood and become capable of reproducing themselves. This net reproduction rate was, for example, 1·3 in 1851 for England and Wales, showing the possibility of a burgeoning population. Mortality too should be explained against the background of food, wages, health, housing and climate, and the calculation demands a knowledge of the death rate of each five-year age group in the population and the average age of death. Survival rate of babies as well as expectation of life among the old are considered here. Immigration and emigration also affect this discussion, often profoundly, and the historian considers the number of people involved, their reasons for shifting, their age and jobs at removal time, the distance travelled and their previous history of wandering.

Since a community becomes economically sound through the sweat of its inhabitants' brows, it is vital to know : the size of the working population by excluding children, the old and sick, unemployed, vagabonds and mothers at home; the length of the working life which probably varied from job to job; the proportion of males to females among the productively engaged. An occupational analysis is simply worked out by choosing general categories such as agriculture, retail trade, industry and professions but any more detailed and worthwhile classification is fraught with contradictions, and there is no agreement among historians about the most satisfactory divisions. The historian must devise his own. Occupations changed their nature and status from time to time. In certain centuries and places a person might both make and sell shoes, be a feller of trees as well as a timber merchant, butcher animals and tan fells, be an innkeeper and a farmer, a money lender, banker and goldsmith, a scrivener and a shopkeeper, a master and a man. Some occupations ran in families, sons hardly controlling their destiny at all. Other boys entered established trades and crafts, having observed folk prosper by so doing. Ambitious venturesome people thought of new ways of earning a living and so by their initiative, faith and decision set the township and possibly the region on a fresh course. Thus the crafts of towns depend on people's will as well as on accessible raw materials, good communications and the convenient location of the settlement. There is no particular economic reason why the manufacture of shoes should be centred mainly in one town rather than in another or spread out among dozens of others in the midlands. The student therefore traces the work of men in that place through generations to apprehend how careful training, skill, capital formation, cultivation of customers over a wide area, determination and other personal factors resulted in that town's predominance. It may also be possible to demonstrate that a town's heavy industry is founded not merely on the region's iron and coal deposits which were of course available to hundreds of places but as much on five hundred years of local men's adept production of metal implements and trinkets in tiny attic and back-yard workshops, on skills and money passed from father to son and on inventions pioneered in the place by careful trial and error. It is essential to consider whether employment was mainly of the master and man type or much more individually organised. This might affect the size of farms, factories and other enterprises, the adoption of modern machinery, the type of agricultural practice and scope for taking on a large labouring force. There are also questions to be asked about the organisation by factory or domestic system, the channelling of profits either at the end of all processes to one capitalist or board of directors or at the completion of each stage to workers actually engaged in production, the tone of relations between factory owner and hands, between farmer and labourers, the formation of unions, guilds, societies or combinations to benefit sections of workers or employers, the community spirit engendered or embittered by the structure of employment as well as the whole problem of law and order.

Housing conditions are an important consideration for nearly every-one in all centuries, and the historian sets himself the task of counting the number of houses available at different dates, deciding why the number fluctuated occasionally at variance with population trends, estimating how many dwellings were occupied and allowing that some large homes would hold a dozen or more servants without overcrowding. The researcher seeks plans and elevations of houses while hoping to judge which places were furnished with acceptable amenities, stoutly constructed and comfortable according to con-temporary standards. He calculates the density of houses on each acre or, more carefully, the density of rooms to the acre since other-wise large mansions affect the average house density considerably. He distinguishes densities for the original settlement, new middle-class suburbs, working-class districts and country areas. He identifies the builder, architect, financier, industrialist or private resident responsible for erecting local housing, questions his motives and examines his profit and loss account. He determines the proportion of houses honestly built, owner-occupied, held on lease or by the week or on mortgage. Mortgages especially should be examined in detail because they have long been an important means of paying for the development of a district and it is worthwhile knowing from what sources the money was raised. Villages almost entirely owned by one landlord whether aristocrat or Oxford college may prove to have less available building land than freehold settlements. The latter also possess larger farms and might have decided nonconformist leanings, though this statement must be checked in more cases before it can be asserted confidently because there are exceptions. Towns whose property is held on lease of an estate could well seem less bustling than freehold towns, though in certain cases a wealthy landlord naturally has the power and money to develop and industrialise his estate faster than conservative, independent, moneyless and jealous freeholders.

Hardly a single community since the conquest has been entirely cut off from contact with its neighbours. Hence it is the historian's task to study some wider area which supplied his township with goods and which was itself in turn provisioned in part by the township. The means by which men transported material must be studied in all periods. Even the peasant ploughing a strip of the demesne was probably working a portion of a large estate whose produce stewards moved by road or waterway to central storehouses. Survival and prosperity depend on ease of communication, on the existence of roads, bridges, rivers, hostelries, ports and staging-posts along the route, on the conquest of mountain, marsh, forest and fen barring the way, on law and order in the countryside, and on men's determination to improve facilities rather than accept passable or wretched conditions. Whenever communications are developed the landscape is altered. Thus a canal usually encourages the construction of wharfs and warehouses, a road means inns, a railway needs embankments, cuttings, sidings and factories. The student therefore maps the pattern of communication existing at the start of the relevant period, the means by which these routes joined community to region and nation, the size of the effective economic region round a settlement or hinterland of a port, the resulting improvements in land or water communications and the drawbacks to progress in the shape of water pollution, cluttering of the countryside with buildings and the upsetting of harmonious relations between organisms and their environment.

He goes on to discover reasons for all changes and to describe the process of construction, trying all along to discern behind the legal verbiage of documents which men financed the schemes, whether locals or outsiders, perhaps fat merchants eager for a killing at the expense of and against the wishes of township people. The historian is able to describe the effects of development on the region and also on the landscape, economy, population, even politics and religion, of the township. Thus a railway not only destroys a rural setting but brings in navvies whose radical politics and Catholic religion may alter the local way of life unrecognisably.

A community is held together partly by a common feeling about religion, education and social welfare. Different places exhibit a variety of concerns. The thoughts of Victorian Blackpool turned mainly to the encouragement of holidaymakers whereas men in Hanley were anxious about conditions of employment in the potteries and collieries. Eighteenth-century cottagers near Blackpool talked in all probability about fishing, tourism being far from their minds. Medieval men might gossip as much about the holy days of the church as Georgian parishioners pondered on the intractable problem of the poor. The kind of government in operation in a community reflects to some extent the needs and concerns of the people. Thus a vestry which devotes itself mainly to the suppression of crime and payment of constables serves a society respectful above all of property, plagued by thriftless wanderers, fearful of a return to days of civil disorder and the interruption of commercial activity. The historian thus begins his probing by asking how the affairs of his locality were managed and how interests of the community were safeguarded or even furthered by various departments of government. He selects specific aspects such as poor relief, education, religion, control of unrestricted private enterprise or law and order and then identifies the officers who dealt with these matters and examines their qualifications and work. Engaged in matters of concern there will be official government agencies created and paid by common decision such as guardians of the poor after 1834; informal or voluntary agencies such as church or charity groups; commercial enterprises like water and gas companies or private schools; as well as individuals. During many periods self-help was of the greatest importance, people never being able to rely on the agencies of government. It is, however, necessary to describe how the groups carrying out poor relief and other work were structured, how their decisions were arrived at and what importance they assumed in the community at different times in history. The student often wonders why one person or group seems to exercise extensive influence in a community, why for example the local squire controls all land as well as decisions of the vestry, why the local colliery board of management governs wages, prices, opening hours of inns, schools and housing. Such authority sometimes descends by inheritance or depends on wealth, custom, education, professional status or simply the general acceptance, even apathy, of inhabitants. The researcher goes on to ask how many people helped in making decisions that affected the community, what proportion of the population was entitled to vote for members of Parliament and how many of this number actually cast a vote, whether people's involvement in local government benefited the cause of education or the poor and how far control by the lord of the manor or select vestry effected the general good. The level of rates to support various government bodies should give some idea about the ordinary person's opinion on the work of these authorities, provided that the town meeting had any say in fixing rates. If you know the names and interests of people forming the membership of the agencies, whether formal boards or private charities, you can guess the type of attitude they will show when dealing with matters of concern. It will however be necessary to discover how active each member proved to be, which men controlled meetings behind the scenes, what kind of person offered himself for hire as officer to carry out the orders of the authorities and whether members or officers could claim any really vital interest in solving the problems. The constitution of such a body may set out high claims while resolutions usually read very impressively but the practical effect might yet be nothing. The historian therefore debates and pries into the role of the overseer in actually eliminating poverty or at least in preventing the poor from becoming poorer, the constable's work of suppressing crimes of violence and the manor court's success in regulating the social life of the village. No statement even in the most formal document ought to be taken on trust because the actions of people, in so far as they can now be discovered, speak louder about motives and intentions than words.

Men and women were in one sense bound together but in another held at loggerheads by the influence of the Christian religion, and the researcher attempts to assess how far in any period this faith was accepted, by what proportion of the population and by what types of people. The groups left outside the fold may well have been very significant especially if they included teachers, journalists and factory owners. Uninterest in religion can effectively colour a town's character and bear upon its style of government, people's concerns, architecture and other matters. The existence of sects undoubtedly embittered personal and business relationships in many a community. Hence the researcher traces the origin and growth of sectarianism from the sixteenth century with an occasional glimpse of medieval revolts against the Catholic church and describes how sects felt about each other, the spirit permeating and motivating each body and the kind of person dominating the denominations. He must also know something about the ordinary members of churches and the relative strength of sects, whether the siting of buildings reflects the social or economic standing of worshippers and how frequently nonconformity flourished only where the established church was weak. Religious groups also actively engaged in charitable work, some members turning to education and politics to further their efforts. It is worth considering the direction in which aid flowed, perhaps only to poor members, perhaps to anyone in the town, possibly to national societies. One job the local historian cannot complete is to assess the quality of religious life. He writes about membership numbers and good works but he has few means of looking into members' souls to learn about sincerity, compassion and other Christian qualities. His chapter on religion is necessarily superficial.

Relief of the poor shows a community's concern, and the researcher deals with the size and kind of problem involved, the authorities responsible for relief and the commitment of ordinary townspeople to the elimination of poverty. He attempts to define words like poor and needy and tries to stress that a wage of two shillings a week in one century could mean prosperity, in another century poverty, that lack of running water in a kitchen in 1900 indicates need for home improvement whereas absence of a pump in the cottage of 1600 is unremarkable. The definition of poverty demands a consideration of money, wages, housing, diet, work, health and other factors. The poor is a term embracing the old and crippled, invalids, orphans, widows, the unemployed as well as the penniless. Each town acted to relieve poverty in slightly different ways from its neighbour, one place perhaps relying on wealthy charities, another on the local industrialist, a third being forced to raise money and appoint an overseer of the poor. It is therefore important to assess the contribution of the various bodies that worked in poor relief, to state how each was organised and financed, who were its officers and how it was regarded by the inhabitants at large. Sometimes more people are receiving relief than are paying rates, and the net result of all efforts is a disheartening stagnation. Generally however the agencies succeed in a number of their aims perhaps on account of the employment of efficient, educated, full-time officers who served long enough to learn their jobs and to dispense charity without favour. Occasionally the reverse is true and officers fall behind in their tasks, leaving the poor poorer.

The historian of law and order first asks which people made laws and appointed officers to enforce obedience. Obviously the government by national legislation and local rulings in quarter sessions lays down a code of conduct. But the researcher also examines the part played by such authorities as the town meeting of community leaders, churches, charitable trusts and industrial companies anxious to preserve stable conditions. Individuals are probably important too, the parson, squire, innkeeper, schoolmaster being men able to influence their fellows, though the daily conversations and practical example set by these people will not generally be recorded for the historian. Officials like manorial steward or county sheriff would supposedly serve as forces for stability. Their careers are worth investigating if documents survive, especially if such men seem to stir up trouble in the locality rather than bring peace. Occasionally private trusts are created to uphold the law, keep the district quiet and capture criminals. Acting mainly on behalf of landed and industrial interests, these bodies kept an eye on the common sort of person, so to speak, whom higher wages, schooling, lack of religious devotion, mobility, shorter working hours and unruly families might lead to unrest. It is instructive to consider what proportion of ordinances at quarter sessions were aimed at the suppression of activities by farm labourers, craftsmen and industrial workers. The effectiveness of law enforcement is shown when a town is quiet especially in times of famine, plague and civil unrest, though there may be many other reasons for this peace. The historian inquires into the effect of harsh punishments, manorial control of police work and unpaid untrained constables. He takes note of the stages and methods by which people mitigated the severity of the law, the extent to which inhabitants approved of these changes and the various experiments in law enforcement over the centuries that provided security for the township man.

He discusses the cost of policing the neighbourhood, the names and positions of ratepayers on whom the financial burden fell heaviest and how this affected the kind of laws imposed, the number of cases settled locally in manorial court or landowner's home, the frequency with which townspeople were arrested and taken to higher courts and the help given by township officers towards the capture of fleeing criminals. Punishments will be considered because they indicate something of the mind of a community, though it is hard to know if fines, whipping and hard labour represented the wishes of inhabitants or merely the unthinking execution of law handed down from elsewhere.

When the historian writes about education he necessarily disregards the works of well-known theorists and seeks the attitude of his own local people in centuries past. Generally no direct statements by ordinary folk remain for such an assessment but indirectly the researcher guesses opinions from the way people organised educational affairs. Schooling sometimes seems to be established in practice for the very young, the helpless, the inactive and imbecile in order to keep such unproductive persons out of mischief, to be established possibly for the poor to help them be content with their station in life, occasionally for the bright boy with pretensions to the church or law, usually for the squire's son to enable him to serve as magistrate or member of Parliament, not often for girls, rarely for the budding technician, inventor or engineer, hardly at all for the young adult desirous of attending university. The investigator identifies boys that went to university prior to 1914, analyses their family and school background and discusses their financial means, courses of study and subsequent career. He counts the number of schools and scholars at various dates, stating wealth, social standing, age and sex of children, and diagrammatically marks any relation between new school building and increasing population or standard of living. It is always profitable to follow where possible the school career, if any, of men who later became politicians, manorial stewards, merchants or inventors and to judge the appropriateness of the curriculum as a preparation for their career and for everyday living. The effectiveness of schooling can be deduced from a knowledge of the identity and qualifications of teachers, the number of children each must instruct, the appointment and employment of monitors and pupil teachers, the names and occupations of managers, governors or trustees of the school, the type of school building and its location in the parish. The historian lists the subjects taught but determines the content of reading, writing, arithmetic and religious studies at relevant dates. He may even be able to say what proportion of the day was spent on each activity. The stern but excellent teaching of a particular master ought to be recognised in the hands of scholars as later they write out manorial accounts, charters or vestry minutes, occasionally in a stilted old-fashioned way that makes dating difficult. The level to which pupils aspired, any subjects out of the ordinary introduced by certain masters, the regularity of pupils' attendance, the influence of seasonal activity like harvesting on classes, the attraction of neighbouring industries and towns on the length of stay at school, passing of examinations and discipline problems must also be mentioned. The student reviews the demand for adult education that originates from persons either left unsatisfied by uninspired primary schooling or stimulated to further endeavour by inspired but inadequate elementary lessons. He will doubtless discover and wonder at the fact that education was of little concern to the majority of folk before 1870, the matter being left to town grammar schools, usually privately founded and maintained by charity or church. Charities, philanthropic individuals and church groups paid for many of the minor local schools. A dame school was normally organised by a woman with much time and little money or by a group of women with many children and little time. The teacher himself, though not under the eyes of vigilant inspectors, would naturally try to advance the cause of education because if he did not he might find himself without a school and a job when people decided that the value of education was overrated. It is interesting to know how often, though more usually how rarely, a whole community supported better educational facilities by paying for a new school and teacher. The historian works out how people financed and governed their school, what area the school served and how far if at all the vestry, manor court or other authority became involved in its daily running.

The researcher inquires into the need for leisure activity by investigating the length of the working day, week and year. After all if a man works fourteen hours a day, six days a week his leisure time will be spent sleeping and (if the church is active) worshipping. Holy days and holidays, saints' days, bank holidays, religious and national occasions, all furnish some relief from work. The type of provision for leisure will vary with the community. A mining village probably wants public houses, games halls and chapels whereas a fashionable seaside resort might demand hotels, gambling establishments, bathing machines and a race course. In Victorian times the prosperous suburbs of a city usually asked for a library and created a debating society. Opportunities for leisure activities will occasionally be provided by the local government in the case of libraries, often by charities or religious groups in the case of mystery and mumming plays, temperance meetings and church feasts, by individuals seeking profit in bookshops, bear-baiting, theatres and inns or by people helping themselves (debating society, card playing, dancing, bagatelle and cricket).

CHAPTER 2

Research and writing

THE historian undertakes his research projects in a certain order which is to some extent reflected in the arrangement of this book in so far as fieldwork precedes delving into archives. The wise researcher accepts that local history begins in the locality itself with a survey of the lie of the land, of fields, hills, woods and streams; roads, houses, public buildings, stocks, animal pound, market cross; furnishings of homes, implements about farmyards, machines in factories. The researcher meets people and learns traditions or memories that produce valuable clues for the recreation of past societies. He discovers archival material lying about in attics, cellars, parish chests, deed boxes and offices. While examining the locality he also journeys to the city, town or county library to consult works in print or typescript on his village or town, perhaps discovering in the process that the history has been partly written already by another student. Whenever no specific book exists there is bound to lie on the shelves a regional study that mentions the settlement or states some useful background information. An article dealing with the place should have appeared in the local historical society journals or in the local newspaper files. The third port of call is the borough, city or county record office where are preserved original documents relating to the locality. Every settlement no matter how small occurs somewhere in archival material, even villages long since deserted. Record offices usually now include the important diocesan repositories whose registers, court papers, probate records and licences form priceless contributions to local studies. Fourthly, the researcher goes to a large reference library such as Manchester Central, the Bodleian at Oxford or London University Library. Here he is able to consult printed parliamentary papers as well as older works of history and topography, directories, obscure and learned works, even unpublished theses. Few city, county or university libraries are in fact good enough for really advanced research so the historian prepares himself for a long journey at some stage to the first-class library. He may even find it necessary to work in the British Museum reading room or Guildhall Library, London. It is as well to enquire about special conditions of entry to some of the great research libraries and to be prepared for lengthy queues of students at busy periods. The researcher normally travels to London at some point to consult national archives in the Public Record Office, British Museum, Guildhall Library, House of Lords Record Office or those held by government departments such as Customs and Excise, religious societies, Church Commissioners, the British Transport Authority, College of Arms, Society of Genealogists and industrial companies. Finally he looks in libraries, museums, country houses and other locations for collections of documents that have not yet been deposited in county or borough record offices. I myself have come upon documentary information in the most surprising places from the sideboard of a widow's cottage to the cabin of a canal pleasure cruiser.

RESEARCH METHODS

Historical research today requires the organisation of material as well as a dedication to detail; a regard for method and also for truth. The scientific approach to fieldwork and archives combined with an artistic way of writing produces an acceptable local history. The local historian surveys every inch of his chosen ground and writes reams of notes on his investigations. Books and manuscripts add to the accumulation of material. He speaks with as many knowledgeable people as possible but checks all reminiscences against documents and independent fieldwork. One old man told me he remembered when the manor farm was first built about the time of Queen Victoria's Jubilee of 1887. He had, as a small boy, helped carry bricks to the foot of the labourer's ladder and had fallen down the new staircase from top to bottom. This caused him to miss the royal celebrations so there was no mistake about the date. But it was an easy matter to survey the farm and to consult surviving farm accounts in the possession of the landowner. This investigation showed the demolition of the old wattle and daub timber-framed house in 1886 and the substitution on the same site of the present brick and slate dwelling. Memory was thus reasonably accurate about date and event but had not quite correctly recalled the whole story.

When material of any sort is considered, the historian usually sifts at the outset what is going to be of use and significance. I wrote about one canal settlement from 1775 to 1845. I did not write many notes about canals in general or even about my own canal except to gain some background knowledge of the subject and period. I did not investigate in detail canal locks because there were no locks on my stretch of canal. I did however note down an old boatman's description of legging through tunnels in Staffordshire because my settlement lay at one end of a long tunnel and I might find men of my place working as leggers of boats through tunnels. As it happened I did find written records of local men as leggers but not once did I come across anyone who had actually thus pushed boats through my tunnel. In this sense the boatman's description proved invaluable. The methods of taking notes from fieldwork, manuscripts and books will be discussed in later sections of this book that deal with those matters. For the moment reminiscences alone will be dealt with. I suggest that the researcher employ single sheets of quarto-size paper, a pencil and an eraser. At the beginning of an interview the informant's name, address and subject of interest are recorded together with the date of interview. Permission should be sought of course since some people do not like to think they are being directly quoted in print. As the person speaks, his statements can be written in long or short hand, or relevant points may be noted from memory (if that is good) at the end of an interview. If the informant is not frightened of a microphone then the talk can be recorded on tape or cassette. An interview might be jotted down as follows :

SOURCE NOTE 9

Interview with George Barker, Macclesfield, on canal navigation; taken July 1957.

Worked as canal boatman 1883-1920 between Lancashire and midlands; cargo various but included tea, slate, bricks. No family on board. Recalls going through my settlement but stopped only at inn (Reaper's Arms?) and does not recall meeting many people. Describes life of boatman, various types of boat, midlands factories— seem to agree with printed accounts and no particular relevance. Legging—stretched plank across back of boat from wall to wall of tunnel; two men lay on backs on plank over water, one on each side; pushed with feet against wall to propel boat.

If the interview with George Barker had been recorded on magnetic tape it would have been possible to preserve the whole conversation with its employment of dialect and old-fashioned words for future reference. A shorthand typist could also have transcribed the interview for publication, eliminating of course all hesitations and regional or local peculiarities in grammar or syntax.

As research continues from year to year the historian creates a frightening stack of paperwork. Unless notes are neatly written or typed from the beginning and filed in orderly fashion, this research archive will grow unmanageable. Here is one reason why it is important to use as far as possible a standard size of paper which can be boxed, filed or piled in one sequence. A small scrap of paper placed over two larger ones is very hard to locate. The wise student thus heads each set of notes with a source number and numbers each page of the set so that should any one become detached it is easily refiled in the correct position. He is careful while researching to copy accurately and to write legibly, and if he is working from memory, on scrap-paper or in shorthand he sits down at the end of the day to rewrite his notes. All kinds of mistakes creep in if this immediate tidying is neglected. The object is to enable another researcher to use your notes in order to produce your history should you be struck dead next day. In the same spirit when the historian completes his work or decides he has had enough he preserves all his notes at his home, in the local library or at the county record office. Even when the history appears in print the files are never destroyed because they always contain something of value to later researchers. You will, for example, have taken a complete copy of the tithe apportionment of rent charge which will help a neighbour to write the history of his house. You have copied out the chancery law cases relating to the town but their significance can be assessed very differently by another student.

As work proceeds a mass of notes will build up. It is almost essential to card index the information as an aid to memory. For this the student needs a small filing cabinet or drawer with some white indexing cards five by three inches in size. He first makes a numerical card index of sources, one on each card, and keeps notes stacked in the same order.

1. Parish church records.
2. County record office : quarter sessions : petitions.
3. Title deeds to Leigh estate.
4. Field survey of Bankes watermill.

In the course of writing the researcher may recall a relevant death certificate. It is no long task to sort through the card index to learn that death certificates are number 153. Relevant notes are then more readily found. By the time I had reached source number 153 my notes occupied a whole chest of drawers making it almost impossible for me to find a specific set without my index.

It is equally advisable to create one alphabetical sequence of cards showing names, places and subjects mentioned in the detailed notes. Cards are useful in bringing together information from many sources in the following way.

ROPERY—Bankes farm	
Owned by Thos. Bankes 1816	(4/5)
On tithe 1843	(21)
Owner Mary Bankes 1818-31	(34)
Sells to Coventry 1810	(41/71)
Shed & tools surveyed 1959	(42)
Apprentice 1805	(51)
	TURN OVER

(In the above 4/5 refers to source notes 4/5 being title deeds to Bankes farm; 21 tithe map; 34 land tax; 41/71 settled accounts among records of local solicitor; 42 field survey; 51 overseer of poor's accounts.)

THOMPSON, William, labourer	
c. 21 May 1801	
b. 16 Jun 1864	
son of James, gardener, & Elizabeth	(15)
tenant 1826-31	(17)
tenant 1843	(21)
married Mary Bates 1820	(89)
in court, theft 1823	(101)
	TURN OVER

(15 parish register; 17 land tax; 21 tithe apportionment; 89 diocesan records, bishop's transcripts; 101 county record office, quarter sessions, indictments.)

FARMING—arable	
corn & vegetables 1620	(13)
strips ploughed in open field 1527	(19)
peas in enclosure 1672	(29/7)
dispute about bounds 1630	(42)

(13 manorial survey; 19 landowner's survey of township; 29/7 farmer's inventory accompanying a will; 42 Public Record Office, chancery, law case.)

WRITING

My book claims to advise the historian how to write local history. In a sense it cannot do this so it is essential to confess as much at the outset. The researcher will not then reach the final chapter on government records and expect to find an appendix on how to put pencil to paper. For the same reason the depressing situation about publication is soon to be stated. To be warned prior to commencing work is to be forearmed against disappointment. Most of this book's chapters confine themselves to the simpler task of pointing to documentary and visual sources of local history; of saying 'this is how to write notes, to transcribe, to card index'. The process of putting history on paper depends very much on individual capabilities, taste and interests. The most admirable of all works are Sir Francis Hill's *Medieval Lincoln* (1948), *Tudor and Stuart Lincoln* (1956) and *Georgian Lincoln* (1966) published by Cambridge University Press. It is both easy and true to hold these up as an example of how local history should be written and to tell the researcher to model himself on Sir Francis Hill's style and planning. Yet other excellent books resemble *Medieval Lincoln* in no way. I find the styles of Professors Finberg and Hoskins so pleasing that I study with enthusiasm the history of places I have never heard of. Other people may find these styles displeasing. Some historians have obviously a naturally attractive style and clarity of mind while others need the discipline and red pencil of a professional tutor. It would be wrong to print rules that might limit the exuberance and freshness of approach of another Richard Gough. But it is at least safe to assert that a local history should be based entirely on good evidence, be carefully set out and above all be readable.

The local historian no longer adopts the romantic style reminiscent of some historical novels. At one time the writer would take the single fact that Sir Geoffrey fought in a battle as an invitation to embroider : 'bold Sir Geoffrey rushed into the thick of the fight, conscious only of his golden-haired bride and lively children; for them he had come so far . . .' The historian cannot prove that the knight was bold; was in the fight at all; ever thought about his family on the field; or had joined the army for his family's sake. The bride is nowhere described as golden-haired and the children may well have been the opposite of lively. Noting the number of misprints in the work one wonders if the author had in fact written lovely rather than lively. Words like 'probably' or 'possibly' alone can justify the historian's use of reconstruction of thought and action : 'probably Sir Geoffrey actually went into battle that day but we know only that he accompanied the king on the field . . .' Not many local histories now rely on legends when documentary and archaeological evidence can readily be called on for authentication. The following type of story should not appear in a local history for it dates from after 1710 (by internal evidence) when parish registers, family muniments and court records are all available for checking.

> One tells of an early Lord Barrymore who visited Egypt and there met a young lady who later followed him back to Marbury. She was accepted by the family and at her request they promised that when she died her body should remain at Marbury Hall. When she was murdered on the stairs this promise was forgotten and she was buried in Great Budworth churchyard. Soon afterwards service bells rang for no apparent reason and villagers saw a fine ghost-like lady riding on a white horse. The apparition was seen for many years until the body was at last moved back to Marbury Hall.

Also out of favour is the antiquarian type of history, really a book of appendices rather than a coherent story. It details the descent of the manor, pedigrees of notable families, coats of arms, ownership of hall, names of parsons, mayors, aldermen and members of Parliament, famous events year by year. Local histories are all too often completely uninteresting to the outsider, without value for the student, lengthy, formless, verbose as well as seemingly ignorant of economic affairs, fieldwork, demography and statistics. Chapter after chapter tells what happened but not why, and no consideration is given to the possibility that the events might have any effect on the lives of people at the time and on the course of town history. It is a pity that so much effort should go into books that sit as dead weight on library shelves gathering grime.

The local historian first determines to tell his story as concisely as possible. A length of forty thousand words should be adequate for a village and could appear as two short paperbacks if need be. Every researcher has his own plan of campaign when deciding on chapter divisions. One person will concentrate on the middle ages, another on industries, a third on politics, a fourth on a feature of the locality that is significantly out of the ordinary, and there will be more chapters relating to such topics of interest in one book than in others. In general the following chapter headings will be applicable :

Lie of the land: geology, natural features of the district.

Settlement: reasons for settling in the area and for setting out the township in a certain way.

Population: reasons for growth or decline.

Work: trades, crafts, retail, market, farming, wages, prices.

Transport: inns, post office.

Property: owners, occupiers, estates, type of house and standards of living.

Government: politics, councillors, officers, rates, work undertaken.

Social welfare: poor relief, employment, health, hospitals, protection of one section of community against others.

Education: culture.

Law and order: crime and punishment.

Society: structure of community by social and economic class, gentry, middle class, labouring population.

Religion: customs, superstition.

Recreation: sport, leisure activities.

Some historians choose the chronological approach dealing with all aspects of local affairs century by century or reign by reign. This method enables the reader to grasp more clearly the entire state of the community at various specific dates and suits the person specialising in a particular century. On the other hand the student of education or housing prefers the topical approach outlined above.

When the subject of each chapter is established the writer then chooses subheadings before finally selecting the contents of each paragraph. After the whole book is thus planned the paragraphs are written out in full from the source notes. A small section of the plan of the book could look like this, the chapter heading being capitalised and subheadings italicised.

SOME FEATURES OF THE LOCALITY

Forest and parks

forest clearings (source notes 24, 156)

hunting forests (24, 36, 62)

parks (26, 102, 107, Shirley)

Estates and demesne
    Saxon estates (28, Anglo-Saxon Charters, Dr Hooper)
    demesne farm (36)
    country hall (42, 164, Pevsner, RCHM, MHLG)

I write the first draft on one side of quarto-size paper using pencil and eraser. I make many mistakes, have afterthoughts and need frequently to delete so an eraser saves much untidy crossing out. I add whole sentences and paragraphs to my first draft, if need be, by the simple device of snipping with scissors the original page and taping the additional matter in place.

No local history ought to be published without at least one map. Quite obviously the reader cannot be supposed to know every feature of the locality even if he lives locally. The map therefore shows the lie of the land, important natural features, roads, waterways, hamlets, churches and all other places mentioned in the text. Wherever this policy leads to an overcrowded unpleasing result the historian must provide two or more maps arranged perhaps chronologically, perhaps by subject: medieval Puddlecombe, transport in Puddlecombe, Victorian expansion of Puddlecombe. It is hardly necessary to emphasise the need to draw maps clearly, to distinguish roads from rivers and houses from factories, to use plain and legible lettering, to add a scale and to show a compass pointing north. Contour lines and height above sea level are useful in most non-political studies. If the historian is not a draughtsman he is well advised to seek the services of a professional cartographer rather than produce a cheap but second-rate job. He should certainly ensure that the blockmaker does not reduce the original map to illegibility just for the sake of squeezing it on to one page of the completed book. If the printer does specify one-page maps then it is best to draw many maps containing few details on each one. Whenever the map is large it can always be folded into a pocket inside the back cover of the book or fixed to a page of the book in such a way that it can be unfolded to be consulted whilst the book is being read. The map must be strong enough not to tear, even at the folds, when opened, perhaps by being liner-backed like the expensive Ordnance Survey maps though this would increase the thickness and price of the book.

Illustrations help the historian to speak more clearly to the reader and should form as important a part of the historical evidence as statements in the text. Often pleasing to the eye, pictures and graphs provide some relief from the multitude of words. The historian generally chooses as many contemporary paintings, prints, woodcuts, sketches and photographs as he can lay hands on subject to the publisher's stipulation about cost. Unfortunately glorious coloured pictures normally appear in black and white plates so it is imperative to photograph the original as sharply as possible, sending to the blockmaker a glossy unglazed print half-plate size. Photostats lack the sharpness demanded by printers. It is usually good policy to reproduce manuscript maps and plans of the whole township, of field systems, estates, houses, factories and communications. These are, however, somewhat difficult to photograph and print especially if drawn in faded ink and paint on dark parchment. Nineteenth-century plans are generally so expertly finished that reproduction presents few problems. Unillustrated manuscripts exist in thousands but only a handful are worth printing in the book. Perhaps one ancient charter with seal could be pressed into service as an indication of the antiquity of the settlement, though readers may not be able to decipher the handwriting or the Latin without the aid of a transcript. It is probably best to reproduce only specially eye-catching documents or those that can be tackled by readers themselves. Examples could include the 1642 return of protestation signed by dozens of villagers, a page from the 1851 census, an eighteenth-century quarter sessions petition in round hand, part of the tithe apportionment or an extract from the minutes of the guardians of the poor. The writer himself makes up for the lack of historical pictures by commissioning drawings and photographs of important features in the locality usually embracing the church, castle, oldest houses, market-place and industrial premises. An air photograph of the township is always a useful and instructive companion for maps while pictures revealing ruined or vanished sites are specially pleasing.

Diagrams and graphs when carefully planned and acceptably drawn save much explanation in the text and of course ought to impress their message quickly and clearly on the reader's mind. There is no point in employing this means of communication unless documents have yielded accurate statistics as basis for these drawings. Simple statements like 'membership of Puddlecombe chapel rose from sixteen in 1815 to eighteen in 1825 and twenty-two in 1830' do not require explanation by graphs. There will, however, be room for a logarithmic graph to illustrate rate of population growth and graphs setting out the number of people in each house from 1801, totals of baptisms and burials smoothed out into five-year averages, growth of literacy and poor-relief expenditure. Diagrams might help the reader appreciate the problem of migration in the Victorian village, the age structure of the community, distribution of occupations at each census and voting patterns at parliamentary elections. Tables consist almost entirely of numbers, fractions and decimals dealing with such matters as population, harvest yields, production totals, prices of goods and acreage owned by various people. It is essential to produce accurate tables with numerals aligned perfectly and additions of columns of figures correctly calculated. Most tables are in fact reset by the printer who copies the typed original exactly.

By consulting the works of other historians the writer soon realises which type of information is most susceptible to diagrammatic and graphical treatment and the very real problems involved in drawing bold clear diagrams. Nineteenth-century history is regularly illustrated by these methods on account of the abundance of (admittedly often suspect) statistics and a number of examples appear in Alan Rogers's guide book, *This was their World* (1972). Statistics collected prior to the last forty years are sometimes unsatisfactory because the definition of the science and methods of work have changed rapidly since Victorian times.

The printer asks for sharp drawings in heavy black ink on white paper. These will probably be prepared at double the size needed in the eventual publication and details must be capable of bearing reduction. All must be clean, free from erasures, finger marks, construction lines and corrections. The historian types a list of all illustrations numbered in correct sequence and showing the full caption. The drawings and photographs are numbered on the back and there is an indication in the typescript where each illustration belongs.

Writers employ footnotes to state the source of information in the text, to add a few more words to the text by way of parentheses and to save cluttering the text with minor but worthwhile points. Footnotes at the bottom of the page have been eliminated by many publishers partly to save expense, partly to provide a page more pleasing to the eye. References are now given at the back of the book. It is usual to number notes from 1 in each chapter though I prefer to number from 1 to 600, or whatever, disregarding chapters. A typical footnote referring to a book shows the author's surname and initial, the short title of the book underlined in the manuscript and typing stage to indicate italics and the page number on which the information is to be found.

[21] P. Hinschius, *System des kath. Kirchenrechts*, i, 291.

Here i means volume 1 while 291 is the page number. A quarter sessions petition dating from 1691 and held in the county record office could be quoted by symbols as follows, a key to abbreviations being provided at the front of the book.

[36] CRO, QSP (1691).

Repeat the full reference to each new footnote. Do not say :

[38] Hinschius, *op cit.*, i, 286.

This entails the reader looking back through the notes to find the first occasion when Hinschius's book is quoted by title. The object is to make all references crystal clear. I was recently given as reference to a statement the words 'Faddiley, Henhull'. I looked in the library catalogue to see what the author H. Faddiley had written but had no success. I wondered if somebody Faddiley had produced a book called *Henhull*. It was then I guessed what had happened. I checked. The note should have said :

'J. McN. Dodgson, *The Place-Names of Cheshire*, part 3 (1971), p. 145.'

The writer quoting from printed calendars of manuscripts should give details of the edition and page numbers. He should never pretend to be using the original material if he is not. One reason for this rule is that the printed book may contain errors in translation or interpretation. The historian claiming to be reading the original adds the authority of a second researcher to any errors. If he is using documents themselves he should not just refer to 'document at the Public Record Office' but must give the exact detailed reference number so that later researchers can find the manuscript again.

It is essential somewhere in the book to provide a glossary of unusual or dialect words that occur in the history. If the work is to be read by people outside the district or unfamiliar with history, it cannot be assumed that readers know such terms as inquisition *post mortem*, assart, terrier, honor or peculiar. Admittedly there are difficulties in the way of adequately explaining to the layman what a common recovery is, without stopping to qualify nearly every word used in a technical sense, while the description of certain machines or processes in industry in simple words is clearly impossible. Necessarily detailed explanations should however be placed in appendices, the glossary being confined to one or two sentences for each unusual word.

If space permits the bibliography should refer to all books mentioned in the text or studied and found useful by the author in the course of research. It includes all documentary sources and field monuments relevant to the project. The bibliography of one of my local studies runs to eighty-six typewritten pages. Here are some extracts.

Manuscripts : at John Rylands Library, Manchester

    DDC1 Cornwall-Legh of High Legh muniments

    286 Inquisition *post mortem* of Matthew Leigh of Swynhead, gent., concerning three messuages, one cottage and 130 acres of land in Barnton, 27 Mar 1623

Books :

    DUGDALE, James *The New British Traveller, Cheshire,* i, London 1819

Fieldwork :

    Survey of lanes and tracks

    Shuttes and Brammows lanes, abandoned by 1830 after the new river cut was completed, survive unrepaired with traces of sidestones, cobbles, hedges and ditches

Indexing is a skilled and demanding task and cannot be adequately dealt with here. It consists of much more than extracting names of places and persons as will be evident from studying the index of any good reference book. It is wise to establish first of all how large an index will be needed or allowed by the publisher. Should there be no limit then the writer may index all names of people and places, all authors and titles of books, all events, all ideas like beauty and justice, all subjects such as poor relief, administration and postal services. Footnotes, foreword, illustrations and appendices must also be indexed. The rules for indexing would run to many chapters so only one or two points can be mentioned now.

When I index a book I have by me some thousands of pieces of paper about three inches by one inch in size. I read through the book and decide what type of entries I must index in order to satisfy all possible classes of students. I then begin again and write each entry on a fresh piece of paper with its page number.

Acorn wood 1

Thompson, Henry 1

poor relief 1

At the end of each chapter I put all the papers in alphabetical order, combining cards with identical entries.

poor relief   1, 10, 13-14, 21-2

I arrange entries of more than one word by what is termed the word-by-word method rather than in alphabetical order all through. All but the first word is ignored and entries are placed in the alphabetical order of that first word. Thus Dog Wood precedes Dogs' Home because dog comes before dogs in the alphabet. By the straight alphabetical arrangement Dogs' Home would come before Dog Wood. When I accumulate several entries with exactly the same first word and all connected in subject matter such as poor law, poor relief, poorhouse, I arrange them in this way :

poor
   house
   relief
   law

Of course if the entries are not closely connected each has its own position in the alphabetical sequence. In this case since the first words are the same these are ignored and the entries alphabetised according to the second word (or third if need be).

poor
   house
   law
   relief
Poor Tom's Wood
   enclosure of
poor widows' charity bread 1702

I try never to place more than a dozen page references against one word in the index. In order to save the reader some tiresome searching I subdivide important entries as follows.

agriculture
documents relating to
open-field
Saxon
Tudor pamphlets about

When I have indexed the whole book I interfile all the cards. It is now that it is vital to ensure that *agriculture* has not been used as a heading for one part of the work while *farming* has taken over for another section. All page references should be under one word, say *agriculture,* and a *see* reference employed in this way :

farming, *see* agriculture

When I use various interrelated headings, none of which can be eliminated I make a *see also* reference.

architecture, vernacular 4, 7, 26-9, 87-97. *See also* farm buildings; houses; Grey, Thos., carpenter

The choice of key words is obviously a skilled task. These ought to be chosen with the need of prospective users of the index in mind. Will readers look under vernacular architecture first or architecture, vernacular?

When a subject covers more than one page continuously the first and last pages should be given, as in the example above : 87-97. But if the topic is just mentioned on page 87 and then forgotten until the bottom of page 88, next mentioned on page 89, the numbering ought to appear as 87, 88, 89.

There are different ideas about dealing with abbreviations, numerals, sets of initial letters and hyphenated words when placing these in alphabetical order. The books recommended below will provide the reasons for and against certain rules, but it is essential to adopt one rule and keep to it. The number of columns per page, entry layout, punctuation, indentation of headings and subheadings, use of capital or lower-case letters to begin headings and similar important aspects of presentation will depend largely on the publisher's instructions, though if the writer is himself publishing the work he will have to learn the various possibilities and decide for himself.

Most publishers can arrange for a professional indexer to deal with a book but this has to be paid for out of the historian's pocket. On the other hand the author undertaking to index a book for himself must realise that much time and patience are called for. He ought in addition to become familiar with at least the three books that follow : G. V. Carey's *Making an Index* (1951), R. L. Collison's *Indexes and Indexing* (third edition, 1969), British Standards Institution's *Recommendations for the Preparation of Indexes of Books* (periodically revised).

Typing the manuscript is one step nearer publication and is necessary before any editor or publisher should be asked to judge the work. The typist must be asked to use white quarto paper of good quality, type at least one top and two carbon copies and leave at left and right hand side of the page at least a one-inch margin. Double spacing is essential. Nothing is underlined save what will appear in italics in the book. Figures [45] indicating footnotes are typed half a line above the text without punctuation but footnotes themselves are placed one after another on separate sheets rather than at the bottom of the relevant page. Quotations are usually typed with the text within single quotation marks. Most historians capitalise chapter headings in the centre of a page but remove subheadings to the left-hand side of the page and employ lower-case letters. In all events it is essential to be consistent in this as in such matters as spelling, hyphens and initial capitals. This is the writer's job, never the typist's.

PUBLICATION

This book is about the writing of local history rather than its publication. I can hold out little hope that work will ever go into print let alone be published and sold in bookshops. None the less I urge the writing of the history. My own village history lies in a box at home. The manuscript does not await publication. It was, however, fascinating and informative to write, disciplining my thoughts and theories and clarifying my mind on some matters; it is available to students and villagers; and it provides instances and illustrations for lectures, broadcasts and books on local history in general. It would be a public-spirited action to type three copies, one for myself, one for the county record office, one for the county library. The local historian who is committed to provide copies of his work for sale or gift should consider the possibility of having a stencil typed. Copies can be run off on a duplicating machine whenever needed at modest cost. If the local researcher goes to a printer and pays to have his book printed, even in paperback or by offset duplicating processes, he will probably lose money. Some three thousand copies must be sold to cover printing costs (assuming that photographs and maps are included) and this is nearly impossible. People that promised to buy the book will in fact borrow a copy from the library or from friends, or even from the historian himself perhaps on the excuse of services rendered during research. Many local histories have of course appeared in this way and are often as admirable as any published by university presses. I think for instance of Robert T. Clough's study of *The Lead Smelting Mills of the Yorkshire Dales* published privately by the author in 1962.

Local historical societies might help with publication. These bodies issue annual transactions which contain articles of varying length on aspects of local history. The study of a town or village could hardly be contracted to article length but different centuries or subjects can be studied and the results of research published article by article over the years. Most editors have, however, plenty of material awaiting publication so this method is not very practicable. National journals like *Local Historian* do not take histories of specific places but articles of general application such as 'how to read title deeds'. A local society does consider sponsoring the publication, as an independent volume, of any local history of merit. It would also be worth following the plan of the Hatfield branch of the Workers' Educational Association by issuing the history in thin paperback parts. If the first couple did not sell, the project could be abandoned with modest losses. One part could be published before Christmas each year and a comparatively faithful clientele built up. It is easier for the customer to spend a few pence each year than two or three pounds all at once.

Some historians have managed to have their work printed with the aid of subsidies from local councils or industries. More often than not it is the university press nowadays that takes local history. I contributed to a history of Congleton that was published for the local historical society by Manchester University Press with the help of a borough council grant. A local university would certainly not disdain to publish the history of a village provided that the author's standard of research and writing were high, his maps and photographs clear and relevant, his list of consulted books and documents impressive. Every book is accepted first and foremost as a work of scholarship and of educational value. It is not taken merely because the author is willing to pay some or all the costs. Of course subsidies are very welcome since local history is of a specialised nature with a limited audience and occasionally demands complicated printing work. Thus Cambridge University Press produced Sir Matthew Nathan's history of West Coker in Somerset in 1957 and accepted the author's offer to give a substantial sum to the cost of his book in order that the work could be sold at a price within the reach of potential users. This press is technically a charity and recognises an obligation to use resources to publish books which could not appear commercially. It does not therefore demand a subsidy for even the most uncommercial of works. Other university presses adopt similar attitudes so the local historian might be successful in his search for a backer. Leicester University Press published H. J. Dyos's brilliant study of Camberwell called *Victorian Suburb* in 1961, and the reader can readily see why after delightedly examining two or three chapters. This latter press has become renowned for its local history publications partly because the Department of English Local History is within the university. This naturally attracts to Leicester many manuscripts, some of which appear in the series of occasional papers issued by the university press, a few as full-length books.

Leicester also offers an annual prize named after the historian and publisher John Nichols. This is for an essay some twenty thousand words long on any local history subject chosen by the researcher and approved by the university.

It is virtually impossible to find a commercial publisher for a local history. Although the subject is booming and thousands of students enrol for courses and even write studies, published works deal with regions, industries or subjects of more than parochial relevance. The local historian desiring above all to burst into print ought to study the types of books now being published so that he can extend his researches in the right direction. The firm of David and Charles in Newton Abbot publish much local history and archaeology of a certain kind. Their city and county history series is aimed at the general reader, college student and sixth former and includes books about conurbations like Tyneside and the Potteries. All books have maps, graphs and bibliographies and can obviously be read by people who have never even visited the places in question. Volumes about industrial archaeology concern whole counties, canals, railways and industries. My own manuscript on one canal settlement would not be taken by this firm but could form a basis for a work on canal settlements in England or a history of the Trent and Mersey Canal.

The simplest way to find a publisher is to ask the county archivist or librarian for names and addresses. He may suggest you supply material to the editor of the *Victoria County History* of the shire should this not already be in print. Each township in the country is surveyed in this work and your notes could save the full-time researchers much effort. You might be asked to write the necessary article as long as you abide by the strict rules about content and style. The archivist or librarian will most likely send you to the university press or local historical society. It is also a good policy to find a recently published book that resembles yours in subject or district, to note the name of the publisher of that work and then obtain his address in library reference books. You can send the publisher a synopsis of your work or the typed manuscript itself, enclosing a stamped addressed envelope if you want the book returned should it be unsuitable. There are advantages in finding a publisher before the work is typed because each firm has its own ideas about length, style, capital letters, arrangement of chapters, punctuation, footnotes, index and bibliography. A study written with the Oxford Historical Society in mind will look very different from a book for Messrs David and Charles.

If the book does appear for sale in some form, it is essential to publicise it. An excellent work sells not at all if nobody knows it is available. Review copies must be despatched to newspapers and historical journals over as wide an area as the book is expected to sell. The local bookshop should be persuaded to take copies on a sale or return basis, and a special exhibition could be arranged in the shop at publication time. It will obviously cost money to produce posters and leaflets. Most books nowadays are introduced to purchasers by means of neatly printed leaflets or brochures coloured and illustrated if possible. Even if the book itself is economically printed the advance leaflet should be expensively laid out. This is cynical but is modern business. The leaflet introduces the author and book clearly and concisely and sets out some interesting, attractive and pertinent extracts from the text and illustrations. The price is stated and a rebate could be offered for early orders. An order form is enclosed. This is all frequently managed on a single sheet of glossy paper printed both sides.

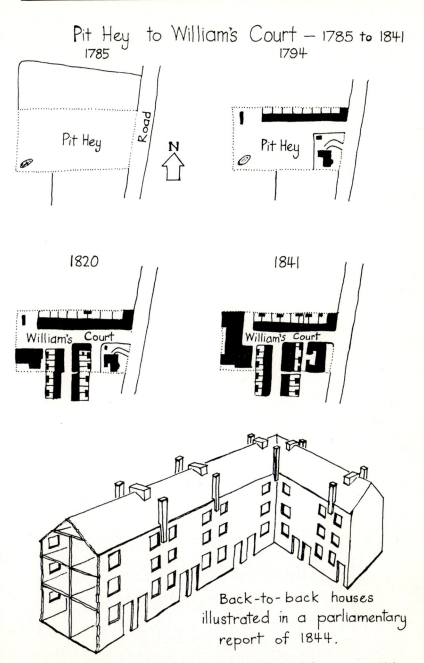

Pit Hey to William's Court — 1785 to 1841

1785

1794

Pit Hey

Road

N

Pit Hey

1820

William's Court

1841

William's Court

Back-to-back houses illustrated in a parliamentary report of 1844.

1. Pit Hey to William's Court: houses in Nottingham of the type erected in William's Court, from the first report on *The State of Large Towns and Populous Districts* (1844). (Drawn by Trevor Dennis)

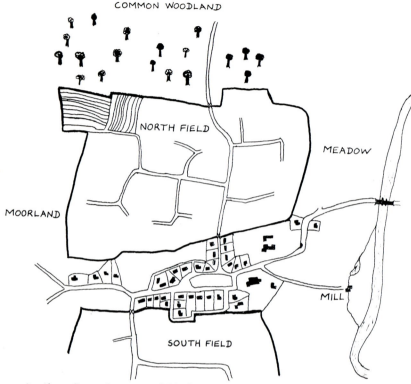

COMMON WOODLAND

NORTH FIELD

MEADOW

MOORLAND

MILL

SOUTH FIELD

2. *Above* Part of an open-field village showing North Field with access roads to furlongs and two furlongs complete with strips. Beyond the field is common woodland while the open common lies to the west. The corn-mill straddles the stream to the east, and water meadows adjoin the river. The sketch is not drawn to scale.

3. *Below* Farming activities illustrated in the Luttrell Psalter. Manorial records concerning village agriculture complement these rare pictures. (British Museum)

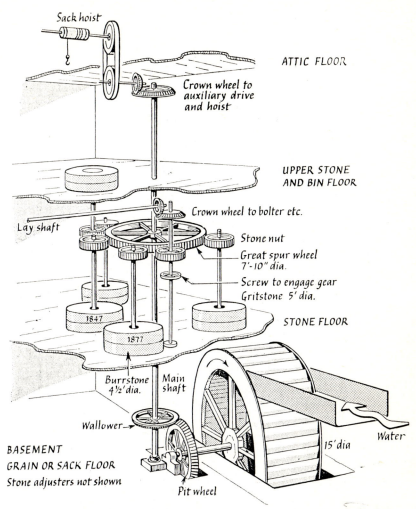

Sack hoist

ATTIC FLOOR

Crown wheel to auxiliary drive and hoist

UPPER STONE AND BIN FLOOR

Lay shaft

Crown wheel to bolter etc.

Stone nut

Great spur wheel 7'-10" dia.

Screw to engage gear
Gritstone 5' dia.

STONE FLOOR

1847

1877

Burrstone 4½' dia.

Main shaft

Wallower

15' dia

Water

BASEMENT
GRAIN OR SACK FLOOR
Stone adjusters not shown

Pit wheel

4. Water corn-mill at Bainbridge, Yorkshire, of seventeenth-century design but rebuilt in 1797 and overhauled in the next century. (Drawing by Neil Hyslop in Dr Arthur Raistrick's *Industrial Achaeology*, 1972)

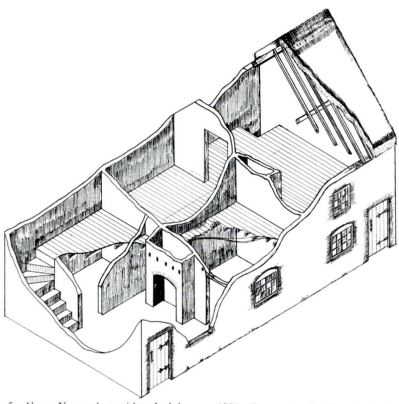

5. *Above* Yeomen's semidetached houses, 1775. (Drawn by Geoffrey Buchan)
6. *Below* see opposite.

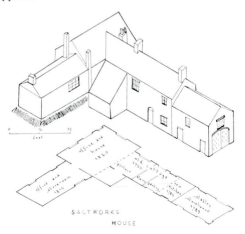

SALTWORKS
HOUSE

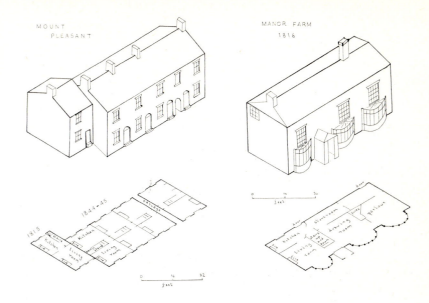

6, 7, 8, 9, 10. Drawings of houses in an industrial settlement.

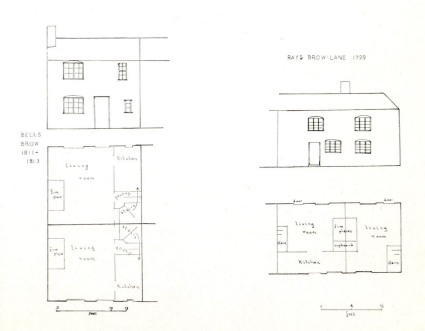

11. The second explosion at the Oaks Colliery, Barnsley, Yorkshire, vividly drawn in the days before newspaper photography (from *Illustrated London News*, 22nd December 1866).

12. The sheet and rolled plate glass works of Messrs Pilkington, St Helens, 1879. St Helens Crown Glass Company established its earliest glass cone in 1826 on a site just off the left-hand side of this picture. Notice the use of horses, sailing boats and manual loading. The canal, a branch of the Sankey Navigation, was opened in 1757 and filled in in 1898

Name	g	b	bn	c
Thompson Thomas, watergate-street, cordwainer				c
Tylston Samuel, boughton, slater	g	b		
Tylston Samuel, jun. ditto, combmaker	g	b		
Taylor William, nun's-lane, cordwainer				c
Taylor William, weaver's-lane, combmaker	g	b		
Tylston Joseph, foregate-street, cordwainer	g	b		
Tylston Thomas, St. john's church-yard, ditto	g	b		
Thornton Henry, dee-lane, ditto	g	b		
Tyrer John, barker's-lane, ditto	g			
Trape John, bridge-street, blacksmith				c
Tapley Henry, northgate-street, cordwainer	g	b		
Tapley John parson's-lane, taylor				c
Tyrer William, foregate-street, cordwainer	g	b		
Taylor Thomas, boughton, yeoman	g	b		
Thomas John, handbridge, roper	g	b		
Tylston Charles, foregate-street, mason	g	b		
Thring Samuel, bridge-street, victualler	g	b		
Tamerlane John, northgate-street, ditto				c
Turner John, watergate-street, cordwainer				c
Thornley John, bunt's-lane, combmaker	g	b		c
Taylor John, horn-lane, news-carrier				c
Towsey John, northgate-street, hosier				c
Tonna Samuel, pepper-street, glover				c
Tonna William, king-street, druggist				c
Thornton Henry, northgate-street, slater	g	b		c
Tonna John, werburgh's-lane, butcher				c
Trevor William, bridge-street, skinner	g			c
Tonna Richard, king-street, brewer				c
Trevor John, eastgate-street, peruke-maker	g	b		
Taylor John, watergate-street, cooper	g	b		
Townshend George, foregate-street, esq.			bn	c
Thompson Owen, watergate-street, grocer			bn	c
Townshend Edward, stanley-place, esq.			bn	c
Townshend Thomas, abbey-court, esq.			bn	c
Turner William, northgate-street, hairdresser			bn	c
Taylor Jonathan, northgate-street, combmaker	g	b		
Thomas John, ditto, chandler	g	b		
Towsey Thomas, ditto, hatter	g	b		
Turner Joseph, roodee, architect	g	b		
Townsend Gerrard, foregate-street, gent.	g	b		
Thomas John, hawarden, ditto	g	b		
Townsend Robert, chester, esq.	g	b		

13. Part of Chester poll list, 5th-16th April 1784. The letters in the right-hand columns refer to the four candidates: g—Thomas Grosvenor, b—Richard W. Bootle, c—John Crewe, bn—Roger Barnston.

CHAPTER 3

Working at the library

THE local historian begins his work in the library. After all, if Puddlecombe is already served by a recent and satisfactory study the researcher would be well advised to find and read this before commencing work all over again. It is an advantage to visit the nearest library that stocks an adequate supply of reference works and local histories and has a trained librarian in charge. The libraries of most large cities, some universities that allow in members of the public, the British Museum and county library headquarters should be suitable for research purposes. Local libraries cannot hold a wide enough selection of general reference works as well as local histories from all parts of the country. Thus the student easily gets a false impression of what is published and what needs yet to be done after looking at such inadequately stocked shelves. It is essential to seek an interview with the reference or local history librarian who will tell what the historian should read. He can save the student time because he knows what is available and where this is found. He immediately realises that the county Domesday survey is translated in the *Victoria County History* for the shire. He will probably find in print a large amount of material suitable for the project.

The British Museum was founded in 1753 following Hans Sloane's bequest and sale of his library and museum to the nation. Books and manuscripts of the Cotton, Harley, Egerton and other families were placed in the museum. These refer to most places in the country and include muster lists, sketches of villages, petitions to Parliament, charters, maps and valuations. In 1757 George II donated the royal library with its privilege of compulsory deposit of all copyright books published in Great Britain. It is rare indeed for the museum not to be able to make available any book on local history that the student requires, though pressure on space and staff tends to mean slow service. In order to work on books and manuscripts in the museum reading room the historian first needs plenty of time and must secondly obtain a reader's ticket by post after filling in the relevant form. A character reference is required.

Printed books that the historian uses in his work are compiled from original documents, fieldwork and reminiscences as well as from other books. It is all too easy for an author to misquote a source, to turn out old-fashioned theories or to copy correctly a previous writer's incorrect transcription of a document. A book's value may be judged not by its date of publication or format but by a reading of any footnotes, bibliography and index. The index should be as thorough as space allows and the list of books consulted will include standard reference works as well as the most recent publications. Footnotes ought to indicate that the author has delved into all relevant sources of information. Works that purport to be editions or transcripts of documentary material are in general reliable. Volumes of local record societies normally maintain a high standard. It is not too serious if an editor misses a comma here or wrongly spells an unimportant word there. Occasionally however an editor leaves out what he considers uninteresting, obscene, indecorous and embarrassing material. Even worse he may not even note what he has done in the text so that the reader gains a false impression of the original document and the writer.

When I read a book I write down at the head of my notepaper the next source number, the name of the author, title, place and date of publication. I read a book and make notes on a piece of scrap-paper of the places where I find relevant information. Thus 16 2t means page 16, paragraph 2, top section. At the end of every chapter I stop and, using the key, make my notes quoting in full or in précis form as I think will prove of most value when I write the history itself. My notes might appear like this.

SOURCE NOTE 197

George BORROW *Wild Wales* (first pub. 1862), London 1955

p. 41 Llangollen in 1854 'small town or large village of white houses with slate roofs'

p. 50 children of the lower classes 'great pests to visitors'

p. 54 description of Llangollen ale

p. 55 no papists; abbey of the vale of the cross now farmhouse

Each set of notes is card indexed for the numerical index of sources and then people's names, place-names and subjects are extracted and indexed because most local histories will revolve around men, women, houses, fields, industry and suchlike.

The historian should start his reading with general works that ought to include three books by Professor W. G. Hoskins: *Local*

History in England (1959), *Provincial England* (1963), *Fieldwork in Local History* (1967); the short but exhilarating work by Professor H. P. R. Finberg and V. H. T. Skipp on *Local History: Objective and Pursuit* (1967) which contains Professor Finberg's classic lecture on *The Local Historian and his Theme* (1952); J. J. Bagley, *Historical Interpretation* (1972); F. G. Emmison, *Archives and Local History* (1966); J. West, *Village Records*, well illustrated (1962). Professors Finberg and Hoskins have both headed the Department of English Local History at Leicester University, the first and so far only university faculty of its kind in this country. R. B. Pugh's *How to Write a Parish History* (1954) sets a high standard for the local historian. Other useful books are listed in the Historical Association's *English Local History Handlist* which is periodically revised. Periodicals include *History*, *Local Historian* and *Economic History Review*.

The *Victoria County History* if available for the shire should be the first local work consulted. Introductory volumes deal with education, agriculture, Domesday survey, geology, industry and similar subjects. Then each township or parish is dealt with : descent of manor, history of church and hall, famous families, buildings of interest, industries and charities. Because the great project of writing histories of all townships in the country was commenced early this century, historical outlook and ideas have changed as volume follows volume. Modern surveys concentrate more on archaeological investigations, economic conditions and vernacular architecture and less on the squire and his relations. After this, volumes of county historic and record societies must be studied, and these will be further mentioned later. Books specifically about the historian's own locality might be seventeenth-century classics like Sir William Dugdale's *The Antiquities of Warwickshire* (1656) or modern paperbacks like the twelve-part *Hatfield and its People* (1961-4). There will be books dealing with subjects of local importance such as coal or the Great North Road and with families of the district. Model local studies include H. J. Dyos, *Victorian Suburb* (1961), dealing with Camberwell, and J. D. Chambers, *A Century of Nottingham History, 1851-1951* (1952).

Many old works of history and travel provide pictures of England as seen by contemporaries. Thus John Leland (1506-52) in his *Itinerary* describes the country at the time of the destruction of the monasteries. Daniel Defoe in *A Tour through the Whole Island of Great Britain* started his journey in 1722. John Wesley's *Journal* illustrates a locality's attitude to religious revival. Arthur Young (1741-1820) in various *Tours* speaks of farming practice in specific areas. J. Aikin's *Description of the Country from Thirty to Forty Miles round Manchester* (1795) was reprinted in 1968. This book shows the spread of industrialism. The brothers Lysons wrote an excellent work of topography and history in their *Magna Britannia* (1806-22). Samuel Lewis's *A Topographical Dictionary of England* went through several editions from 1831 onwards.

Charles Hatchett (1766-1847), a scientist who knew the European industrial scene well, has left us a short but excellent diary of a tour he undertook. This was published in 1967 as *The Hatchett Diary; a Tour through the Counties of England and Scotland in 1796 visiting their Mines and Manufactories.* John Britton's autobiography (1849-50) is as informative about English society and economic life as about the author. John Hassell's *Tour of the Grand Junction Canal* (1819), a classic illustrated work, was reprinted in 1968. Industrial and country activities are surveyed in *Picturesque Scenery of England and Wales* (1805) by P. J. de Loutherbourg. For an illustrated account of Victorian London—its high society, slums, underworld and working conditions—see Gustave Doré and Blanchard Jerrold, *London: a Pilgrimage* (1872). An earlier work pictures the metropolis in great detail, describing trades and street scenes and local characters. This is the celebrated *London Labour and the London Poor* (1851-62) by Henry Mayhew in four volumes.

John Britton and E. W. Brayley produced a work in twenty-five volumes entitled *The Beauties of England and Wales; or Delineations, Topographical, Historical, and Descriptive of each County* (1801-15). The engravings often show buildings and scenes that have disappeared while the text deals with a country hardly touched by industrialism. For delightfully accurate pictures of everyday activity in Georgian times—sheep shearing, washing, wheelwrights—consult W. H. Pyne's *Microcosm* (1803-6), two volumes. A similar, very famous work is George Walker's *The Costume of Yorkshire* (1814). James Dugdale's *The New British Traveller* (1819) and J. G. Kohl's *England and Wales* (1844) are two interesting records of tours which covered some places now altered almost beyond recognition. Throughout the nineteenth century topographical and statistical information of a useful kind is to be found in county and town guide books issued for the benefit of travellers rather than commercial interests.

Published reminiscences about local life are often enlightening if treated intelligently and critically. Richard Gough's hilarious *Antiquities and Memoirs of the Parish of Myddle* displays human nature in his seventeenth-century Shropshire parish through shrewd observation of his fellow villagers. This book was privately printed in 1834, published in 1875 and reissued in 1968. Flora Thompson's classic *Lark Rise to Candleford* (1945) deals with local life in late Victorian and Edwardian times. The historian might profitably copy some of the methods employed by G. E. Evans in finding out and recording local crafts, customs and lore. This author's books include *Where Beards Wag All* (1970).

ILLUSTRATIONS

Paintings, prints, drawings and photographs frequently help the local historian to gain a clear picture of his locality in times past. He ought to be able to discover a number of sketches and photographs dating from 1880 onwards that relate to most villages and towns, though churches, mansions and monuments tend to be represented more often than ordinary homes, street scenes and industrial buildings. But a photograph taken in 1880 may well show a row of cottages erected in 1540 and demolished during town improvements in 1885 and therefore long forgotten. Illustrations in general even when not dealing with the place in question do create an atmosphere in which the local historian can more sympathetically work. He cannot fully imagine his village as it was in 1740 if he merely takes away the telegraph poles, sealed roads and other clutter of modern life, changes the dress of the people and reduces the population by one-quarter. Paintings of the period indicate how much greater the changes have been than we at first realised, how superlatively beautiful the country-side seemed, how green with meadows, woods and leafy lanes, how wild with untamed and mysterious fens and marshes and mountains. Pictures record wide parkland, magnificent mansions newly built, cottages seemingly growing out of the rich earth and foliage of surrounding gardens because they were constructed largely of material on the spot. Other sketches hint at the noise, dirt, steamy fog and depressing poverty of town life in the industrial period. People are in rags, houses are unkempt, horse manure and sewage are strewn in roadways. On the other hand the historian notes with Victorian eyes shining new railway stations, factories, bridges and terraces of houses and appreciates his forebears' pride in the fine country they had created in a couple of generations. Joseph Wright's haunting illuminated industrial scenes, J. Constable's 'Hay-wain' of 1821 and J. M. W. Turner's 'Rain, steam and speed' of 1844 are examples of paintings that recreate for me the calm and unhurried, or alternatively the exciting, atmosphere of the past and show how some people, perhaps the folk of my community, might see their environment.

Among the many illustrators whose work since the eighteenth century has shown places all over the country may be mentioned Johannes Kip (1653-1722) who drew some splendid views of halls, parks and villages in Stuart days. Samuel and Nathaniel Buck engraved scenes of towns, abbeys, mansions and castles between 1720 and 1753. During the first half of the nineteenth century John and Charles Buckler drew hundreds of pictures of schools, towns and church buildings. Some are in print, others in the British Museum. A collection of seaport illustrations relating to the whole country is held at the National Maritime Museum, Greenwich. The National Monuments Record, London, collects illustrations of all types of historical structure and has absorbed the archive of the National Buildings Record. Because pictures of any one locality are never numerous, it is important to employ every picture fully, identifying and explaining each detail wrung from the work. Are those hedges and trees still growing in the same position? What happened to those cottages on the river bank? How was that mill converted into the Victorian factory? Look for instance at S. and N. Buck's prospect of Bath, an excellently drawn view of 1734. Examine with a magnifying glass every square inch until at least one object of unusual importance emerges. Tucked away to one side is a railed-way, and this is in fact one of the earliest pictorial representations of an industrial railed-way.

AIR PHOTOGRAPHS

Photographs taken obliquely or vertically from the air are valuable aids during research. It is helpful to see an area in relation to the surrounding district or to study at a glance the entire village or town. Older photographs show sites since destroyed by industry or housing while new ones preserve a picture of the town as it is today before altered by further development. These pictures help the student to distinguish field patterns, farm sites, course of streams, roads and paths, position of swamp, wood and hill, the plan of settlement and the relation of house sites to waterway, well, main road, wharf, castle or church. Some photographs are better than the largest maps in clarifying problems of local history such as the reason why a village lies where it does, why a road zigzags, why fields are situated in such a portion of the township and woodland elsewhere. Various marks in the soil and vegetation reveal sites of villas, old farming systems, deserted villages, abandoned factories and tracks. Photographs taken obliquely, late in the afternoon, after dry weather and over cereal crops produce best results. Air Ministry photographs shot vertically are excellent if read with a stereoscope. This collection has been taken over by the Ministry of Housing and Local Government which is now part of the Department of the Environment, though copies are held in some libraries and may be purchased at reasonable cost from the department in London. Air photographs may also be purchased from Messrs Aerofilms, or borrowed from the local council planning department. It is advisable to contact the Curator in Aerial Photography, Sidgwick Avenue, Cambridge, concerning any detailed historical problems that air photography might solve. The present curator, Dr J. K. S. St Joseph, has among other works edited a wide-ranging pictorial survey on *The Uses of Air Photography* (1966).

NEWSPAPERS

Newspapers and magazines may date from the eighteenth century onwards. Numerous local papers sprang up after the abolition of obnoxious duties in 1855-61. Early newspapers, say prior to 1800, contain little local news partly because this passed by word of mouth in the coffee house or inn while the town remained small. But advertisements and announcements are of great importance as a source of local history because they mention sometimes in detail the disposal of estates, house sales, tradesmen's stock and prices, requests for labour as well as births, marriages and deaths. Later papers report on crime, trials, riots, local history and antiquities, politics, building plans, the economic situation, transport projects and religious disputes. When I wrote the story of canal building in one village, company records proved useless but the local newspaper of 1775 carried advertisements for labourers to dig the canal and for miners to build the two tunnels. These are the only references anywhere to the construction of the canal in the locality.

Nearly every town has supported one or more newspapers which have survived independently or in union with former rivals. Copies should be sought at newspaper offices though some proprietors have sent old files to libraries or record offices. The *Handlist of English and Welsh Newspapers 1620-1920* published by *The Times* in 1920 indicates what local papers would be available for research. Newspapers are generally not indexed so the historian has to study each issue page by page. This is not too burdensome till about 1860 because earlier papers are usually only weekly and contain few pages. Their layout can be readily learned and columns that normally furnish information which is irrelevant for the local historian, such as foreign or court news, should be ignored in every issue.

There exists a number of useful periodicals. The *Gentleman's Magazine* dating from 1731 exhibits material of interest to genealogists, archaeologists, antiquarians, students of prices and the weather, travellers and researchers into ecclesiastical affairs, 'More in Quantity and greater Variety than any other Book of the Kind and Price'. The *Methodist Magazine* prints biographies and religious news concerning the growing and influential sect whose members are so typical of the early industrial community. The state of industry and the development of modern machines are reviewed in the files of *The Engineer* (from 1856) and *Engineering* (from 1866). *The Builder* (1842 onwards) and *The Ecclesiologist* (1841-68) deal with new and altered buildings of all kinds. The *Illustrated London News* from 1842 contains much local news and pictures; it is quite well indexed.

There is no swift method of adequately studying newspapers and periodicals apart from enlisting the help of a group of dedicated enthusiasts. It is not sufficient to choose a couple of issues annually because this does not produce a balanced view of all seasons of the year. Nor should just a few picturesque or interesting items be extracted. Accepting this then it must be realised that the search page by page over a couple of centuries takes time. Even if a volume every five years is chosen this still leaves twenty huge files to study each century. The historian reads this material and makes notes in the ordinary way, either word for word or in précis form. But so bulky are the completed notes that it is essential to card index the information by categories corresponding to various sections of the intended history. Suppose there is a long report about a meeting which planned the local canal. Notes from this reach five pages in length. This should be briefly indexed under category 4 (transport) **as follows :**

Canal meeting 2 Jul 1793 p. 76 (This page refers to your notes; the date to the issue of the paper.)

The following categories are useful in most histories :

1. Topography of the settlement and any items of use in fieldwork projects.
2. Property sales and leases.
3. Trades and crafts : including fairs, markets, farming and factories.
4. Transport : including roads, inns, coaches, post office and waterways.
5. Professions : including surveyors, lawyers and doctors.
6. Society : a general topic which embraces gentry, army, navy, sport, coffee houses.
7. Education and culture : schools, bookshops and libraries.
8. Religion.
9. Social welfare : poor relief, employment, health and hospitals.
10. Politics.
11. Local administration : vestry, corporation and town meeting.
12. Crime and punishment : law and order.

The cards of material relating to category 4 are bundled together. When the chapter on transport is written the cards readily point to the detailed notes from which the account will be produced. If time allows the historian extracts people, places and subjects from his newspaper jottings for inclusion in the general card index of sources. This ensures that the main card index is comprehensive.

DIRECTORIES

Printed directories from about 1780 onwards are local guides to towns and villages. Each book usually sets out a history and general description of the district with details of post office, churches, trades, industries and gentry as well as a list of the more substantial inhabitants. Some books arrange people in alphabetical order stating occupations and addresses while others put types of work in alphabetical order and place people in these categories. Directories occasionally contain legends, misprints and outdated statistics so it is as well to check information from other sources. Among the best works are the nineteenth-century directories by Baines, White, Pigot and Kelly. Kelly bought the copyright of the *Post Office London Directory* in 1836 and his publications continue to the present day. Most directories after 1840 are very detailed. There are lists of these books in C. W. F. Goss, *The London Directories 1677-1855* (1932) and J. E. Norton, *Guide to the National and Provincial Directories of England and Wales, excluding London, published before 1856* (1950). The careers of local men may be followed in directories of schools and colleges. P. M. Jacobs prepared a list of *Registers of the Universities, Colleges and Schools of Great Britain and Ireland* (1964). Professional directories referring to clergymen, lawyers and army or navy people are occasionally useful to the researcher, though most date from 1820 onwards.

RECORDS IN PRINT

Important documents are available in printed form. It is usually easier to consult records that are printed rather than in manuscript, partly because any local library can obtain books on loan where it cannot borrow manuscripts. Most books are supplied with indexes of place, subject and people which lessens the burden of research. Evidently, then, the historian always ensures that relevant manuscripts are not in print before he journeys to the archives. He finds this information by consulting the catalogue of a reference library, the multi-volume printed catalogue of the British Museum library and E. L. C. Mullins, *Texts and Calendars* (1958). During the nineteenth century the Record Commissioners published works such as *Valor Ecclesiasticus* of 1535, showing the wealth of English monasteries, dioceses, hospitals and parishes; *Taxatio Ecclesiastica,* taxation of Pope Nicholas IV on the English church, 1291; and rolls and acts of Parliament. The Public Record Office issues calendars of charter, patent, close, fine and liberate rolls; calendars of state papers domestic; and a catalogue of ancient deeds in the public records.

National societies publish documents of general interest. The Harleian Society specialises in heraldic visitations in Tudor and Stuart days; indexes of persons named in chancery cases 1385-1467; Anglican church registers such as those of Canterbury Cathedral from 1564 to 1878 and of many London parishes from Tudor to modern times. Other societies that deal with specific types of documents which may interest the local historian include the Huguenot, Catholic Record, English Place-Name and Selden (legal) Societies.

Local societies publish documents relating to certain areas. Thus the Oxfordshire Record Society produced up to 1956 thirty-seven volumes including *Wheatley Records, 956-1956.* The Northamptonshire Record Society's publications provide a model for would-be editors who should for instance consult *A Descriptive List of the Printed Maps of Northamptonshire* (1948) by Harold Whitaker and

Sir Christopher Hatton's Book of Seals (1950). The book *Texts and Calendars* sets out what calendars and transcripts have been issued by these local societies. Many historical groups however prefer to accept articles on local history showing the fruits of research rather than transcripts of records. Such volumes mention industry, politics, social welfare, education and other aspects of local life as well as nearly every settlement in each county.

HERALDRY AND PEDIGREES

Heraldry helps the local historian to piece together family histories. Coats of arms were granted by the king to specific persons and to their direct descendants. By a process called quartering people added to their own coat of arms the arms of families with whom they had intermarried or from whom they claimed descent. If your local squire seems to exercise undue influence look at his coat of arms for a clue to his relations.

During the years 1530-1688 heralds visited English counties to record pedigrees and the right to bear coats of arms. Original returns are at the College of Arms in London. Many heraldic visitations are in print though versions are none too reliable. For a guide to authentic pedigrees see Sir Anthony Wagner's *Records and Collections of the College of Arms* (1952). Pedigrees of thousands of families appear in Burke's *Landed Gentry,* Debrett's and Burke's *Peerage, Baronetage, Knightage, and Companionage,* and Walford's *County Families.*

REPORTS

The farm historian studies the Board of Agriculture's county series of *General Views* (1793-1817), the annual *Annals of Agriculture* (1784-1815) edited by Arthur Young and the journal of the Royal Agricultural Society (1839 onwards). A locality's public buildings, houses and fortifications are surveyed in reports of the Historical Monuments Commission for England (and similarly for Wales and Scotland). The provisional list of buildings of architectural or historic interest prepared by the Ministry of Housing and Local Government for each district mentions even modest structures. Ancient monuments are subject to reports issued, often in pamphlet form, by the Ministry of Public Buildings and Works. Old parliamentary papers on local affairs are becoming more generally available in libraries either on microcards or as volumes reprinted by the Irish Universities Press.

CHAPTER 4

Fieldwork

'THE Duke of Wellington banqueted in my mine with members of the Royal Society.' My dentist friend beamed as he handed me his industrial archaeology report.

'What, underground?' I enquired.

'Yes. They illuminated the cavern with ten thousand lamps, set wax tapers and flowers on the tables and provided wine and meat in plenty.'

The industrial archaeologist had been studying a Cheshire salt mine.

'I've read old newspaper reports of activity down the mine, and several books mention the place too. It's a pity that no documents exist apart from general figures of production for the whole district printed in parliamentary papers. I spoke to the former manager who'd worked there for forty-five years and he didn't know of anything but was most helpful in describing daily routine and processes.'

My friend's account turned out to be what I should term business history based on printed or manuscript sources rather than an industrial archaeology report from actual survey. In fact the very substantial remains of the works above ground were not investigated at all. Pansheds, storehouses, items of equipment and wharf were not photographed or sketched, probably because everything seemed ruinous and insignificant. This attitude is understandable since tumbled bricks and rusty machines say very little to the man untrained in engineering and industrial processes. But if the investigator had penetrated into what was once the men's lunch room, he would have come upon two small metal boxes that had been used, according to the manager, for at least forty years as additional seats for the apprentices. He might have opened these by force and found account and minute books, letters and plans relating to the works from 1812 onwards. He would next have been referred to the office of the local solicitor, where were preserved other records about the mine and works. He could then have related ground plans, purchase orders for machinery and building accounts to structures remaining on the site, most satisfactorily by calling in an engineer. The study of old industries and other survivals from the past, houses, churches and canals does demand fieldwork; detailed investigation on the site with measuring tape, camera and sketch pad as well as a keen eye to pick out every possible item of significance.

As a fieldworker you will get to know the neighbourhood as it looks today, seek traces of the past under or on the ground and interpret all discoveries to show just what happened years ago. Where possible you will show the reason for such events, the effect the happenings created at the time and their significance for succeeding generations. The fieldworker is an archaeologist as he digs for an ancient burial, a student of vernacular architecture as he tries to follow the various additions to a local farmhouse, an industrial archaeologist as he surveys the colliery engine-house. He plots the position of open-field strips, deserted moated homesteads and boundaries of Saxon estates. Naturally the extent of fieldwork will be governed by the features of your district, the scope of your study and the period of history that interests you. But it is almost impossible to produce a local history unless you are a walker and enjoy the open air. Because as a walker you move slowly and poke around in back alleys, under hedgerows and in ruined mills you are able to discern many points of interest that would escape the motorist. At times of course you will find it an advantage to use a motor car in order to reach outlying areas while a boat for examining navigation works and a light aeroplane for air photography and surveying would not come amiss.

So begins some important but time-consuming work on the site which should never be neglected. Indeed if you live in the district there is no excuse for not keeping your walking shoes handy, your eyes open and your notebook available the whole time. The researcher first enjoys numerous walking trips around his locality to learn where every stick and stone lies, recording all he sees. He does not need to be an historian to recognise that a woodland lies to the west, a waterway to the south, a place of worship here and some tumbled weed-grown bricks there, though eventually he will know that the woodland consists of firs, a recent plantation; that the waterway is a canalised river; that the church is a chapel; the ruined bricks a decayed textile factory. He plots on sketch maps exactly where village houses and streets lie in relation to hills, rivers, meadows, woods, marshes and cultivated fields.

It is important to point out whether the land is mountainous, fen or rolling plain, rich heavy soil or chalky upland, blessed with minerals, harbour or river. A relief model of the area or the Ordnance Survey map with contour lines will be essential for this work. The geological structure of rocks and soil should be known from the various series of geological survey maps (especially the modern one-inch set) and from *Memoirs of the Geological Survey of Great Britain*. At this stage it might be feasible with the aid of maps, conversations with local farmers, reference books and personal walking visits to construct a conducted tour of the area to whet listeners' appetite for the historical explanation.

Every local historian should begin with this description of the lie of the land and face of the parish, employing words, photographs, drawings and maps to enhance the description of fields and woods, church and manor house, homes, workshops and mills, wharves, ponds, rivers and bridges, guildhall, school, gaol and theatre. This first study may take years if the researcher fully surveys the community as it merits and the resulting account can be the most interesting and valuable of all in showing to the knowledgeable historian why, for instance, few people settled in the area prior to the industrial revolution. The work will explain how the pattern of settlement in a region of rich pasture or arable differs from that of the fens, marshes, mountains, dales and heavy forests and the description may lead archaeologists to exclaim, 'Surely here is a perfect site for a new stone age settlement.' Never underestimate the importance of your daily walks and carefully recorded observations.

Now you will again have to look closely at your district, at all features whether a grassy mound on the high common, decaying stones of an old cotton mill, handsome town church or overgrown waterway. Your work at this stage is not merely descriptive but interrogative. What are these structures? What needs did they meet? Who built them? When? What changes of purpose have these places seen? So comes the question behind all local history : by what stages have local people created from the original marsh, heath and woodland the present landscape?

Britain is divided into two geographical zones whose pattern of settlement has been very different. The local historian in the lowland zone, country south and east of a line from Tees to Severn, will be dealing mainly with pleasant rolling land of sandstone, gravel and chalk, not difficult to farm but open to invaders. Here lay compact villages surrounded by the open-field system of agriculture. In the remainder of the country settlement has been sparse, scattered and late. Rocks are old and hard, soil heavy, climate cold and wet, mountains bleak, forests thick, agriculture and cattle raising unrewarding, communication by land and water hazardous. The pattern of settlement growth within the two zones has naturally not been uniform and various sub-regions, lately appropriately named as fen, forest, field and fell parishes, are readily recognised. In the highland zone field patterns, vernacular architecture, farming produce and population growth vary significantly in Devon moorland, Yorkshire dale and Cumberland fell parishes. In the lowland zone fen, forest, arable and pasture (field) regions provide interesting points of comparison. Probably forest or fen villagers would be independent, seldom susceptible to unwelcome influence by landowners, sheriff or church, mobile and sturdily proud of their free if undynamic way of life. Open-field villages may well be more tightly controlled by landed gentry or parson and possibly more faithful to established political and religious doctrine, prosperous if docile and somewhat set in their ways. But the historian studies his own locality to know for sure whether such generalisations are acceptable. During your extensive field trips contrive to bump into farmers, schoolmasters, postmistresses, road-men, people who are able to provide clues about local affairs and history. These men and women often see the landscape with a new eye. 'If I were founding a village that's where I'd build, on the hill by the spring not down here in the marsh.' Investigate. Was the hilltop indeed the original village site? But reminiscences and gossip of local people should be sought, sifted and compared with your own findings. Much will be nonsense or confused memories and can lead to serious mistakes if not thoroughly checked by independent observation.

Much of this work will require archaeological training and knowledge because so little history is in fact recorded in documents. Be very careful, however, because it is easy for the amateur to overlook significant remains through ignorance or while excavating to destroy without making proper records. In many ways it is better to call in an expert from the county or university museum if there is any digging or other disturbance necessary. The trained archaeologist will in any case make a report explaining the origin, growth and decay of the structure. Of course many sites are already the subject of archaeological digs and reports. Read any relevant reports and place the information in your history, acknowledging in footnotes or bibliography the source of your information.

But archaeology is perhaps the wrong word for our purpose, implying the systematic study of what lies buried beneath the ground. Fieldwork is a better word for the work carried out by most local historians : the study and description of men's still-visible handiwork from the beginning until yesterday. Local historians do not as a rule find time or opportunity to undertake digging whereas every student surveys old cottages, industrial undertakings and field tracks.

Visiting museums greatly helps the fieldworker. Social history and archaeology as well as science and industry are well-illustrated in English museums. You can therefore see for yourself artifacts from the past like a spinning jenny or a Saxon dagger or an Elizabethan clock. Moreover the good museum sets objects in their proper context, reconstructing the society that produced and used the tool or trinket. The development of industry, houses, ports, artistic life and much else is traced by skilfully created exhibits. South Kensington Science Museum is one of the richest sources for technological and industrial history. There are preserved very many early machines. The Victoria and Albert Museum shows period furniture, household goods and costume among its varied collection. The Castle Museum at York has a reconstructed Victorian street, corn-mill and prison while at Abbeydale (Sheffield) an industrial hamlet may be viewed dating from the period of Britain's predominance in iron and steel manufacture. For Welsh students the National Museum at Cardiff and the Folk Museum at St. Fagans (Cardiff) try to recreate what life in Wales was like in years gone by. The specialist historian researching on, say, railways would naturally visit the transport museums in Swindon and York, the student of glass manufacture must go to the Pilkington Glass Museum at St. Helens, the farmer to the Museum of English Rural Life at Reading University, the archaeologist to the Ashmolean at Oxford.

Getting back to the land again the fieldworker provides himself with notebook, pencil and rubber. This is equipment at its simplest but is adequate enough for noting the course of a path through formerly open fields and for sketching the shape of a cottage roof. More complicated equipment will be discussed in connection with industrial archaeology but for the time being it is good to concentrate on general observation of the district and on correctly explaining the reason behind what is seen and its meaning. Eric S. Wood's *Field Guide to Archaeology* (1963) should be carried around on expeditions. This book provides a concise description of most field antiquities from megalithic tombs to staddle-stones and a section on the technical and legal aspects of archaeology. A few most useful pages are planned on the pattern : 'if you see . . . it could be . . .'. Important sites in each county are listed.

Whenever a site is surveyed, however cursorily in the first place, it is essential to make notes in the following fashion, leaving blank spaces where information is not yet available.

NOTES ON SITE

1. Precise location of structure (parish and grid reference).
2. Name of site and general type (this need only be a couple of words : Abbeydale industrial hamlet).
3. Dates when built, altered, abandoned.
4. Purpose for which used at various dates in the site's history.
5. Description of remains, exterior and interior, including notes on building material, dimensions, surviving furnishings or machinery. (Drawings and photographs may accompany this description.)
6. Details of any excavations and reports on the site; reason for present investigation.
7. Name and address of site owner.

The information provided in these fieldwork notes should be condensed on to small white cards. Place-names, subjects and names of people are extracted for the alphabetical card index. In this way comes together on one card what has been learned from books, fieldwork and documents. On the card below, source note 84 is a survey undertaken with virtually no digging. The detailed notebook stated among other matters that bricks of the panshed wall seemed to date from 1805 being in appearance exactly like bricks used in two rows of cottages erected in 1804-5 and 1806.

SALTWORKS	
In operation early 19th c —	
from 'Salt in Cheshire'	(52)
Survey reveals pansheds 1963	(84)
Land taxes 1804-31	**(96)**

Fieldwork investigation will provide notes and sketches about all kinds of structures and implements. The local historian needs all these facts and more. But it is essential for him to interpret the material for his reader. What light is thrown on social conditions by these discoveries? What does the presence of a round barrow tell of a man's life in the neighbourhood a couple of millennia ago? Fieldwork is only really worthwhile if as a result our picture of local man's development over the ages is the clearer. Fieldwork is about men and men's handiwork.

SETTLEMENT OF THE LOCALITY

Your first fieldwork project seeks reasons why men founded the settlement in a certain place and not elsewhere. Look for adequate drinking water, the basic and most important requirement of a community. Lack of springs or wells means no sanitation, washing or cooking and soon leads to disease. A town like Old Sarum whose water supply peters out ceases to expand and may be deserted. In some cases water is piped from afar but this is expensive and rare. Water as a means of power or transport is also an important consideration right up to the present century.

Could virgin land easily be cleared? Was the natural terrain damp oak-ash or chalk beech; misty moorland or boggy heath; marsh or sterile thin-soiled furze? Would pioneers need the axe? Or could vegetation be burned? Or is the land such that only advanced tools and methods can make an impression? Is the site sheltered from prevailing winds and storms? Could men create defences against flooding, wild animals, enemy invaders? Did Saxon invaders tend to found towns a mile or so away from any rivers and Roman roads that enabled marauders to attack suddenly? Find out from farmers and geologists whether the soil is fertile in its natural state. Is there sweet grass for animals? Can grain and vegetables, those staples of medieval diet, grow easily? What raw materials are available? Is there timber for building, fuel and fencing? Lime-pits and sand-pits, marl, salt, peat, walling-stone are between them essential for fuel, building, fertilising and cooking. Where could fish be caught to vary the diet and obey the priest's commandment prohibiting meat on Fridays?

Then consider the site in a wider context. Men may have settled in the place with an eye more on the surrounding country than on the soil or raw materials of the town itself. Is the settlement in the heart of rich farmland, at the junction of ancient trade or military roads or by the most convenient river ford? Did the town, lying between two differing economic regions, cater for the exchange of goods? Seaports especially come into this class, connecting hinterland with other ports in Britain or abroad. Large numbers of market towns began life as informal open-air sites, usually at river crossings, where men met to trade. Considerations of fertile ground, sheltered site or building material thus played hardly any part in the founding of such settlements.

But why did men lay out the settlement in a particular fashion and not otherwise? Can the original plan be discovered by stripping away, in the mind's eye, later features? What does the original layout tell about the lives of these pioneers? At this stage it is essential to read two books whose titles are self-explanatory: Joscelyne Finberg, *Exploring Villages* (1958) and W. G. Hoskins, *The Making of the English Landscape* (1955).

A typical community lies round an open space or green near which are grouped vital structures such as the well. Houses around the green look on to an encircling back lane at their rear. Sometimes this plan is defensive in origin, dating from the early days of Saxon invasion but the green may be just an animal stockade, the ring of houses and yards forming a wall.

The street village stretches along a main road, often a busy trade route, where each house owner wants to face the traffic for commercial purposes. Sometimes the local landowner or village meeting may forbid building on the land behind the street, creating a settlement of great length. A road leading to a bridge, monastery or castle usually attracts houses.

A village whose houses are scattered almost certainly results from individual squatting on common pasture, mountain side, drained fen or in woodland clearing at any date from the seventh century onwards. Some industrial places in Lancashire grew in this haphazard way during the years 1680-1820. But the rather modest dwellings though physically separated are not normally isolated farmsteads. They form a definite community connected by tracks. This type of settlement somewhat resembles on the map the scattered villages created at the time of enclosure of open fields when farmers moved out of the old village centre to build in their own compact holding of fields. Large houses and outbuildings, erected very nearly at one period, strewn across a hedged or walled landscape characterise such an enclosure-period village.

Most settlements were not laid out according to a master plan. Settlers added house to house as need arose. So meandering streets that still survive date from earliest Saxon times. Is there any rhyme or reason behind the meanderings? Why do lanes bend, seemingly inexplicably, or halt suddenly? What obstacles like castle, church, burial mound, stream or marsh diverted these streets?

Town planning demands that one man or corporation own the whole site and possess sufficient wealth and foresight to carry through the project. There must be reasons for the planning of a new town : port facilities, a market or fair centre, a strategic situation, proximity to minerals or manufactures. Local lords founded Hedon in the East Riding because Hedon Haven lay only two miles from the wide Humber estuary. Ships sailed right to the town quay. The neat grid-iron pattern of streets usually indicates a new town either from the years 1066-1300 or from the modern industrial period. A useful county gazetteer with a list of source material is provided by M. W. Beresford's *New Towns of the Middle Ages* (1967).

BOUNDARIES

Community boundaries are among the oldest features still discernible. The earliest bounds became necessary when neighbouring communities disputed ownership of grass and woodland. From such outlying areas villagers acquired timber and food for their animals. So people determined upon prominent and clear features for boundaries to follow or dug what now appear as sunken trackways between banks of earth spoil. How old are the boundaries of your town? Can these be traced back to medieval or Saxon times? If so, why do they follow such and such a course? What features like stream, round barrow, valley or ridge-way would be visible to the men of the Saxon community? Why do boundaries make curious detours and zigzags? Can they have followed edges of fields that were already ploughed? Or do they take in a corn-mill or a detached field belonging to the manorial lord? Is it possible that a Roman road or more ancient trade route delineates the edge of the settlement even though no track now remains evident to the fieldworker's eyes? Is there a Saxon charter, manorial extent or village survey describing the bounds of the town at any date prior to the introduction of adequate maps? The county archivist or reference librarian will be able to answer this question. Such documents should be read in transla-tion alongside an Ordnance Survey map. The bounds must of course be walked on foot in order to recognise the features mentioned in manu-scripts : 'from the ford over cotebrook to the merestone at the head of the valley, then west past slochtrenhus to the lane between the banks, past the oak tree to the ditch . . .'

DESERTION AND DECAY

Village sites and shapes alter to suit men's need. Houses that once were conveniently situated for farmers and traders may eventually be abandoned after the enclosure of open fields, silting up of a river or the opening of a new market. For such reasons Roman Southampton was abandoned and the Saxons moved west of the Itchen. Medieval Southampton is still further west. If a parish church stands alone away from any settlement it could be that the original village lay near the church. But why did families abandon their old homes and desert their village? The answer is as often found by observation of the landscape as by searching documents.

Look for traces of the two thousand deserted villages of England, destroyed for royal forests and parks (from 1066), by Cistercian monks seeking solitude (1120-1200), after economic and climatic deterioration, by the Black Death (1310-1420) and by sheep farmers during the century 1450-1550. Study M. W. Beresford, *The Lost Villages of England* (1954); M. W. Beresford and J. G. Hurst, *Deserted Medieval Villages* (1971); and the aerial survey by M. W. Beresford and J. K. S. St Joseph, *Medieval England* (1958). In the first two books are county lists of lost villages with short histories of the sites. Communities have been destroyed more recently by landowners' landscaping (1660-1790) or when local industries such as lead and coal suffered reverses (1880-1960). Many rural settlements have been slowly decaying since 1850 because people have gone to the towns while farms have been mechanised and the labour force reduced.

On the ground it is sometimes possible, when sunlight and grass co-operate, to recognise deserted sites in parcels of rough pasture. The medieval house and croft site appears as a raised platform surrounded by sunken boundary ditch. Only in stone country can any house foundations be expected, as at Gainsthorpe in Lincolnshire. The town street, back lanes and tracks to fields and neighbouring villages show up on air photographs. The church, built in stone wherever possible, with the manor house are seen without excavation. Old kilns, mill-races, mounds on which windmills stood and fishponds survive though usually overgrown with bushes and nettles. It is these ditches and hillocks that can all too readily be labelled as castle hills and moats (and of course vice versa) unless observation is keen and backed up by documents. At least one village fishpond has in a local history been upgraded as an iron age fort, despite its most inconvenient siting for defence or offensive action. A deserted village site regularly bears a name like town field, though this was also the usual name given to the first of a settlement's open fields. The old place-name may survive relating to what is now just an enclosed field. The tithe map is a useful source for such field names. Alternatively a farmhouse, constructed to take in the village lands after depopulation, may retain the village name.

New Towns and Villages

Comparatively few new villages appear after the period of Domesday. A growing population therefore won land from wastes within existing parish boundaries. Improved techniques pushed ploughed areas to the margin of cultivable land. By 1350 some villages had reached their limits of expansion, exploiting poor scrub and throwing out isolated squatters' houses or hamlets (often called Newton). Pennine valley communities especially found difficulty in cultivating land far uphill. Houses tended to spread irregularly along the valley floor over a considerable distance. New towns of the middle ages and industrial period provide instructive study. The local historian tries to find out if any development on the site had taken place prior to the new town's foundation. He wants to know the reasons behind the appearance of a settlement at that period and on that site.

Markets

Some men deserted old villages when a market developed nearby. Markets frequently were held in churchyards (prior to 1285 when church authorities forbade it) before traders moved stalls on to a convenient piece of open country. Others doubtless took place on village greens or in main streets. Stalls were converted into permanent shops with dwellings attached, filling up the empty space, though there was resistance to such encroachments where the market was mainly for sheep and cattle. Animals needed much space, the problem being solved by opening a new cattle market away from the town centre. Building on the old market explains why in some towns two main streets, separated narrowly by an island of shops, run parallel. In other towns a maze of alleys occupies the former open space. Can you trace the bounds of the original open green or market?

Markets in open country attracted people. During the twelfth century communities appear as at Ramsey Abbey's new town of St Ives lying between the old village of Slepe and the abbey gates near a new river bridge. Next comes the paved market-place with adjoining church. Since the townsfolk remain members of the original parish in whose territory their new market lies, the church is a mere chapel of ease without burial ground, at least till quite recent times. Look for such a church, enclosed by lanes and houses, near a market-place. Explain the reason for the course of the boundaries of the new town.

Markets have of course decayed as traders moved elsewhere perhaps to a larger centre or to one situated nearer a busy road, waterway or railway. Directories of the period 1780-1860 indicate that hundreds of what are today quiet villages had then a weekly market and one or two fairs. Since markets in the midlands and south had been established generally before 1340, the period 1340-1780 saw the decay of many other market settlements. These lost markets are sometimes recognised, as Professor A. Everitt suggests, when local property is held more or less equally by resident freeholders rather than by a large magnate; where nonconformity in Victorian days was strong; and where small industries like basket-making or pottery continued up to about 1914. Occasionally there survives the plain market cross or at least its stone base and shaft; an open green once used for the market; and place-names like Market Hill, Cheapside or Chipping meaning 'cheap' or 'shop', Cornhill and Bere or Barley hill where grain was kept dry prior to sale. The market may be surveyed in the papers of the royal commission on market rights and tolls (1888-91).

SUBURBS AND SLUMS

Distinguish the various suburbs created by expansion of the old town. An ancient town centre may include parish church, castle and market-place, though the two last named sometimes lie just outside town bounds. A second market, granted by charter on a different day from the first market, is founded in a new suburb. If you can date the various church buildings in a town you have an idea of the order in which new sections of the town were built. Many suburbs were founded when wealthy families moved from the centre, when industry needed room or if water supply for power proved inadequate in the old town.

The building of houses and shops on every piece of land in the town centre is most noticeable during the periods 1160-1340,

1700-1890. Houses acquire four or five storeys. Alleyways stretch back over former gardens. This becomes very necessary nearly everywhere because it is impossible in practice to destroy open fields and pastures and so abolish common rights and the farmer's livelihood. In some cases great landowners objected to town expansion and refused to grant building leases.

Despite in-filling, towns remained for centuries very compact. It was the age of steam, bringing industry back from remote valleys to towns, that created slums after 1810. Manufacturers settled down near canals that brought coal and took off products cheaply. Canals ran round old towns, sometimes on flat low-lying ground, so workshops and factory houses were built in that neighbourhood. Sanitary conditions became appalling. The word slum perhaps means foul mire. Can you trace deteriorating workmanship, smaller floor area, common privies and water pumps in houses put up in 1810-45? Do Victorian streets follow lines of strips and tracks in the newly enclosed former open fields as at Nottingham? The creation of a slum is illustrated in the sketch maps of Pit Hey (plate 1). This land was enclosed from the open fields about 1710 when surveyors also laid out the straight new road to Grange Farm to the north. In 1785 the owner of the farm sold Pit Hey to a local manufacturer who in 1790 erected for himself a house adjoining the road. In 1792 this man disposed of most of the remainder of the enclosure to a carpenter and speculative builder, and the latter put up eight houses with cellar and attic dwellings and a tavern by means of a mortgage in 1794. The same man built ten four-storey houses with backyard privies and cellar premises and, for his son's use, a small textile factory. This took place by 1820. By this time a new street of houses stretched to the town centre. About 1830 the property passed by sale to a tanner who extended the factory, converting part into single-roomed dwellings, and turned six of the houses into back-to-back homes. A builder purchased the manufacturer's residence which was no longer in pleasant surroundings and put up a four-storey block containing eighteen tiny tenements in its place. By 1841 Pit Hey now called William's Court was crowded with houses and people, a depressing alley of poverty as the census returns of 1841 and 1851 testify.

CHAPTER 5

Some features of the locality

NEARLY every parish in the country should be able to provide examples of at least three or four of the features mentioned in this chapter. It is not always easy to recognise a structure for what it is. Indeed the majority of historical remains can hardly be seen at all without excavation. Nevertheless the effort should be made to record what survives in sketches, words or photographs. Even if the features cannot at the moment be explained the researcher hopes that future historians will read his report and come to some conclusion. In the chapter below only a very few structures are mentioned and these are summarily dealt with in the hope that the researcher will read for himself specialised studies on features that interest him. If work is to be undertaken on remains dating from before the thirteenth century or thereabouts the wise student consults first with an expert from his local museum and also reads widely on archaeological methods and discoveries. As a start he reads J. and C. Hawkes, *Prehistoric Britain* (1947), a clear and concise account, and O. G. S. Crawford, *Archaeology in the Field* (1953). The Ordnance Survey's *Field Archaeology: some Notes for Beginners* (fourth edition, 1963) is most useful, not least for its reading lists. He should also buy I. A. Richmond's *Roman Britain* (1955) and Dorothy Whitelock's *The Beginnings of English Society* (1952).

FIELDS AND ENCLOSURES

Early stone age people were nomadic hunters and have left virtually nothing for us to find. But before 3000 BC the first farmers came to Britain. Stock-breeders and wheat-growers, they still used only flint tools and settled in high chalk or oolite fertile naturally drained lightly wooded areas such as Wiltshire and the Cotswolds. There may be traces of their stock enclosures or assembly places. Two or three concentric circles of banks and ditches are crossed by causeways. These camps are not usually hill-forts.

Invasions after 1900 BC brought an energetic people who introduced copper and then bronze and so settled in highland areas such as Cornwall in search of tin and copper. These bronze age people traded and farmed. They built round cottages and farmhouses, the remains of which are seen in such areas as Yorkshire and Cornwall. With dry-stone walls backed by earth and pebbles, cottages are small one-roomed places associated with the nearby rectangular enclosures for cattle raising and crops. The people themselves preferred to settle in upland valleys, the Yorkshire Wolds and Salisbury Plain where soil and woodland were not too heavy.

Successive waves of invaders introduced iron in the sixth century BC as well as trading links with the European mainland. These people were farmers. Their fields are rectangular, possibly to allow for cross-ploughing. Air photographs reveal Celtic fields in areas like the chalk uplands that have never been intensively ploughed since the disruption of ancient society about AD 450. Cultivation terraces or lynchets may be noticed on sloping ground on the upper and lower sides of ancient fields that climb the hill. Boundary banks limit these fields on sides running uphill. Many lynchets date from later centuries. Thus Anglian settlers in the highlands have left ploughing strips ranged in terraces along the dales. These follow contours and cross modern stone walls.

The Romans completed the task of integration by taking Britain into the empire in AD 43. Towns, villas and roads were built. But the highland zone was never properly subdued and here are found many military camps alongside enclosed fields. In the peaceful country-side British farming continued, centred on the farmstead (several structures in a walled compound) and surrounding enclosures. In the highland zone on the other hand men lived in small hamlets of stone huts. Some Roman villas may be built on the site of older farmsteads but may stand in hitherto untouched districts. Villas often lie on sloping ground facing south or east, near water, sheltered from winds and on light soil. They are revealed when farmers or builders disturb the ground, throwing up a litter of potsherds, rusty nails, tesserae from masonry pavements, tiles and central heating flues. Air photographs reveal square rooms grouped round a courtyard.

From the fourth to eleventh centuries of our era invasions brought Anglo-Saxons and Norsemen to a Britain that was in the main still an untouched wilderness. These new people preferred lowland farm-ing and hitherto unsettled river valleys but pressure of population sent many into the hills. Settlers sometimes occupied new sites, some-times took over old towns. The former inhabitants, the Celts, survived in certain areas so that agricultural pursuits went on, possibly uninter-rupted, from iron age to middle ages. Until about 1780 agriculture provided the basis of wealth. Men pushed back the bounds of forests and heaths at first in most districts of the lowlands by a system of communal ploughing in open fields. They grew grain and vegetables. They kept sheep and cows. Wool became a source of good income in areas like the Cotswolds and East Anglia. Some communities grew rich but others were destroyed to make way for sheep runs. Monks who pioneered the cultivation of desolate wilds like Yorkshire and the Wye valley also razed villages to the ground in the interests of extensive farming.

Beyond the bounds of most towns even in Victorian times lay open fields, pastures and wastes. Because the wealth of many places came almost entirely from agriculture it is important to identify, for instance, the pattern of open-field farming in your area. This is most readily seen in the midlands where the distinctive traces of ridge-and-furrow still show up. In air photographs these sweep across modern additions to the landscape like hedges and railways. *The Open Fields* (third edition, 1967) by C. S. and C. S. Orwin tells the agricultural history of Laxton in Nottinghamshire, a place that has kept its old system of farming to the present century.

Villagers created the open fields as they cleared forest or heath. Working alongside each other through much of the farming year to produce arable crops, they created intermingled unfenced strips of land. This is enclosure from the waste for arable, meadow and pasture. As such it is looked on as a sign of progress and well-being. The peasant in ploughing his strip or acre had thrown soil towards the centre, eventually creating a high ridge. The strips vary in size according to the lie of the land and nature of the soil. A bundle of several people's strips all running in the same direction made up a furlong or *cultura* (possibly surrounded by a low bank). Wide green balks or occupation roads (best shown up by air photographs) give access to all strips. Dozens of furlongs compose one open field, with a fence occasionally all round the outside but none round individual holdings. If you plot all the ridges and furrows or strips on a map you will gain an idea of how the area of arable was slowly extended over the centuries, furlong by furlong.

Enclosure of open arable fields has continued from medieval times. Evidence of the revolution is traced by deserted villages; newly created parks and sheep runs; neatly hedged, privately owned fields, five to ten acres in extent. Hedgerows of full-grown hawthorn, stone walling, wooden fences and gates, ditches and field drains of brick are also significant. Enclosure from about 1730 creates new roads with verges on both sides some fourteen feet wide bordered with trees and hedges. These run straight across country to new farms situated way out in the enclosures. Farm names follow the news. Around 1770 they will be Quebec, Belle Isle and New York. Old yeoman houses in the town centre become rows of workers' cottages especially in the period 1760-1850.

FORESTS AND PARKS

It is instructive to work out the chronology of forest clearing wherever possible. The latest enclosures will be small irregularly shaped fields on the edge of high moor or undrained marsh, and such names as Brackenthwaite, the bracken clearing, provide clues to what has happened. Isolated barns and monastic granges or store-houses may indicate areas of comparatively late clearances, possibly from after about 1320 when pressure of population in old settlements eased and farmers felt no urge to move their homes to remote spots. Cistercian monks of course deliberately chose desolate uninhabited regions for their abbeys, farms and granges from the twelfth century. The drainage of fens is marked by ditches and dikes. Roads on the top of these banks still meander from hamlet to hamlet above surrounding low flat fields.

Not all land was cleared because wild country sheltered beasts for hunting. The king indeed created royal forests as hunting preserves and took wide areas of arable and pasture as well as woodland. Inhabitants were subject to harsh laws which in some respects retarded economic growth in those districts. Interminable medieval legal disputes and detailed perambulations of forests from about 1230 until Victorian days may be studied in chancery and exchequer records in the Public Record Office.

Wealthy people enclosed with massive hedge, bank and ditch extensive tracts of countryside for parks, destroying communities if need be. A park is an enclosure where the lord kept deer for sport and meat. The history of parks is found in E. Shirley's *English Deer Parks* (1867). Usually created under royal licence the medieval park might enclose former waste heath or woodland at some distance from settled districts, though many founded in the centuries before the Black Death actually encroached on arable, pasture and villages. Pressure of population eased after 1340 and landowners extended parks without much difficulty. Tudor and Georgian squires purchased these properties but, finding the area too small, the hunting unsatisfactory or the view imperfect, decided to alter the landscape. They therefore removed villages, planted avenues, dug lakes and erected sham ruins. Some parks still survive in one form or another, though others have been returned to farming use or sold as building land. In old parks the historian could come upon fossilised features from centuries ago like Roman road, deserted village or castle mound that in ordinary circumstances would be ploughed out or built over. The ha-ha or deer leap is a low wall and ditch round the garden of a hall to prevent animals straying from park to garden or round an entire park to trap animals in the park enclosure. This type of boundary does not interrupt the view from the house. Ha-has have been built since medieval times and ought not to be mistaken for castle mounds, moats or other fortifications.

Estates and Demesne

To discover the whereabouts and boundaries of Saxon estates is a skilled but rewarding task. A boundary bank and ditch though well-disguised usually survive in the shape of a sunken lane or hollow way between hedges. More recent hedges abut but do not cross these bounds. The historian may follow the suggestion of Dr Max Hooper of the Nature Conservancy and estimate the date of hedges and banks by counting the number of species of shrub in the hedge and expecting one species for each century of unmanaged growth. Saxon boundaries sometimes explain the origin of later parish or county frontiers. More important, they indicate early settlement and the beginning of the field pattern of the district. As an aid to locating estates the researcher should study Saxon land charters that mention boundaries : 'from the stone on along the highway to the ditch, thence down to Wealdenesford, thence on to the hollow way, thence down the brook to Hunburgefleot . . .' These features and names might be recognised in today's landscape or on Ordnance Survey maps. The location of charters is given in the Royal Historical Society's *Anglo-Saxon Charters* (1968).

The lord of the manor's house and lands, the demesne, should be identified. This farm ought to be the largest in the village, naturally occupying rich land. In open-field districts the lands will be scattered throughout the township and difficult to recognise, but the chief house may still show old work. The farm name too normally contains such elements as great, church, hall, court, barton or town. Ancient farm boundaries coincide with parish boundaries, edge of woodland, streams or ditches but are recognised only after many walking expeditions and the thoughtful study of Ordnance Survey maps.

Eventually the lord's house may even become a pleasant country hall or famous mansion. The architectural history is worth investigating. Which owners could afford alterations and why did they consider these worthwhile? Does this mean that local rents produced a good income or was there money from other sources? Did the owners follow London tastes in building or employ craftsmen and designers from the neighbourhood? Books on the architecture of halls are numerous. Most large houses are individually discussed in Professor N. Pevsner's *Buildings of England* series, in the reports of the Royal Commission on Historical Monuments and in lists of buildings of architectural and historic interest issued by the Ministry of Housing and Local Government.

TOMBS AND TEMPLES

Most common and noticeable of field monuments are what appear on Ordnance Survey maps as tumuli. These are bronze age earth or stone round barrows or burial mounds. They are most readily recognised in chalk or stone country where the plough has not been so destructive as in clay and sand regions. There is an account of some of the twenty thousand barrows in the country in P. Ashbee's *The Bronze Age Round Barrow in Britain* (1960). A barrow is a mound shaped like an inverted bowl usually with a ditch and occasionally a surrounding bank. The bermed barrow may have considerable distance, called the berm or ledge, between mound and ditch. Disc barrows and others that have been nearly ploughed out are very flat but the berm and ditch should leave traces for careful investigation. Round barrows date from 1800 BC to Saxon times. Their excavation is the job of archaeologists and may reveal rich grave goods as well as a miniature 'house of the dead' ring of posts. Beauty, symmetry and size of barrows with associated objects indicate a high level of civilisation and organisation. In some cases archaeologists have traced the houses where builders of barrows lived and worked and so we gain an idea of the way of life of these distant people. It is possible to recognise the trade roads, between areas where the bronze age people settled most thickly, as surviving paths and banks or as field marks on air photographs.

Neolithic (new stone age) tombs date from 2800 BC to 1900 BC.

They are of earth, chalk rubble or pebbles depending on the district. The building material is heaped up to form a long cairn or barrow, flanked by a ditch, with higher broader end eastwards. Burial is by inhumation. Sometimes bodies were stored on the site till the cairn could be built up, and many barrows therefore contain dozens of bodies. Earthen long barrows survive in Wessex, Lincolnshire and Yorkshire. But more numerous are the stone-built long or round chambered barrows. Walled and roofed in stone with entrance and passageway, these megalithic (great stone) tombs have to be raised before burials take place but allow successive or collective burials over a period of time. Burial chambers, occupying the eastern end, have usually long since been plundered.

From about 2500 BC to 1500 BC men constructed sanctuaries such as Stonehenge and Woodhenge possibly for ritual purposes in connection with burial mounds. An embankment with interior ditch ordinarily surrounds a setting of posts or stones. Such monuments are greatly embellished during the bronze age after 1900 BC. Some isolated standing stones may date from this neolithic period especially in the highland zone, indicating settlement in nearby dales and possibly marking tribal meeting points.

CHURCHES

The parish church is more often than not the largest and oldest of local buildings and the story of its original foundation, building, alterations and rebuilding reflects town history. In other words a settlement that has always remained backward will usually possess but a mean church whereas a place that has prospered at some particular period may boast of a fine church dating from that time. The first church in the settlement could result from the missionary enterprise of a holy man or monastery, and in such a case the foundation need not mean that a large thriving community existed thereabouts. A visionary builds a church in strange quiet spots. On the other hand a church normally appears because villagers feel prosperous enough to support one. A pre-conquest church would generally be situated in an important military, commercial or religious centre, perhaps in a pagan earthwork or Roman camp, near a holy well, on a burial mound or at a crossroads. The historian should work out which churches in the district were founded first. Original or mother churches from Celtic or Saxon times served wide areas, and their site is sometimes marked by a place-name ending in *church* or *minster*. They are almost always mentioned in Domesday and remain centres of large parishes in medieval times. I can see the tower of one such church for miles directly ahead of me as I plod across field paths from outlying settlements in the parish, following in all probability the footsteps of Saxon villagers. A church that is not one of these very ancient centres will be a daughter chapel of ease and be founded almost certainly at a period when the population of the subordinate settlement grew quite large. The dedication of the church gives clues about history. Thus Celtic Christians adored St Michael the archangel and churches dedicated to this saint might have histories stretching back to pre-Saxon days. Devotion to St Helen seems to date from crusading times. A church dedicated to St Thomas of Canterbury may have been first built at any time after the late twelfth century though the dedication of an older church could easily have been changed. That must be worked out by excavation, for traces of the older building should still be evident.

A cross antedating all religious buildings and set up on a holy or central site marks many of the sites where Christianity started locally. Carved with symbols, designs and even words that enable an approximate dating to be hazarded, the cross could now be built into a churchyard wall, used as a farm gatepost or employed as a stream bridge. Celtic and Saxon crosses, richly decorated with carving, should be sought possibly in the county museum as evidence of early Christianity in the district. The medieval market or crossroads cross still stands on its pedestal in quiet villages and towns. It is of stone or timber and very plain. The font may be as old as any cross, and could be the oldest object in the district, at least above ground. Because the right to baptise was prized by early communities, parishioners carefully preserved the symbol of that right. Celtic, Saxon and Norman fonts survive to indicate that settlement of the area was thriving at those times.

The historian needs a concise but accurate structural history of the church. It should not be too difficult to find one already in print, perhaps in Professor N. Pevsner's study in his *Buildings of England* series, in the *Victoria County History* or in any general architectural guide. The chancel where the altar is sheltered should be an old part of the church. Originally the priest lived over or beside the chancel. Villagers have long been responsible for erecting the nave for their own comfort and use. Since they paid the bill they often employed the wide covered area for secular purposes. A medieval guild possibly built the side aisle as a place where its meetings could be conveniently held. People met in the porch to make contracts about marriage and disposal of lands. They fortified the tower as a defence against invaders especially in the north country.

The style and various building dates of churches is a reasonably sure guide to local history. A poor moorland parish is served by a low, dark and undecorated building. A prosperous fourteenth-century town added a delicate spire to its church, perhaps copying Salisbury cathedral. Most towers date from the fourteenth and fifteenth centuries when wealth especially from wool allowed a good deal of alteration to churches. Local styles are very evident in towers and spires. Many Devonshire towers tend to look tall and slender and have an enclosed staircase clearly visible at one corner. A number of Gloucestershire towers boast of decorated battlements and pinnacles, tall windows, arcading and buttresses. Where wood is plentiful belfries exhibit carved woodwork, as in Essex. When prosperous villagers rebuilt their church they often raised the nave roof high in order to accommodate clerestory windows that caught the daylight. The perpendicular gothic style with soaring columns and windows, handsome towers, gilded rood screens and carving in wood and stone dates from 1380 to 1540. This most magnificent architecture appears in the south-west, Suffolk and the Cotswolds, despite the ravages of the Black Death, because of local wealth from tin or wool. Some churches are constructed with materials like Caen stone brought from abroad while skilled masons from afar worked on the project and left their individual marks in the stonework. Occasionally a mason's name and the location of his other buildings may be learned from recognising his mark. Such men could use local building material of no great beauty or strength to produce magnificent tracery, arches, buttresses and quoins. Payment for this work should be recorded in vestry accounts, or in the estate muniments of the landowner that financed the project. L. F. Salzman discusses the work of masons and other builders in *Building in England down to 1540* (1952).

Church furnishing reflects village or town outlook in the matter of religion. Obviously much dates only from the last restoration or change of religious opinion. A medieval church might be without pews but its altar would be imposing and its plastered walls covered with coloured paintings. In the sixteenth century the altar was removed and stained glass windows smashed by zealous reformers. Any decorated medieval seats could be destroyed to make room for very plain box-like pews. Conservative parishes managed to ignore the worst excesses of Protestants and furnishing may well survive even now from medieval times. Villagers in the seventeenth century usually moved the pulpit and reading desk into the centre of the church in front of the communion table. Georgian churches seem austere with box pews and gallery rather like a town hall meeting room. Victorians restored many old churches according to their own ideas of what medieval gothic looked like, but their efforts are some-times sufficiently careful to lead the cursory visitor astray in his dating. Churches affected by the Tractarian movement would elevate the altar, push the pulpit to one side, add decorated pews, place coloured glass in the windows and lay on the floor tiles of medieval design. There are many good guide books for the local church historian including M. D. Anderson's *Looking for History in British Churches* (1951).

One church has been studied and its features noted in the follow-ing note form.

c. 1080-1100	Church in Domesday; base of tower, south doorway, font, part of cross.
1280-90	Chancel, north wall (base) of nave.
c. 1320	Second stage of tower, nave, roof, wall painting.
1689-95	Altar, pulpit, floor paving.
1780	Pews, gallery, spire on tower.

It is obvious that this village prospered after the conquest, possibly because of the energy of the new resident lord. The forty years 1280-1320 saw a rising standard of living perhaps on account of the wool trade, another new lord and a quickly increasing population. Then, if the church development is any guide, there is stagnation until the period of industrial revolution when population growth necessitated a gallery and new pews. The community probably did not thrive in the nineteenth century because it could not afford or at least did not desire a fashionable restoration. Church features suggest the course of local history as satisfactorily as any other type of evidence but the resulting account must be checked in docu-ments as far as possible.

BURIALS

From the end of the Roman period till about 1550 most graves are unmarked. Pagan Saxons at times used old and new barrows, burying with the body weapons, ornaments and household goods.

But Christian graves are often impossible to date because of the lack of grave goods and headstone. None the less the presence of a cemetery helps to locate a settlement site and to show its century of origin. Burials demand expert investigation of course. On top of the ground the historian can readily survey the graveyards of churches and chapels mainly to read monumental inscriptions from Tudor times onwards. Gravestones usually give information about village surnames, dates of birth and death, possibly places of residence, occupations and achievements. Surnames reveal the original homes and jobs of some families and their study leads to some knowledge of migration. Each area has its own typical names and a strange surname stands out. In one churchyard I noticed names like Boston, Wilton and Lancaster indicating that these families had once belonged to those towns but had migrated at some period probably after 1350. I noted on later stones European surnames indicating a substantial immigration after 1815 to local works. Tablets, carvings and effigies inside the church reveal biographies of local worthies, occupation, armour and clothing. Medieval craftsmen loved to carve likenesses of villagers in stone and wood about the church. Among the most valuable of monuments are the brasses on floors and walls. Because the material is latten, a brass-like metal, detail is normally very fine. Portraits are regarded as quite accurate and show styles of dress and armour of the period. Inscriptions name the deceased person. The best brasses are medieval. There is an account of this type of monument in Mill Stephenson's *A List of Monumental Brasses in the British Isles* (1926).

Casual burials outside churchyards need not be very ancient. Stranded travellers, criminals from a crossroads gallows, soldiers from a skirmish and outlaws may be buried in this way up to, say 1750, especially if the parish church is a distance away. Look for shreds of clothing, coins, signs of decapitation, binding of hands behind the back and bullet wounds as dating aids.

COINS

The study of coins may yield relevant pointers for local history if interpreted correctly. Coinage has been used in this country for over two thousand years and the discovery of coins in your locality could indicate settlement contemporary with the coinage. The standard reference book is by G. C. Brooke *English Coins from the Seventh Century to the Present Day* (third edition, 1950). If you find a hoard of eighth-century Saxon coins you may be able to prove that the Saxons settled locally, or there might just have been a traders' route nearby. Do the coins belong to a local ruler?

Private coinage tells an interesting story. When money is issued by local lords spiritual and temporal in the middle ages this indicates the weakness of royal authority. But during the industrial revolution manufacturers issued tokens on account of the shortage of small coins of the realm. These tokens were exchanged in the company's shops for food and drink but often circulated over a wide area when the firm was famous and soundly financed. The pictures and inscriptions on these tokens are remarkably clear. The penny token issued by Priest Field Furnaces in 1811 perfectly illustrates the works in Staffordshire.

FORTIFICATIONS

Iron age defended sites, mainly hill-forts, are widely distributed. Some structures lying on rocky promontories or on the edge of marshes need walls on only a couple of sides but most stand on hills, surrounded by one or more embankments to enclose from one to dozens of acres. In the lowland zone grass-covered banks, ditches almost filled with soil and in-turned entrances of forts may be visible especially from the air. But in the highlands stone walls and rock-hewn ditches formed the defences which should present fewer problems of recognition though in fact stones nowadays are tumbled in confusion about the site. Few forts are earlier than 450 BC and a significant number probably date from after the Belgic invasion of around 75 BC.

Cross-country stretches of bank and ditch were built for defence and as boundaries in the centuries before the commencement of our era. On Stockbridge Down (Hampshire) a continuous bank separates grazing land from a system of enclosed cultivated fields. The Belgic people opened up new areas of the country with their heavy wheeled plough, creating estates that called for delineation. The Belgae also settled river valleys and founded thriving small towns and ports which were later inhabited by the Romans and English as regional capitals. They took Britain culturally and economically into Europe.

Roman fortifications are so soundly constructed that hundreds of sites are excavated and well documented. Forts, permanent bases of legions and units, are rectangular with rounded corners and gates in each side. Stone walls are backed by earth ramparts and fronted by ditches. Corner towers, a shrine and headquarters built of stone stand in an important fort while bank and ditch seem sufficient for marching camps. The Romans generally protected entrances to forts with traverses.

The Saxons probably built strong forts only from the period of the Danish invasion in the ninth century. Alfred the Great and Edward the Elder constructed forts at such places as Wareham and Cricklade. Banks and ditches have usually been destroyed by later development so both Saxon and Danish works are somewhat difficult to trace on the ground though literary sources indicate where archaeological remains might be expected.

The earliest Norman castles from the century after the conquest have left only the earth *motte* or mound surrounded by a ditch and, possibly, an embanked enclosure called a bailey, tower and stockade. Castles are confused with barrows or windmill mounds if the investigator does not carefully search for remains of the bailey, access road, the well and the levelled top of the mound. Later stone castles are excellently documented in standard histories partly because royal licences were necessary for fortifications. For any type of royal building whether castle, gaol, bridge or monastery information is to be sought in H. M. Colvin's *History of the King's Works* (1963- in course of publication).

Moated homesteads and halls are very numerous. Usually built in the period 1220-1420 and abandoned by 1580, the rectangular sites may now lie amidst open countryside. Only the weed-ridden moat might be visible if the house was of timber. The moat served as defence against men and as a source of fish. There is an interesting discussion on 'Moated settlements in England' by F. V. Emery in *Geography*, volume 47 (1962).

Forts have been built to counter threats of invasion by Philip of Spain (1588) or the two Napoleons (1802-70). Trenches, pits and mounds have been constructed by the army and these should not be labelled as remnants of medieval castles or halls. Architectural follies and sham castles built in parks or on hills to please the eyes of Georgian or Victorian gentlemen ought soon to be identified for what they are.

Townsfolk erected walls round their settlements whenever possible until late in medieval times. Walls protected homes, workshops and markets but also restricted the spread of streets into the country and encouraged men to overcrowd crofts in the town centre. It is important to know when the town was first walled, at what date builders ventured beyond the town limits, the density of housing and population within the walls and the reasons for the decay of the fortification.

ROADS

The study of local roads usually tells something of the economic development of the district. Pre-Roman trackways like the Harroway and Icknield way on ridges of open country served as trade routes between river valleys or different economic regions. Roman roads were trade and military routes and are marked on the Ordnance Survey map or described in such works as I. D. Margary's *Roman Roads in Britain* (1955-7). Roads did not generally follow ancient tracks because so many Roman centres were new towns. They therefore headed straight across country and are remembered today in the lines of main roads, parish boundaries, hedges and field paths. Their foundations, paving and side ditches have not entirely disappeared even now.

Medieval ways were often entirely local in purpose, leading to fields, mill, meadows, church and pastures. A number wound further afield, like the green lanes built for such specific purposes as linking a village to its lord's court or a grange to a monastery. Salt ways and drove roads were not usually specially planned for salters and cattle-men who moved along old ways and through long usage gave their names to the tracks. Pack-horse roads cross wild moors and climb steep hills, their route marked by pillars or crosses and by flagstone bridges. Some tracks whose twists and turns seem puzzling today may once have wound to a now deserted village or to its open fields. Old ways may be discovered by noting the course of parish boundaries along hedgerows and paths.

Not many new main roads were laid down in England after Roman times until the present century. Medieval roads often followed local tracks or Roman routes and even roads constructed by turnpike trusts in the years 1730-1830 did not ordinarily break fresh ground save to cut out long detours, cross drained marshes and avoid steep gradients. Turnpike records are reasonably complete so there should be no confusion between new stretches of turnpike and ancient main roads. Post-enclosure lanes, however, tend to be deliberately planned and bounded by ditches, grass verges, walls or hedges whereas medieval tracks followed wide courses over open land, altering position as ruts grew deep and wet. The route of all roads should be plotted with the help of contemporary manuscripts or printed maps. In John Ogilby's *Britannia* of 1675 (facsimile edition, 1939) is a survey of all main and cross roads then in use. John Cary and Daniel Paterson drew maps of roads during the great coaching era, 1770-1820. For a list of useful maps and guides see the somewhat outdated *The Road-books & Itineraries of Great Britain, 1570 to 1850* by H. G. Fordham (1924).

RIVERS AND PORTS

Medieval traders used rivers and seaways frequently on account of the wretchedness of roads. Many rivers were navigable far inland because of the shallow draught of boats, and little ports may be discovered in surprising places. Some ports can be found from a study of place-names : *hythe* meaning 'landing place'. Others still have grass-covered wharves, boat basins or floodgates. Remember that the river or sea may have changed position during the centuries leaving works high and dry as at New Romney. Here the main quay forms a ridge in an orchard near the church. From 1565 the government began to compile a list of all English ports. The list of 1575 names over five hundred creeks, ports and landing places, many lying miles from the coast. These lists are in State Papers Domestic at the Public Record Office where also are numerous port and trade records.

BRIDGES

Bridges have been built since Roman times where traffic and trade justified the cost. The existence of a bridge greatly stimulated the local economy : shops, houses, even a market and fair might appear near an important river crossing. Stone bridges begin to appear about 1180-1250. Early bridges have pointed arches, ribbed vaulting, stout piers and triangular cutwaters. Many were widened and strengthened, especially in advanced areas like the wool country, during the fifteenth century and even more so after the 1531 Statute of Bridges. The more frequently your local bridges were repaired, the more traffic probably used the route. Look too for bridges along country lanes and pack-horse routes. These are narrow, single-arched structures without parapet. Some will have been originally wooden bridges, renewed in stone only a few years ago. Others may once have carried traders and travellers across country on some now bypassed route.

CORN-MILLS

The corn-mill was a feature of nearly every settlement, partly because families found it most convenient to have their corn ground swiftly by mechanical means rather than laboriously by hand querns; partly because the lord of the manor often insisted that people patronise his mill whether they wished to or not. Mills figure in manorial records, in legal documents and on early maps as important structures alongside the church, hall and castle. They are worked by wind or water power. A water-powered corn-mill (plate 4) will be situated near the lowest fastest-flowing portion of a stream within manorial bounds. There is usually a small stone clapper bridge nearby at which paths from every direction converge. The mill building itself will probably have been rebuilt since medieval times and may now consist of a ground floor on a level with stream and wheel, a second floor where millstones are turned to grind corn and a loft with a sack hoist and external jib for raising loads. To increase the flow of water the main stream is dammed and a special mill-race or canal is cut to lead through the waterwheel pit. There is often a mill pool to ensure that a regular supply of water is obtained at all times of the year. The wheel-pit is shaped to the size of the wheel and even when the wheel is gone the pit usually survives as a guide to the wheel's original dimensions. The waterwheel engages through a bevel gear wallower or wheel with the main vertical shaft which then by means of its crown wheel turns all minor wheels. The latter move millstones which grind the corn. All this equipment would be wooden in medieval times but iron parts were inserted after about 1760. Waterwheels were not ousted by steam power at an early date, partly on account of the cheapness of water power, partly because wheels may be started and stopped without trouble whereas engines must be warmed up. The sites of corn-mills are rarely difficult to locate, but the trained engineer can learn much from even the slightest of remains. Sites of windmills being less wooded and boggy have more frequently been erased by later buildings.

KILNS

A kiln is an oven that can be heated for the purpose of hardening, drying or burning any material. Men have used kilns for drying grain, for burning gypsum, for making bricks, tiles or pottery as well as for reducing limestone to lime. Kilns are locally constructed and so differ from place to place. Wherever a site is identified fragments of waste material usually indicate the type of manufacture undertaken; while place-names like Kilnloont, Artillery field, Tilery meadow, Potterpits, Limekiln lane and Brickyard show exactly what activity went on there. Since farmers found lime of great value for enriching the soil, lime kilns were built in nearly every parish. These should be studied in connection with the source of supply of coal and limestone. Early medieval kilns are normally ten to twelve feet in diameter, three to four feet high with draught tunnels at the base and a fireplace for wood or coal. Limestone was fed in at the top, so kilns are quite often built against a sloping hillside. They are built in strong stone which may now have been taken away for other construction work. Most surviving kilns probably date from after about 1760. The modern running kiln is a large stone-built bowl, some ten feet in diameter, tapering outwards from the bottom before becoming parallel-sided for eight feet or more. There is a grate at the base for drawing out lime and ashes. The whole is placed in a structure perhaps eight feet thick through which a tunnel penetrates as far as the grate. The top of the kiln is level with a quarry floor or a sloping hillside so that limestone may be wheeled to that position and tipped in.

PLACE-NAMES

The historian finds that place-names often yield the surest evidence about the earliest period of settlement and other aspects of local history, though there are many pitfalls awaiting the unwary researcher. Guesswork from the appearance or sound of a name is always dangerous, and most students must rely entirely on reference books to interpret names and elements. The English Place-Name Society is publishing volumes relating to each county while Professor Eilert Ekwall's *Concise Oxford Dictionary of English Place-Names* (fourth edition, 1960), definitively surveys names of towns and villages all over the country. A. H. Smith's *English Place-Name Elements* (1956) deals with the portions or elements into which most names may be analysed and interpreted. Also useful will be P. H. Reaney's *The Origin of English Place-Names* (1960) and J. Wright's *Dialect Dictionary* (1898-1905).

The settlement's name may embody the personal name of the founder or clues about the original landscape that the first immigrants saw. It can tell the historian to expect Roman occupation with the element *chester* meaning 'camp'; pre-Christian Saxon settlement as at Weedon, the 'hill with heathen temple'; or tenth-century Vikings as at Wigston, the 'Viking's town'. Many Newtons mentioned in Domesday are probably of early eleventh-century origin. Some places have of course been renamed by successive waves of invaders so it is never safe to assume that a village with an English name is no older than the sixth century. Biddisham in Somerset is, according to its name, of Saxon foundation but its earlier name, Tarnuc, fortunately preserved, indicates Celtic occupation. The Normans occasionally added their own family names to older village names, creating combinations like Stoke Mandeville.

Place-names provide one of the clues by which historians date the settlement of a region. The earliest Saxon names dating from about the sixth and seventh centuries, depending on the region under discussion, end in the elements *ing* or *ingham*. Later come endings in *ham* and then in *ton*. Danish places with the element *by* must date from after about 870, unless there has been a renaming of an older settlement. Subsidiary Danish settlements from the tenth century end in *thorpe*. Finally as far as medieval places are concerned there are settlements, often of post-conquest origin, with the elements *hurst* (wood), *den* (pasture), *cot* (cottage), *ley* or *leigh* (clearing) and *wood*. When the place-names of a region are plotted on a map with different symbols for each type of element, the pattern of settlement emerges reasonably clearly. The earliest towns from about 550-700 are situated near a point of entry into the country or a navigable river. Later settlements lie further inland or on higher stony poorer ground and may always have remained small in population.

Some names of villages, fields or lanes help in the reconstruction of the old landscape. The element *ey* meaning 'island' seems inappropriate when related to an inland town but at one time the settlement lay on a low hill within wastes of damp forest, bog or lake. A field with the element *hey* was once an enclosure out of the forest or heath. The name Sweden or Swithland denotes forest cleared by burning especially in the north. Numerous Woodhalls, Woodhouses, Newlands and Newhalls indicate the progress of the post-1066 conquest of forests, forming hamlets in the wood. Names sometimes prove that the land was once forest, waste or cultivated and even the type of crop or vegetation commonly grown there. Lands once within medieval open fields may be traced from such elements as *shutte, acre, selion* or *strip*. Certain names like churchflatt, lordshill and monks-wood refer to former ownership rather than to topography while others like breachesmeadow probably allude to the shape of the enclosure.

The historian ought never to assume that the interpretation of place-names is straightforward. Newton is in a sense the new town though town here means settlement or even homestead rather than urban community, and in the earliest days implies the existence of a fortified enclosure. Newport is the new market town because port means market not harbour. Newhaven is the new port. Saltersgate is the street not the gate used by salters whereas Saltaire is the industrial town founded on the banks of the Aire in 1853 by Sir Titus Salt. The place-name Barnton with which I am familiar is open to a facile explanation, held by some old inhabitants, that refers to the town of many barns. Brick-built barns were until 1920 or so a feature of the township. Since the modern form of the name is found as early as the fifteenth century, people might assume that such prominent buildings would influence the choice of village name and even lead to the changing of an old name for a new form. It is however generally a mistake to interpret a place-name without seeing the earliest examples of spelling. In medieval documents Barnton usually becomes Bert(h)ington and in Domesday of 1086 Bertintune, clearly nothing to do with the word barn in English or its Latin form *horreum*. There is an interesting complication in that the name of a neighbouring but not adjoining place, Bartington, goes back to the same Domesday form leading to the conjecture that the two places were originally one settlement. Names of hamlets in between, Leigh, Shutley and Crumley with the final element *ley* would be later settlements cut from the virgin woodland within the bounds of the larger township of Bertintune. Indeed those hamlets lie near what is still called Bartington Common. It is possible that the original form of the settlement's name was a long word like Beorhthaedingatun or Beorhtgydingatun, the first part of each coming from personal names of the founder of the place. Strongly reduced versions of such names could become Bartington in one case and Berthington (Barnton) in the other. There is no doubt however about the antiquity of the names. Both end in *ing(a)tun*, meaning 'settlement of the people or family of . . .'. This is one of the earliest of Anglian place-name endings, indicating settlement even in parts of the country furthest away from invasion routes by the first half of the seventh century. The antiquity and length of the names might account for the variation of *t* and *th* in forms of the two place-names between about 1150 and 1450. It is difficult to conjure up the shadowy figure of Beorhthaed but his fortified enclosure carved by hard work and by the axe out of unyielding damp woodland, high above the river has its modern counterpart in the occasional isolated farmhouse standing in strips of unspoiled wood.

Evidence of pre-Saxon settlement in place-names is not uncommon. River names are usually Celtic. The British word *ecles* meaning 'church' in place-names like Eccleston generally indicates that a Celtic church stood on the site dating possibly from the third century. Some places called Walton were Welshmen's villages; evidence that a native settlement survived there when the English arrived. The element *stow* means 'a holy place, place of assembly' relating to the missionary days of Christianity. Many *church* elements date from a little later, say the seventh or eighth centuries, denoting early mother churches.

Names prefixed by 'new' or 'old' have no definite date. Newbald in Yorkshire is mentioned as early as 963. The places are new or old in relation to other communities. Thus New Sarum supplanted Old Sarum in the thirteenth century. It is important to establish the reason behind the new foundation. Why was Newport, the new market town, founded? Can the site of the former market be identified or is Newport a completely fresh settlement on virgin soil? Which new towns date only from Victorian times, perhaps growing up round a railway junction or new suburb?

Street names speak of activity there in olden days. Bread, Goldsmith and Baker streets are easily explained. In Horsemilne Street stood the horse-powered mill. The shambles means the lane or row where the meat market took place. Other names may preserve memories of vanished features such as town gates, cross or walls. The element *gate* in northern town streets (Churchgate, Fishergate) means 'street' not gate. When street is applied to country roads, a Roman road will often be found under the modern surface. There will be no need to excavate because the clearcut course of the road should be as evident now as it was years ago to the Saxons who first admiringly or fearfully labelled it *the* street.

Houses too tell a story. A farmhouse quite often takes the name of owner and occupier, and many have not been renamed since Napoleonic times, a golden age of farming, or even earlier. Tithe Barn Row probably refers to cottages converted from a medieval barn where were stored church tithes like corn and vegetables. In Arkengarthdale, the valley where Arnkel, a Norseman, had an enclosure, is a house called Booze. Some people connect this name with illicit whisky distilling in the eighteenth century though the dwelling is Bowehous in a document dated 1473, a word derived from the old English and meaning the house in the curve of the dale or beck.

Since the name is Saxon, it is allowable to assume there has been occupation of the site since the eleventh century. A house called the Grange might be on the site of the granary where monasteries stored produce from outlying farms, but Victorians also chose such gothic-sounding names as grange, hall and towers for their new homes without regard for historical accuracy.

CONTINUITY

The boundary, land use, geology, folk customs, place-name and documents of a locality might well suggest a continuity of settlement. To judge from archaeological remains innumerable sites have sheltered people's homes from time to time, though continual desertion, rebuilding and relocation mean that houses, hedges and highways are occasionally not nearly as old as the local historian might at first think. Some villages perhaps on marginal land such as the East Anglian Breckland have been abandoned. Certain regions of coastal marsh, fen, heavy woodland and high moor have been colonised only comparatively recently, for example, since the thirteenth century. But not a few sites, it might be hazarded, were continuously occupied from prehistoric times onwards. Topsham at the Exe river's broad mouth offers evidence of settlement and trade since the bronze age, fertile soil and pleasant climate. There is little reason why men should ever desert this home.

Peasants do not lightly leave their fields, crops and animals, thereby facing starvation, because even a successful conqueror cannot conjure a lost harvest from a fired landscape. Houses and temples are destroyed but fields continue undisturbed. Thus the peasantry survive an invasion though families might in the long run be completely replaced or absorbed by the new folk whose language and place-name alone lived on. Old boundaries perhaps of the Romano-British villa estate now surround the open field of the Saxon. Ancient landscapes are not necessarily destroyed therefore and, as Professor W. G. Hoskins warns, 'everything is older than we think'.

CHAPTER 6

Houses

THE history of all local houses, inhabited or ruinous, large or small, should be carefully investigated by actual survey with sketch pad and camera. If the task seems unmanageable on account of the number of dwellings in the district the historian may find it necessary to choose only houses built prior to about 1860. The work is worthwhile for several reasons. The community's standard of living at various dates is revealed in its houses. The seventeenth-century houses in one village which I have studied are all soundly constructed and relatively spacious, suggesting that living conditions in Stuart times were comfortable. This is understandable since a now decayed market then brought prosperity to the villagers. But surviving houses tell one side of the story only, because old surveys show that many cottages that once stood along the high street have now been demolished and it is probable that these places were simply constructed and comparatively uncomfortable. Depressing terraced houses of the industrial period, surveyed before destruction about 1955 and standing alongside homes of wealthy merchants, eloquently indicate the wretched conditions of some families in a booming economy. House building often implies population increase as well as economic growth. The rebuilding of old places shows prosperity, ruins show depression. Quality of workmanship can be related to specific craftsmen and families provided that such relevant documents as building accounts and probate inventories are available. The order in which houses were built shows where and when the settlement grew. The sudden appearance of new dwellings away from the village green, for instance, probably indicates the enclosure of open fields or moorland. The process of tracing the history of a house entails discovering evidence about the earliest occupation of the site, though it is often impossible to be sure about this, as well as the period from which the foundations of the present house date. The historian ascertains when the main structure still surviving today was erected, at what date features such as roof, windows and chimney stack were renewed and which owners and occupiers have been connected with the site over the years.

The researcher starts by photographing, sketching and drawing a measured ground plan with elevation of the main structure of the house. It is helpful to dissect the house to reveal the building material and manner of construction as shown in plate 5. The semi-detached yeomen's houses appear from outside to date from the years 1700-20. But neatly fashioned beams only a few inches across, the unusual position of the fireplace and an uncommon ground plan place the house firmly in the industrial era. It does in fact date from 1775. The function of each room should be entered on the ground plan, if this information can be extracted from documents or old people's memories. While engaged in surveying houses, the historian will continually come across references to bays of building, one bay being the length of wall between the main structural supports of the house. Thus a medieval peasant's cottage might be held up by two trees or crucks leaning against each other at the ends of the building, so forming a dwelling of just one bay. With two further sets of crucks lengthways the house becomes three-bay, and the usual arrangement is that the central bay contains the door, the two side bays windows to two rooms. This elevation commonly dates from after 1570 and is typical of many village homes that survived until recently. Bays are referred to in wills and inventories in the following way : 'my house consisting of three bayes of building'.

Regional variations of style and building material make generalisations about the ordinary farmhouse and cottage unsafe. The extent of the problem may be estimated after studying M. W. Barley's *The English Farmhouse and Cottage* (1961). The author surveys in careful detail the great period of English vernacular rebuilding from about 1575 to about 1720, taking the country region by region. Certain points are stated with some sureness. The lowland zone was until 1750 economically more advanced than the remainder of Britain so that houses there may be superior in style and comforts. If two dwellings, one in Oxfordshire, the other in northern England, look somewhat alike in style the former may well date from 1690, the latter from 1750. Northern industrial development after 1750 reversed the roles. Fashions in building usually spread outwards from south-east England prior to 1750, partly because of the influence of the continent and of London, partly on account of the prosperity of this region which allowed innovations in house construction. Features of houses are traced from county to county, decade by decade, so that what Kent started in 1520, Surrey might copy in 1530 and Berkshire in 1540. This process might be even more finely traced within counties as new ideas move from one border to the opposite side of the shire.

General rules about house elevations are difficult to propound. Certainly the narrow single-storeyed cottage, one or two rooms long, usually dates from before 1700; the house with two-storeyed wings from about 1580-1720. Ornate brickwork and curving Dutch gables add distinctive touches to dwellings built in the period 1660-1720. A farm or town house of the period 1720-1820 will often be a lofty, brick structure with slate roof and symmetrically placed front windows and door. The high triangular side gable will be pierced with a garret window, lighting the servants' bedroom. The two-storeyed brick and slate terraced cottage dates from 1780 to 1910.

It is necessary to stress that many houses, especially those with foundation and framework dating from before 1610, are possibly a mixture of several rebuildings because modern bricks can shelter medieval beams. It is generally instructive to identify the rebuilders, to discover the provenance of money and labour for the work and to know why the place was altered at such and such a date. Most English houses date from after 1570, though there are exceptional areas. In East Anglia, for instance, the medieval wealth of wool merchants allowed new construction prior to 1520. But it was Tudor prosperity that spread new houses across the landscape of the lowland zone between 1570 and 1640 followed by those across the highland zone in 1660-1720. Then northern England, London and south Wales were largely rebuilt again in the period of industrial expansion, 1810-1910. Because Victorians tended to copy older styles the unwary historian is often misled in his dating.

GROUND PLAN AND ELEVATION

The single-storeyed cottage is typical of dwellings from medieval times till about 1780. At the centre lies the hall or house, the common living room that might also serve as kitchen and bedroom. In the poorest houses there is just this one room and the chimney might be merely a hole in the roof, though a brick or stone stack may be raised against one wall. Prosperous families added rooms on each side of the hall : a buttery for ale and pantry for food on the lower end, a cellar or storeroom at the upper end. Above the cellar is the solar or best chamber, the master's private withdrawing place and bedroom. The kitchen is often a detached building on account of the danger of fire to flimsy or timber frames.

During the fifteenth century people of even modest means added a second or third room to their dwelling, copying the ground plan of merchants' or landowners' houses. On one side of the hall lies the chamber or parlour. This serves for storing, entertaining and sleeping and is normally at ground level. The third room is the pantry. Usually the family cooked in the hall because here lay the only fireplace. Although the hall is open to the roof, side rooms may have bedrooms above, especially in towns and wealthy country areas like the Weald of Kent. This last development, well-established in Kent by 1500, is most commonly found after about 1580 in outlying counties.

Ground plans alter radically in the lowlands in 1575-1640; 1615-1700 in the highlands. Malthouse, milking shed and (upstairs) corn-room and cheese chamber are added. The house might acquire one or two wings, usually two-storeyed, and become shaped like an H, E or L. The hall may be open to the roof, though by 1600 owners preferred to insert chambers over the hall lit perhaps by dormer windows. In the south the chimney stack is centrally placed at the axis of hall and wings so that both hall and parlour have fireplaces back to back. Alternatively the fireplace backs on to the through passage and the parlour then possesses its own stack. Highland homes sometimes have stone stacks built like buttresses on the front wall near the main doorway. Stone or clay ovens too are constructed to protrude beyond the thickness of the wall.

Even the poorest homes usually possess a separate sleeping chamber or parlour by 1650 and by 1700 a third room, often called the buttery. These rooms, arranged lengthwise, form a rather long narrow dwelling with the hall still the centre of the house, the living room and kitchen combined. Only after 1700 did the buttery become the kitchen and the parlour a sitting-room.

The square or double house becomes popular about 1680. With a central staircase opposite the front door, this house balances parlour and drawing room on each side of the front entrance with kitchen and back parlour at the rear. The same hipped roof sloping on all four sides and pierced with dormers covers the whole edifice so that, like many Georgian buildings, the square house exhibits a pleasing elegant and symmetrical façade. The door flanked by columns is probably set between tall twelve-paned sash windows.

Terraced houses rarely date from before 1680. London has its late seventeenth-century brick two- or three-storeyed, narrow-fronted terraces where each floor contains two rooms. Later builders add cellars, garrets, bay windows and protruding back kitchens, saving street space by pushing backwards into yards and courts. Country terraces of the eighteenth century consist of small dwellings, possibly with just one living room and a pantry under the stairs that lead to the single bedroom. On these plans are based the majority of industrial houses prior to about 1890. The most common type is the two up, two down cottage with living room and kitchen set one behind the other. Not infrequently in the north speculators erected two rows of cottages back to back, each house of necessity possessing only one door. These rows date from about 1780 to 1840 and speak of the pressure of population, greedy businessmen and local poverty among certain types of workers. They are usually now converted into rows of two up, two down houses by penetrating the pantry wall and removing one staircase.

Regency houses (1795-1840) show traces of a medieval gothic influence. Builders introduced delicate iron tracery, pointed arches, verandas, bay and bow windows. Symmetry is abandoned. Brick is plastered over to resemble stone. Villas looking like country residences stretch down town streets. Victorians also loved gothic details, trying to follow medieval or Tudor buildings. But their doors and windows are too large, their ceilings too high, for the historian to be deceived for one moment.

BUILDING MATERIAL

The walls and roof of a house have generally been constructed from materials easily and cheaply available locally. Thus, for instance, in the timber country covering much of the lowlands a sixteenth- or seventeenth-century house might have a stone or rubble foundation and a strong timber framework. The walls are of wattle and daub (straw, dung, mud). In Devon a mixture of clay, gravel and straw called cob is used. Durable materials like stone and brick were used for chimney stacks in Tudor times. The farmhouse of eastern England might be brick-built by 1660 and this fashion spread westwards during the century 1660-1760. Bricks, locally produced prior to the canal age, tend to be well-burned, purplish, long and narrow. English bond, alternate courses of headers and stretchers, is common in the period 1580-1700. English garden wall bond, three courses of stretchers to one of headers, and Flemish bond, headers and stretchers laid alternately in each course, normally date from after 1690. Many old Tudor cottages were given brick walls after 1700 without any destruction of the framework. Old materials for roofing—thatch, stone and clay tile—are replaced by tiles and slates from the seventeenth century onwards. Dutch S-shaped clay pantiles appear in East Anglia after 1660; Welsh slates are found in the north and midlands when canals were opened after 1775. Pantiles held their own in the lowlands right into Victorian times.

ROOF STRUCTURE

The date of a house may be established from examining the roof structure, if the roof is contemporary with the house. Take with you as guide R. A. Cordingley 'British Historical Roof-Types and their Members : a Classification' in *Transactions of the Ancient Monuments Society,* new series, volume 9 (1961).

CHIMNEY STACKS

Prior to about 1580 the single chimney stack of an ordinary house is small and square. Only later, when an additional stack served the kitchen, did builders adopt the twisted or spirally banded tall brick stacks already favoured by the gentry. Eighteenth-century chimneys are classically proportioned, round or square, brick or stone, and functional. Chimney pots became common after 1800 through inefficiency of flues, and these grew into enormous pot or metal tall-boys by about 1845, dominating the skyline. For illustrations on this subject see V. Fletcher *Chimney Pots and Stacks* (1968).

DOORS

The door of the substantial town and country house of the period 1680-1790 is distinctive. Flanked by pillars and topped by a pediment, semicircular hood or cornice, the panelled door is the centrepiece of a symmetrical façade. A half-moon fanlight and a couple of steps are deliberately added for further effect.

WINDOWS

During the post-1560 building boom, people adopted the mullion as a means of enlarging the area of windows. The window is glazed, and tiny panes are set in lead. One part opens outwards in a case-ment. It is at this date that a glazier first appears in many localities. Northern farmers often replaced casements with sash windows after 1680. One part of the frame slides sideways behind the other. The sash proper, double-framed, sliding vertically by weights, dates from after 1700, often after 1800, and survives till 1914. The dormer window, the sometimes gabled extension of an attic outwards to allow for a vertical window opening, overcame the disadvantage of a sloping roof that restricted garret headroom. Dormers became popular in the south-east from 1575 to 1615. They appear in farmhouses and cottages with attic workshops during the years 1720-1860, though textile workers preferred long strip windows and a full second storey. The half-moon fanlight over doors has its counterpart in similarly shaped panes over windows in Georgian days. Builders of the period 1760-1820 favoured the Venetian window, especially for staircases, with three lights or panes, the central one crowned with an arch of glass. Bay and bow windows are typical of Regency houses in the years 1800-30, probably reacting against the severe formality of Georgian architecture. Windows that are blocked up often date from the days of the window tax, 1695-1851, though just as frequently builders preserved the symmetry of a Georgian elevation by this means whenever a window itself would have proved inconvenient or impossible to insert. Behind the blocked-up window in the drawing of Mount Pleasant cottages (plate 7) is the dividing wall between two bedrooms.

FURNISHING

It is instructive to seek what remains of original furnishings and equipment in old houses. To find nothing surviving need not imply that families were abominably poor or that equipment was shoddily made. But it is surprising how comparatively recently inhabitants acquired amenities now thought to be essential. Thus the water-closet, though known since 1596 and improved in 1775, was not in general use until piped water reached most homes round about 1920. Cesspits and earth privies should therefore have left their traces. Wallpaper came to be widely used only after 1850 when cylinder printing machines reduced prices. Table oilcloth comes in after 1870 and linoleum for the floor about 1885. An efficient oil lamp, burning paraffin extracted from shale oil and petroleum, dates from the second half of the nineteenth century. The combined fireplace, cast-iron oven and boiler—the Victorian kitchen range—dates usually from after 1850. The back boiler may be added by 1885. Gas lighting in towns with gas works was introduced into factories and prosperous homes from the beginning of Victoria's reign.

CHAPTER 7

Industrial archaeology

FROM the seventeenth century onwards men have successfully improved the yield of the soil to feed an increasing population. Exploitation of minerals such as coal and lead has stimulated industry and the export trade. Adaptable workers have learned new techniques and the efficient use of water and steam to produce textiles, pottery and ironware. The financing of new industries and improved transport facilities also helped to create the world's first industrial society.

Industrial archaeology is the science of seeking physical traces of the country's industrial past. The most important remains date from only the last two centuries but any discoveries may well have great significance on account of England's unique position as the earliest industrial society. Machinery in your local mill, for instance, might be the first of its kind in the world.

In order to recognise structures from all centuries back to prehistoric days first get to know about the history of industry and technology. The standard works are C. Singer (editor), *A History of Technology* (1954-8); Sir John Clapham, *A Concise Economic History of Britain from the Earliest Times to 1750* (1949); and W. H. B. Court, *A Concise Economic History of Britain from 1750 to Recent Times* (1954). There is a short illustrated work on *Industry and Technology* (1963) by W. H. Chaloner and A. E. Musson.

Works dealing with specific industries, firms and districts are useful in showing what is known about local sites. Your interest may be in breweries. Read P. Mathias, *The Brewing Industry in England 1700-1830* (1959). Or your premises could have belonged to manufacturers like *The Strutts and the Arkwrights* (1958) whose history is written by R. S. Fitton and A. P. Wadsworth. Regions are well served by works like W. H. B. Court, *The Rise of the Midland Industries 1600-1838* (1938). A large number of local surveys appear in *Transactions* of the Newcomen Society. This society sponsors research on all industrial matters. Many of its members are expert in the fields of science and technology. In order to identify buildings, machines and tools whose function is puzzling look at such works as C. Tomlinson's *The Useful Arts and Manufactures of Great Britain* (1848-50) and *Cyclopaedia of Useful Arts* (1852-4). *The Book of Trades* (first edition, 1804) is simply illustrated and concisely written but describes the most useful trades practised at that date in England.

F. D. Klingender's pioneer work *Art and the Industrial Revolution* (1947) is now reissued with revisions by Sir Arthur Elton (1968). In words and pictures this book shows the connection between arts and technology, illustrating the extent of industrial development and social change. Quoted source material will be invaluable in any historical work. John C. Bourne's illustrations of industry have never been surpassed for faithful detail, liveliness and beauty. Bourne produced drawings of such enterprises as the London and Birmingham Railway construction (published 1838-9). The pictures of the Great Western Railway echo the confidence and pride of Brunel and of Victorian England. Some local industries produced useful, advanced and artistic goods that have stood the test of time. Details of wares may be found in advertisements in newspapers and trade journals. The illustrated catalogue and prospectuses with reports of the juries at the 1851 Exhibition make instructive reading. There are coloured plates of manufactures in Sir Matthew Digby Wyatt's two-volumed *Industrial Arts of the XIXth Century at the Great Exhibition 1851* (1851-3).

Then learn to recognise and record industrial monuments by reading Kenneth Hudson's two books *Industrial Archaeology: an Introduction* (1963) and *Handbook for Industrial Archaeologists* (1967). For local industries look at articles in the journals *Industrial Archaeology, Textile History and Transport History*. Messrs David and Charles are issuing an authoritative series entitled *The Industrial Archaeology of the British Isles* dealing with specific topics and regions of interest to the fieldworker. Of similar standing is Longmans' *Industrial Archaeology* series edited by L. T. C. Rolt. The series includes such works as L. T. C. Rolt's *Navigable Waterways*, W. K. V. Gale's *Iron and Steel* and Anthony Bird's *Roads and Vehicles*. The *Industrial Archaeologists' Guide* provides addresses and information useful to researchers; it is periodically revised. Arthur Raistrick's *Industrial Archaeology* (1972) is an outstanding survey by a geologist and civil engineer.

TECHNIQUES

As a start take photographs of your chosen site. Use a twin-lens reflex camera to produce black and white pictures suitable for enlargement and exhibition. You will find useful an exposure meter, tripod and flash equipment. First record the main elevation of the structure. A photograph may reveal features not actually noticed during your first visit. Blocked-up doors and concealed datestones show up in this manner. Next go indoors to take pictures of rooms and machines. Notice especially types of building material, methods of supporting walls and roof, changes in wall alignment, rooms seemingly converted to new uses. Manufacturers' nameplates aid in the identification of the date and purpose of machines.

Modernisation has at times altered the shape of factories. A large Victorian engine-room may now serve as the staff cloakroom. It is difficult but not impossible to recreate an original factory plan. Do not neglect cellars, attics and waste heaps, for there may be discovered scrapped machines not mentioned in company records but obviously used at one time. It is a good idea to show an approximate scale by asking someone to stand in the picture or by using a rod painted at one-foot intervals in red, white and black.

The surveying of sites and measuring of structures or machines demands common sense and a knowledge of simple geometry. The clearest introduction to this aspect of industrial archaeology is in J. P. M. Pannell's *The Techniques of Industrial Archaeology* (1966). For a classic example of how to survey sites study R. T. Clough's *The Lead Smelting Mills of the Yorkshire Dales* (1962).

In order to survey a site, the equipment need consist only of a chain and measuring rod. But it is advantageous to have at hand the following :

1. A surveyor's chain (sixty-six or one hundred feet long).
2. Linen measuring tape.
3. Markers (arrows, rods and pegs to mark points in the survey).
4. White plastic scales, reinforced with metal, divided into one-twentieth of an inch parts.
5. Field book with waterproof pages, strong cover and pencil pocket.
6. Drawing board and good quality cartridge paper.

The surveyor usually divides his area into triangles whose edges and angles he measures and records. His pencil sketches are converted into permanent surveys with a draughtsman's pen and black drawing ink in the comfort of the study.

Machines seem to present problems to the amateur draughtsman. But the most complicated object is composed of small parts shaped like simple cubes, cones, circles and so on. One difficult job is to imagine the form of all component parts, to draw each unit and to put the whole drawing together accurately. You will need for this certain additional tools :

7. One sliding square with graduated blade and a spirit-level in the stock. (This serves as a depth and height gauge and as a plumb rule.)
8. Mahogany tee-square and transparent plastic set-square.
9. Steel strip tape (six feet) of the self-supporting type and a twelve-inch steel rule.
10. Outside and inside spring calipers for measuring diameters.
11. Bevel gauge and protractor to measure angles.
12. Plumb bob for finding the vertical.
13. French curve for drawing unusual curves.
14. Square-paper sketch pad.
15. Drawing-compasses.

Until about 1914 expert draughtsmen recorded in great detail most machines and structures. These drawings will be found in company records, engineering journals and trade catalogues. If you have to draw machines for yourself begin by sketching important details. This is easier when an owner allows his machine to be taken apart. Then go on to measure the complete machine. Look for suitable horizontal and vertical reference planes from which all measurements may be taken. Floor and walls are unfortunately not always true. Certain main dimensions are next chosen from which other details may be measured. The process is fully explained in chapter five of J. P. M. Pannell's book. There is also a classic though elementary work by A. C. Parkinson *A First Year Engineering Drawing* (sixth edition, 1958).

Buildings too present their problems to the unwary. Never assume that walls are vertical, floors horizontal and rooms square. Should you find walls supported by tie-rods expect some bulging. Walls may be of varying thickness in different parts of a building. Windows and doors are often added or blocked up in the course of time. Yet most structures can be reduced to simple blocks for measuring purposes. Huge cotton mills are therefore not difficult to record being so regular in plan.

So draw up a list of all the industrial structures in the locality that require surveying : railways, furnaces, mines, factories, workshops, waterways, office buildings and windmills. Of course you will not recognise all the buildings immediately for what they are, especially those put to other uses. John Wilkinson's famous foundry at Bersham, sold in 1812, is today concealed within farm buildings.

Whenever you survey any industrial monument, work systematically and record fully :

1. Location of site (parish and grid reference).
2. Usual name of structure and present owner.
3. Industry carried on over the years with date of abandonment if necessary.
4. Present condition of structure and danger of demolition.
5. Detailed description of the site layout with a note of work undertaken and goods produced.
6. Measured ground plan and elevation of main structures; sketches, measured drawings and photographs of architectural features, fittings, machinery, everything from chimney stack to labourers' privies. (Illustrations should be useful rather than artistic. Photographs can save you much sketching and descriptive work though surveying and measuring will still be necessary.)
7. Location of manuscripts, printed works and other materials relating to the firm, the industry or the premises.

You must then organise the information to be of use to students. Assume that your account is to be printed in an article of one thousand words. You must therefore describe concisely. See the model description of the Kennet and Avon Canal in the *Handbook for Industrial Archaeologists,* pages 53-5. Ensure that your summary is so good that if the site is entirely wiped out future historians will still be able to reconstruct it in their minds. Then use the standard record cards issued by the Council for British Archaeology, 8 St Andrew's Place, NW1, to provide a short summary of the structure. Send a copy of this to the National Record of Industrial Monuments, care of the Director of the Centre for the Study of the History of Technology, Bath University of Technology. You can also condense the material to fit your own card index, as mentioned earlier under research methods.

If your fieldwork seems too extensive, concentrate on factories, warehouses, stations and similar structures near a city centre where demolition is an ever-present danger. Then deal with firms that have just been taken over in case the new management decides to destroy or remodel. In highly competitive industries there is much replacing of old premises and machinery, presenting opportunities to the fieldworker. But never exaggerate the importance of structures. Record everything without exception in drawings, photographs and words. Physical preservation in all cases is needless. Indeed museums cannot take anything but the earliest or most worthwhile examples of what survives. Your report should be good enough to replace the original material to a large extent.

FUNCTIONAL TRADITION

The architect usually plans his building after an analysis of the structure's proposed purpose. Results are most easily seen in military or industrial architecture where beauty and style are not a consideration. Of course good planners create buildings which can be efficiently used and also look well. The functional tradition in local buildings should be carefully examined during the great period of industrial revolution. At this time England's efforts were concentrated on communications, mining and textiles. Whereas many countries have older cathedrals, houses and palaces, England's factories, warehouses and dockyards are unique forerunners of modern industrial building. How did builders meet the challenge of new problems like a mill to hold five hundred heavy machines run by steam power? Did they produce ugly but functional structures? How far did attention to embellishment and good taste detract from the structure's efficient working? *The Functional Tradition in Early Industrial Buildings* (1958) by J. M. Richards is a pictorial introduction to this subject.

POWER

Search for traces of watermills by the side of streams. These were once used for corn grinding, metal forging, fulling and similar purposes. Overshot wheels, driven by water falling on top of paddles and buckets, proved more efficient than the older undershot type. Adequate force of water attracted into the countryside cloth-makers from towns like Lincoln during the fourteenth century. As a result by Elizabethan times hundreds of fulling mills lay along the banks of fast streams. Textile manufacturers found it even more imperative to migrate after the introduction of water-driven machinery in the eighteenth century. Consequently they tried hard to improve the waterwheel. About 1778, for instance, John Smeaton introduced strong efficient cast-iron gears and wheel-shafts. Mill-races, wheel-pit and pools, often abandoned, should still be visible on the ground, though liable to confusion with fishponds and old stream courses. In a few mills from around 1840 turbines driven by jets of water began to challenge wheels, the machinery being compact and fast moving. Try to discover if and when in the mill turbines replaced waterwheels. Did this improve efficiency and profits? Is water power still employed? Is the modern watermill used for many purposes besides textiles and grain?

Where water power is not readily available people have since Norman times employed some form of windmill. One type of mill, usually raised high on an earth mound, turned into the wind on a low post. Traces of the post-hole, spoil ditch and access road should be discovered and sketched. The second type consists of a high tower for storage purposes and for machinery. Only the roof section bearing the sails turns. Men used windmills for draining marshes, supplying water to factories and homes and for sawing wood. Quite often shops, sheds and storerooms crowd all round an old mill, leaving well-marked ruins.

Industry employed horses as a source of power more extensively than is realised even in Victorian days. Horses walked round a circular track and turned wheels for winding up coal, draining mines, excavating tunnels and driving machines.

The atmospheric single-acting beam pumping engine using steam power was put to work in 1712 by Thomas Newcomen to raise flood water from mines. James Watt's separate condensing steam engine, over half a century later, provided more power with less coal, enabling manufacturers seriously to consider installing this equipment. Watt also introduced (1781) the sun and planet feature which made practicable the driving of factory machinery. The next year he devised a system of movable rods known as parallel motion to make his engine double-acting, applying pressure above and below the piston to double the power without increasing the cylinder size. During the nineteenth century the beam engine, though improved, began to be replaced with the horizontal or vertical engine whose piston- and connecting-rods were joined directly to the cranks. Several cylinders successively exhausted steam, producing great power economically. Then in 1884 Charles Parsons invented the steam turbine to drive machinery even faster and to produce electricity.

Old engine-houses yield important clues about the introduction of steam power. Usually of stone or brick the earliest buildings are tall and narrow to house the boiler under the cylinder. A chimney forms part of one wall and the large beam protrudes through another wall to connect with winding or pumping gear. Watt's great working beam for pumping work rests on big stones in the lever-wall. Boilers of the waggon, haystack and Cornish types are separated from the engine and stand in low, domed and chimneyed buildings adjoining the engine-house. Beams of rotative engines for driving machinery are entirely within the engine-house. Rope or leather belts transmit power to machinery in the factory or mine. But the engine bearings are supported on horizontal and vertical timbers joined to walls and floor. Boilers are still housed in separate buildings. During the nineteenth century engines became more compact. They are independent of walls or floors and can be placed not in engine-houses but in the factory itself.

A Newcomen-type engine is on show at the Science Museum, London. Here also are original Watt engines of 1777, 1788 and 1797. Nineteenth-century engines may with diligence still be found on industrial sites. For descriptions of various engines consult one of the histories of technology already cited. John Bourne's *A Treatise on the Steam Engine* which went through several editions in the mid-nineteenth century is finely illustrated and expertly written. In the journal *Industrial Archaeology*, volume 4, number 2 (1967) there is an illustrated guide to steam engines. No less than fifty-four types of steam engine are shown and described. Engineers are usually able to describe the type of engine employed in a particular factory merely by studying such likely remains as the cylinder block foundation or boiler seatings.

TEXTILES

The textile industry, at first mainly wool, developed in medieval times, usually financed by wealthy families and organised on the domestic system. Wholesale merchants bought wool and delivered it to a number of households for manufacture, after which middle-men clothiers found markets for the cloth. Sometimes workers congregated in communities or even on the premises of the financier himself. This system continued in the spinning processes until about 1790 and in weaving until after 1830. Houses of merchants and workers occasionally still stand in country areas of the Cotswolds, Wiltshire, East Anglia and Yorkshire where long windows on the upper floor are designed to throw light on the working looms. Textiles remained mainly a village industry during this period of water power, from about 1350 to 1820. But manufacturers next tried to concentrate activity under one roof so that all processes of making woollen, silk or cotton goods might be completed under close supervision. The Lombes' silk mill at Derby, dating from 1718 to 1721, is one of the earliest factories, with five storeys, water-powered machinery, continuous production and specialised functions for the workers. Not all factories were as big, especially those set up in converted corn- or fulling-mills.

The historian discovers factories probably in the remotest districts like the Pennines wherever the water supply might be adequate and tries to explain why men chose and then abandoned the site. He may show how the introduction of steam power meant the moving of the entire enterprise from country to town. He considers the site from the point of view of reasonably efficient transportation of raw materials and finished products. He traces the foundations of buildings, the area of the mill pond and remnants of the iron waterwheel inscribed perhaps with the manufacturer's name. When the researcher deals with factories of later periods, the physical survivals should be more substantial and furnish examples of iron framework to reduce fire risk, boiler-houses, workers' cottages nearby and school or church erected by the proprietor of the mill. Textile machinery may occasionally come to light. The spinning wheel and weaver's hand-loom, once common objects in farm and cottages, are now neglected in corners of sheds. Fulling stocks in the fulling, walk or tucking mill are the oldest power-driven machines, introduced in the twelfth century. Water rotating a wheel drives hammers that fall on cloth lying in a trough of water and fuller's earth, thereby cleansing and shrinking the material. The basic design remained the same even in Victorian days. Arkwright's water-frame, Hargreaves's spinning jenny and Crompton's mule helped to mechanise spinning in the last quarter of the eighteenth century, but weaving was not mechanised for half a century more.

MINING AND METALS

By 1400 coal was being dug in regions like the Forest of Dean, the midlands, Durham and Newcastle, and the industry expanded wherever men found access to the sea or to a large town, though spectacular growth came only after 1770 with the development of canals, railways and steam-powered mills. Old workings, being shallow holes in the ground, are difficult to locate though a number of deeper shafts are known too. But from 1760 collieries leave more traces : deep pits, impressive headstock and winding gear, railed-ways to town or port and miners' cottages. Winding gear is at first a horse-windlass, then about 1790 a simple beam engine run by steam. Railed-ways for horse-drawn waggons have left clear tracks especially in the north-east : cuttings, embankments, possibly wooden or iron sleepers and rails.

Medieval iron mining produced shallow shafts leading to the bed of ore. Waste material was piled round the hole. After the collapse of shafts a depression is left in the mound of waste where trees or bushes take root. Such sites should not be difficult to identify especially if documents are available as an aid to research. The pro-duction of metallic iron demands the heating of ore with other materials like charcoal. Since the iron age men manufactured wrought iron for tools and weapons by direct reduction of ore on bloomery hearths, later with water-powered bellows, and this inefficient method has left the blacksmith's forge and greying cinder heaps rich in iron. After 1490 the blast furnace with water-powered bellows was intro-duced to the Kent and Sussex Weald. A tall eighteen-feet high square stone-built structure, the furnace with enclosed hearth and great height allowed very high temperatures for the making of molten metal. Manufacturers built large dams across neighbouring streams in order to create a sufficient head of water for the bellows and forge or tilt hammers. Slag heaps lie all around and deeply rutted tracks lead to main roads or rivers. In 1709 Abraham Darby of Coalbrookdale began working his coke-fired furnace for producing cast-iron and this has been excavated and preserved by the Ironbridge Gorge Museum Trust. Later in the century Henry Cort worked on the puddling tech-nique converting amounts of cast-iron into wrought iron without charcoal. He employed a reverberatory furnace and rolling mill. Manufacturers were slow to adopt his methods but the stimulus of war after 1793 encouraged investment and works were founded near coalfields. Malleable iron was used where cast-iron could not be, in such objects as ships' anchors. Early furnaces are usually stone-built, square at base but tapering to the top and powered by bellows. Nearby the searcher may find traces of forge-house, pool, stream and waterwheel. Hammers in the forge could well have been run by water since medieval times.

Since early times steel had been produced by the cementation pro-cess which consisted of beating and heating iron bars in contact with charcoal. Wrought iron and charcoal heated in closed clay pots in a cone-shaped furnace by a process perfected about 1690 yielded blister steel. Huntsman's crucible process from the mid-eighteenth century improved on this, employing closed fireclay crucibles and intense heat in a coke-fired furnace to manufacture cast steel. The inventions of men like Henry Bessemer revolutionised steel-making after 1856, and by 1890 steel was replacing wrought iron in most construction work. But factories of this period are so complicated that most industrial archaeologists will have to enlist the services of competent engineers if any investigation is necessary. Small forges of the period 1650-1780 with waterwheels and tilt hammers that produced scythes, shears, hoes and cutlery are numerous near fast-flowing streams. Wortley Top Forge north of Sheffield is documented from 1621 and is being preserved on its site in a bend of the river Don as an example of a typical country forge.

Lead, tin and copper have all been worked since pre-Roman times though copper mining and smelting on any scale start only in the sixteenth century. Medieval tin smelting in the south-west was accomplished in what are termed Jew's houses, small clay furnaces about three feet high and wide, tapering downwards and blown by bellows. The blowing house was introduced in the middle of the fourteenth century, enclosing a granite blast furnace and water-powered bellows. Charcoal replaced peat as fuel after about 1550. Few traces of pre-sixteenth century furnaces, shafts and associated buildings of lead, tin or copper enterprises remain and only from about 1650 can substantial ruins be expected to come to the local historian's notice. A very old shaft ought to be encircled by a horse track for winding drum or gin.

After 1730 tall narrow engine-houses with chimneys appear in Cornwall and the midlands to house steam pumping engines. The entrance to a mine is either by shaft or by level. The mouth of a level is constructed from good-quality masonry, possibly with a date and initials. Sheds are solidly built and may still contain crushing stamps or rollers alongside large waterwheel pits. Lead mine entrances and railed-ways to crushing sheds should be marked on sketch maps of the site. Ore or bouse was washed in buddles, a series of circular or long troughs of timber (to 1825) or of fine masonry. Surviving buddles are about fifteen feet in diameter and date from 1830 to 1880. The smelt mill generally served a large number of shafts because of the expense of production. It lay on a stream powerful enough to drive bellows and near a source of fuel for the ore hearth. The hearth itself resembled a blacksmith's : two feet square, one foot deep, set in masonry with bellows behind and chimney above. Some mills needed two or more hearths for further refining. During the early eighteenth century the reverberatory furnace was developed. This is a large building some eight feet high with fire grate at one end and chimney at the other in which the flames bounce from walls to ore at high temperatures.

To increase draught and to condense dangerous lead vapours manufacturers built long flues from smelter to chimney, high on a nearby hill. The flue itself is a stone or brick trench, covered by a masonry arch, zigzagging perhaps one or two miles up the hillside. This produces an enormous draught, eliminating the need for bellows. Such structures are difficult to destroy and so may be found today on lonely moors.

Try to discover all mine buildings, dams, watercourses and wheels. The tracks and railed-ways leading across the site and to the main road or railway must be sought. Details should be drawn on plans, described in words and photographed. Finally seek the name and nature of the vein of ore, the owner and the lessee, approximate dates of operation, estimate of productivity and location of business papers. For a classic example of recording mining sites see R. T. Clough, *The Lead Smelting Mills of the Yorkshire Dales* (1962).

SALT-MAKING

Salt-making has been an essential industry since prehistoric times. Everyone needed supplies for preserving food and for health's sake, so saltersways and salthouses cover the entire country. Much was produced on the coast by boiling salt-enriched water in metal or clay troughs and then casting salt into blocks. Working places are marked by low but extensive mounds of fire-reddened earth, broken troughs and clay handbricks. Inland brine works in Worcestershire and Cheshire were exploited from pre-conquest days. Manufacturers here introduced wrought-iron pans and coal to replace lead pans and timber by about 1650. Rock salt was found in Cheshire in 1670. This could be mined like coal so premises resembled colliery sites. But there are always refining plants at hand. Brine and rock salt workings have left noticeable scars on the landscape. Many pits and mines collapsed, producing great depressions and lakes into which buildings could easily fall. Derelict boiler-houses, pan-sheds and storage sheds may be found, usually near a canal or river, where also may be discovered a few small harbours for loading salt.

MECHANICAL ENGINEERING

Carpenters and millwrights constructed most early machines in wood, employing costly and laborious hand-tool processes, and these craftsmen survived in places until the First World War. Their workshops and tools may still be found. But water or steam power and the use of cast-iron stimulated the development of mechanical engineering. In the late sixteenth century engineers bored wooden pipes by water power. Two hundred years later they applied steam power to the boring of iron. Machine-tools were produced to build machines with replaceable parts, a vital move in the reduction of the cost of machines, Henry Maudslay (1771-1831) being the key figure in this development.

Steam power in textile factories and on railways in the period 1820-50 raised the engineer's profession to great importance. Machines had to be produced in large numbers with every part replaceable from the factory. Joseph Whitworth's standard gauges and screw threads from about 1835 helped engineers fulfill this need. There is an excellent work by L. T. C. Rolt, *Tools for the Job* (1965), which surveys the growth of the machine-tool profession.

GLASS

Glass is made from a mixture of sand, alkali (soda or potash) and various fluxes. These are placed in fire-clay pots and melted in a furnace. Glassmakers then blow the material to the required shape. Medieval glass works are confined to localities where sand, wood, water and clay were available. The large conical furnace using the reverberatory principle allowed coal to replace wood as fuel from about 1615. Such buildings with warehouses and offices adjoining are easily identifiable. During the eighteenth century plate glass manufacturers worked by casting rather than blowing. The location of works of this era may be found in F. Buckley's researches into old newspapers printed in the *Journal of the Society of Glass Technology*, 8-14.

CHEMICALS

Sulphuric acid is essential to industries like bleaching, tanning and metal-refining. In 1746 John Roebuck introduced the lead-chamber process whereby acid was made in large chambers built of timber but lined with lead. Although some sheds were forty feet high only foundations should be expected to survive because the value of the lead ensured complete stripping. The alkalis, soda and potash, are necessary in glass, soap, bleaching and other industries. Soda was manufactured from salt, sulphuric acid, chalk or lime and coal by the Leblanc process dating from the eighteenth century. The archaeologist could come upon remains of reverberatory furnaces and waste heaps of black ash residue. For use in plate glass factories this black ash was evaporated in lead pans, purified by calcination in reverberatory furnaces and then run into cast-iron pans.

WATERWAYS

The improvement of rivers and the building of canals resulted in an excellent waterways system by about 1810. Some waterways catered for coastal traffic, others merely for tiny tub-boats. Public companies generally undertook the construction and management of these works though branch lines to collieries and factories might be paid for by the relevant owners. Near villages and factories stand wharves for transhipment of goods. The investigator still records a paved track or railed-way, warehouse, inn, canal basin for one or two boats or even a boat-building yard.

Waterways that did not follow natural contours needed pound-locks, sometimes a staircase of three or four in hilly country. Stronger locks of concrete, iron and wood eliminated a number of intermediate gates, especially on rivers, after 1860 but traces of old workings still remain. The archaeologist may recognise the lock-keeper's cottage, now perhaps just an ordinary home, and devices like reservoirs for saving water during the lockage operation. Stop-gates were never locks, merely the means whereby sections of the waterway could be sealed off if the canal burst its banks.

The researcher makes measured sketches of all bridges, tunnels and aqueducts and is excited to find the canal itself running in clay-filled or iron troughs over roads or streams. Engineers did not build internal towpaths through early tunnels so boatmen, or full-time leggers, lying on their backs, kicked the boat through. Special features of waterways include underground canals to mining sites as at Nent Head on Alston Moor and inclined planes to carry boats up and down on a railed-way from canal to road or river. In the late eighteenth century an inclined plane with cranes, warehouse and wharf was carrying much traffic between the River Weaver and the Trent and Mersey Canal in mid-Cheshire eliminating a long detour. Most inclined planes can still be traced on the ground and in documents.

Waterway houses usually date from 1770 to 1880. Each canal company favoured its own design for lock-keepers' cottages, for instance Dutch style on the Droitwich Canal. Toll collectors, wharfingers, lengthsmen and harbour-masters, directly employed by the company, all had to be housed on the banks, especially near waterway ports like Shardlow or Stourport. Boatmen usually built their own houses at convenient settlements. Here you will find terraced houses dating from 1800 to 1880, taverns, the Methodist chapel, stables, smithies, shops, carpenters' sheds and wharves that belonged to the old canal settlement.

Waterways are now well served with reference books. Look at Joseph Priestley's *Historical Account of the Navigable Rivers, Canals and Railways throughout Great Britain* (1831, reissued 1967). An excellent series edited by the expert Charles Hadfield, *The Canals of the British Isles,* contains regional studies written by industrial archaeologists. Charles Hadfield's *The Canal Age* (1968) is an illustrated general introduction for the non-specialist. Messrs David and Charles are publishing a series named *Inland Waterways Histories.* C. T. G. Boucher's *James Brindley, Engineer, 1716-1772* (1968) is notable for skilled drawings of the engineer's work. The illustrations are models for any local historian to imitate.

DOCKS AND HARBOURS

The success of a sea or river port depends on the physical shape of the harbour and the economic growth of the hinterland. Quays, breakwaters and docks represent the continued struggle of port authorities to cater for the increasing trade and bigger ships. It is therefore essential to work out the stages by which men have developed the port. Who provided the money and the plans? What materials were used? When did docks replace open wharves? Why was hydraulic machinery for gates and cranes first used? From which areas did the goods come that passed through the port? How was cargo sent inland? Numerous places even far inland actually built ships for centuries until steam power, the use of iron and increased size concentrated the industry in areas such as Tyneside. Boat-building yards are still traceable along waterways perhaps just as overgrown inlets and decaying foundations of sheds.

WAREHOUSES

The warehouse for raw materials and finished products is probably the most common industrial monument, ranging from the small wooden structure adjoining a local shop to huge dockside buildings. Surviving warehouses are not usually older than about 1780. Efficiently designed premises enable goods to be moved in and out swiftly by manual and mechanical means. Large fireproof places of the period after 1800 usually consist of several floors supported by pillars and beams of cast-iron. The details of ceiling, beams, arches, tops of pillars and doorways provide worthwhile features for sketching and may, after comparison with similar dated premises, be used as one means of dating a particular warehouse. Ordinarily a warehouse of the period 1780-1850 will adjoin a canal (and after 1850 a railway) so that loading bays face the transport facility. On each floor a double door opens straight on to the waterway, road or railway, while, in the gable above, the jib of a hoist or crane should be ready to move merchandise up and down. A few of these hoists have always been operated by horse power. Cranes near a canal may be designed to lift goods from the barge and to swing the load straight into the open doors of the warehouse. All types of raising gear ought to be recorded carefully because some surviving equipment dates from the period 1780-1850. Lifting gear can readily be discovered in warehouses at canal or river ports like Shardlow, Goole or Stourport where warehouses, stables, shops and foundries are often of very pleasing appearance. Old dock warehouses have frequently been demolished in the past half century but there is still great scope in what remains for photographic surveys and measured drawings.

BRIDGES

The use of iron as structural material in bridges marks a significant advance. The first iron bridge was completed in 1779 near Coalbrookdale by Abraham Darby. It consists of semicircular cast-iron ribs spanning one hundred feet between masonry piers. The historian surveys bridges by means of drawings and photographs of details that might reveal why the designer and contractor chose the particular style and materials, what quarry or factory supplied parts and when the structure was erected. He tries to date the replacement of iron by steel and the introduction of swing-bridges opened by hand or machine. His own conclusions are often confirmed when he consults documents relating to bridges in quarter sessions and business records.

RAILWAYS

Railways have changed the face of the landscape on a grand scale despite a modest start as roads with rails for horse-drawn waggons.

Railed-ways in England are probably first found in Nottinghamshire at the end of the sixteenth century, spread to mining districts like Tyneside and Shropshire during the eighteenth century and, with the advent of steam, began to cover all the country from 1830. Tracks were built by mining companies for the movement of their own goods between mine and wharves (staithes) on river, canal or seaside. But in some cases a line belonged to speculators who opened the way to all payers of toll. From 1830 a few industrialists constructed private lines, mainly within factory premises, but most work was undertaken by public companies. Rail trackways or waggonways are most readily recognisable even where the line had been abandoned by 1880 by the tell-tale length of lane or hedge that leads from mine to village or from mill to canal following the path of a former railed-way. Sleepers and rails are of wood, iron or stone, many designs being experimented with prior to 1800 or 1810, and stone sleepers still lie on the track probably now covered by a few inches of soil. Stone or cast-iron bridges, tunnels, cuttings and embankments demand careful surveying. Since some of these works stopped up ancient rights of way, divided fields and farms in two and littered the country with spoil banks, their effect on the landscape ought to be investigated. The researcher records all station buildings, signal boxes, workers' houses, lamp-posts and goes into details about the furnishing of waiting room, the manufacturer and style of water-closets, the size of the ticket office, telegraph installation and lighting.

Railway building convulsed town and country : enormous embankments, deep cuttings, tunnels, viaducts; destruction of houses and roads; erection of railway taverns, stations, lodging-houses, warehouses. What was your district like prior to railway building? What effect had the arrival of hundreds of navvies on local society? How did railways alter the landscape? Some of the monuments are so familiar that we take them for granted. Earthworks of the magnitude of the Wolverton embankment had not been built since the iron age. They are so huge that they seem natural features. Where did the millions of cubic feet of earth from cuttings disappear? Who designed the splendid engineering and architectural features? Indirectly the railways affected every place in the country. Bedford brick, Welsh slate and concrete were carried to every corner of England, disturbing local industries and building styles. National newspapers, fashion, food and manufactures tended to obscure regional variety in the interests of country-wide uniformity. There is a gazetteer of waggonways and tramroads in B. Baxter's study of early railed-ways, *Stone Blocks and Iron Rails* (1966). Jack Simmons in *The Railways of Britain* (second edition, 1968) deals with such topics as equipment, buildings, works and permanent way.

BUILDING MATERIAL

Builders in England have used limestone, sandstone and granite on account of the handsome appearance and durable quality of the material. Stone is not easy to transport hence stone buildings far from quarries are specially significant. For what purpose were these erected and at whose expense? Masons adopted the chisel in place of the axe about 1170 and this allowed them to replace low relief carving with foliage that seems to spring out of the stone.

Methods of stone quarrying altered little till the coming of pneumatic tools and explosives. Tumbled debris and hollow ways worn by traffic mark some old quarry sites.

Timber has until recently been one of the most common of constructional materials. People took whatever type of wood was available locally for ordinary building purposes. They rarely studied the strength and cost of various woods. Where this was undertaken special reasons are to be sought. The carpenter employed tools known to the ancient world. He used wrought iron nails until Elizabethan times and then adopted screws or wooden pegs. The joiner continued to employ iron nails in furniture-making, giving much work to local nailers in town and country. Inventors of machinery tried to mechanise such processes as planing, moulding, sawing and boring, leaving the archaeologist curious and interesting constructions. Builders tried various methods of moving large pieces of timber from wood to saw-mill. Timber became scarce from about 1650 but it was no easy matter to discover alternative means of spanning space. You can thus find evidence of early Victorian stations and factories roofed with massive timber arches. The timber lasted well. But iron fastenings rotted from damp in the wood and from smoke.

Bricks introduced from Europe in the thirteenth century were made in clamps and in up-draught kilns all through the industrial period, though down-draught kilns with tall chimneys were latterly built for quality bricks. Remains of kilns are readily found. Look for a structure with a lower fuel chamber and an oven where products were placed for firing. It is dangerous to rely on brick sizes for dating. Certainly size has altered at various dates, early bricks being about two inches thick, after about 1570 increasing to three inches, but local practice and the reusing of old bricks lead to mistaken conclusions.

Mortar and cement were also produced in kilns, often set into the side of a hillside so that supplies of limestone and fuel could easily be fed into the furnace from above. The lime collected at the base after roasting. By adding a material like clay the maker produced hydraulic lime which set under wet conditions. He manufactured Portland cement (first accidentally produced in 1824) originally in the same way as lime though at higher temperatures. Lime-concrete was used for bridge foundations from about 1760 but modern Portland cement did not gain favour for buildings, foundations and sewers till about 1870. The rotary kiln was widely used only after 1900. Most kilns are found near supplies of chalk or limestone in areas like Yorkshire or the Thames Basin. Reinforced concrete structures date from the end of Victoria's reign.

Builders adopted iron and steel as a precaution against fire. The first factory with both beams and columns of iron was begun at Shrewsbury in 1796. A cast-iron framework became quite common in mills by 1810, mainly for pillars, window-frames and beams. Sections of cast-iron were mass-produced so that the builder only had to rivet these together on the site. Often the framework is concealed by bricks or stone for the sake of appearance or to satisfy building regulations. Steel-framed structures date from about 1910 onwards. You must therefore seek carefully all pre-1914 iron- or steel-framed mills, shops, offices or warehouses in your area as early examples of their type.

BREWING

English ale, a sweet unhopped malt drink, did not keep for long and was therefore produced in small amounts by housewives. But from about 1450 Flemish beer came into fashion and nearly every community acquired a licensed brewhouse. Some can be traced back to Elizabethan times and remnants of the original building (which need be no more than a group of outhouses in a yard) remain, perhaps disguised today as a barn or residence. Germinated barley (malt) is first ground, then mashed in hot water. The extract is run off to be boiled with hops and fermented with yeast. The best-designed commercial brewhouses are tall narrow buildings. The malt mill and boiler lie high up in the roof. The liquids thus run down by gravity from process to process. Is there a tall narrow structure in the district that could be the old brewhouse?

The brewery itself lies along a street. It is pierced with an archway large enough for a waggon to enter the courtyard. Round this yard stretch stables, storehouses for vats, workshops for the barrel-makers or coopers. Brewery offices and the owner's house often rise on one side of the main archway. Because brewhouses were important town buildings the façade follows architectural fashion rather than local custom. This gives the date of last rebuilding, probably coinciding with a period of local prosperity. Maltings where barley is left to germinate into malt and oasthouses where hops and barley dry are not usually located at breweries. Oasthouses are kilns with steep pyramidal roofs, normally nineteenth century in date. Maltings are popular for conversion into cottages.

FARMS

Farm buildings when efficiently arranged and soundly constructed more readily yield profits. Certainly by 1760 farmers produced on a large scale for the market and it was in their interest to create the most harmonious relationship on the estate among men, animals and goods. Some farmers had for centuries decided to achieve this by putting house, barns and dairy under one roof. Other farmers, especially in the prosperous period 1780-1870, have favoured the courtyard plan. The two-storeyed dwelling faced the roadway. Across an archway for hay waggons began the farm buildings that enclosed the whole courtyard without a break. The barn might be as large as a church. All tools and crops could be safely locked away in this type of building which was suitable for arable farmers. Pastoral farmers preferred an open plan, buildings grouped individually round the yard, to allow for tracks in all directions straight from the farm. How many farms in your area were rebuilt in the period 1790-1870? Were these profitable? Did the farmers sell in distant markets?

Look for remains of the steam engine that drove various pieces of equipment (threshers, cake breakers, chaff cutters). There might alternatively be a horse gin or a waterwheel in hilly districts. Some Victorian machinery was so large that it still stands on the farm. What was the purpose of each piece? Did the work done justify the cost? Would not the farm workers complete as much work in as short a period? You can see all kinds of machinery and farm designs in J. C. Morton's *Cyclopedia of Agriculture* (1855).

CHAPTER 8

Archives

A DOCUMENT sets out evidence or information. In form usually a unique handwritten paper or parchment, a document may well state what can be learned nowhere else, certainly not in printed books or newspapers or reminiscences of the local soothsayer. When a document is drawn up or used in the course of some public or private transaction and thereafter preserved in the custody of the people responsible for the transaction it becomes part of an archive. An archival document is stored with its fellows in the archives, the government or private repository often nowadays called a record office because here are stored parish, legal and official records. Authentic evidence of a matter of legal importance is known as a record, a marriage register at the church being one example. A muniment owned by a family or borough evidences rights and privileges.

Although documents are stored in many archives offices ranging from the solicitor's office to the British Museum, only a small proportion of centres are adequately staffed to cater for the local historian. A few libraries employ resident archivists to calendar large collections of documents. But for most purposes the local historian relies on the county or borough record office. English and Welsh record offices have been established to care for the heritage of documentary material scattered through every shire. Borough and city offices normally developed from the department that preserved corporation charters and freemen rolls during the late nineteenth century. Full-time municipal archivists were not unknown at this period but were never numerous. County record offices grew as part of the department of the clerk of the peace, the officer in charge of quarter sessions records. In 1924 Bedfordshire County Council established the first county record office with a county archivist, Dr G. H. Fowler, in charge.

After the Second World War county record offices were established in all counties. Many establishments share responsibilities with city or borough record offices especially in populous counties like Lancashire. Other counties, like Sussex, have two archives centres for the two county councils. In a few cases the county and county town joined to set up one record office : Norwich and Norfolk Record Office is an instance. Cumberland, Westmorland and Carlisle united to establish one service for the Lake District. The Greater London Record Office covers the heavily populated areas of the former London County Council and Middlesex. Some buildings (as at Durham) are new, others old (like Chester Castle).

Each record office exists to preserve county records. The oldest documents are from quarter sessions, dating from Elizabethan times, and these may be exceedingly voluminous. Large numbers of documents have been created by the sessions every year. In addition the archivist accepts records of the county council itself, beginning after the act of 1888. These take up much room too. Then come the archives of bodies whose functions the council has assumed, such as local boards of health.

It would be hardly surprising if the archivist confined himself to sorting and calendaring these records alone. But it is his duty and aim to care for all manuscript material in his area whether archives proper or just single documents. The county archivist thus enquires about the location of manuscripts in the county, investigating by letter, personal call or agent all sources discussed in the following chapters. This work demands tact and persistence. The archivist follows up all clues concerning collections, provides free advice on repairs and storage facilities and even calendars archives in private custody. Eventually when owners trust the archivist and his record office they will agree to deposit records on terms of permanent loan.

The county archivist visits factories, churches, solicitors, mansions, schools and private homes. He investigates waterlogged cellars under solicitors' offices and rat-infested attics in council chambers. He collects small bundles of deeds from the widow's sideboard and chests of documents from the lord lieutenant's stables. He discovers manuscripts which are damp, eaten by mice, congealed by fire, rotten from silverfish, brittle, musty smelling and layered with grime. With the owner's consent he piles the whole lot in boxes or sacks and transports the archive back to his county record office.

No matter what condition new accessions arrive in, the documents are unloaded into a sorting room where preliminary cleaning and accessioning takes place. In the accessions register appears a one-line description of the archive with name and address of owner or depositor. Then damp documents are spread out to dry naturally and slowly in a current of air blowing from window to window across the room. Documents afflicted by mildew are fumigated. Insects and silverfish are usually destroyed after treating documents carefully with DDT powder. Dust is removed with a duster or vacuum cleaner and dirt with a Hardmuth grey rubber or artist's gum eraser.

Next the preliminary rough sort is completed so that the collection may be put into boxes labelled 'title deeds', 'letters', 'official records', 'account books' and 'maps'; or 'medieval' and 'modern'; or 'Exeter', 'Truro', 'Plymouth'. This job of cleaning and sorting must necessarily be swift to allow the archive to be put for the time being either in the main strongroom or in a special strongroom for uncalendared material. Because the archivist has assumed official custody of the documents he does not want any to be lying around unguarded in his daytime sorting room. In this way they could, for example, be tampered with and become valueless in court. It is at this point that the boxes are also given the archive's accession number which serves to identify the collection until classification and calendaring are completed.

The skilled repairs technician with correct and delicate tools and materials can deal with paper and parchment documents. His adequately equipped laboratory is an essential and interesting part of the record office, and it is worthwhile to seek permission and watch the repairer at work. To see the technician carefully treat each document emphasises how valuable such material is. The repairer always must 'leave the nature and extent of his repair unmistakably evident'. He does not attempt to complete missing words of documents and seals nor does he try to make his new paper and parchment look old. A repaired document looks as though it has been repaired.

CLASSIFYING

In order to make a collection accessible to students it must be arranged in orderly fashion. The entire collection is first placed in one of three general classes.

1. Official, such as county council or quarter sessions.
2. Semi-official, such as board of guardians, turnpike trust, river navigation.
3. Non-official such as family archives.

The archivist asks: who created this archive? The depositor could be an army colonel. But the documents are not his or his family's. They were created and for long preserved by the village vestry meeting. Hence they are parish records and are given the class letters PR.

Each class of records has its own code letters which vary somewhat from place to place. You will know that any archive whose code begins with PR is a parish collection. Other important codes are :

CC	County council.
Q	Quarter sessions.
PC	Parish council.
PU	Poor law union.
BC	Borough council.
DD	Documents deposited by families or businesses.
DR	Diocesan records.

The detailed sorting and arranging is skilled. Some collections are nicely arranged into sections by owners : title deeds, maps, leases, correspondence. Since these divisions may well be almost as old as the archive itself, a product possibly of hard thinking on the part of a long-dead estate agent, it is dangerous for the archivist to rearrange the collection. Indeed archivists never disturb the arrangement of an archive without positive reasoning. Whenever a bundle is broken up or a document transferred from one section to another or if strays are collected to form a new section, a clear note is made in the calendar of what has been decided and why.

It is therefore essential that the archivist learn as much background information about the collection as possible : families and estates represented, business interests, offices held, various places where the archive has been stored, previous attempts at sorting and calendaring. So the collection is further divided up, documents being placed in boxes labelled with class and section :

Q	Quarter sessions records.
QS	Court in session.
QSR	Rolled files of documents received or created by the court in session, 1574-1642.

The collection now lies in the accession strongroom in cardboard boxes neatly labelled with section names or numbers. One box at a time can be removed for detailed calendaring. At this stage too the boxes could be made available to the reliable researcher. The archivist usually arranges documents chronologically within each section, hence the word calendar meaning list or catalogue of documents. An example of an archivist's calendar will be given later when we discuss research methods. Boxes are removed to the main strongroom when all stages of accessioning, classification and cataloguing are completed.

SEARCH ROOM

Students work in the search room. Here they find lists and calendars of many collections, possibly a guide to the record office and a card index of persons, places and subjects occurring in documents. An archivist is always at hand to help students and to supervise the proper use of archives. The small library contains the most relevant local histories as well as the *Victoria County History* for the shire. There are books on national history, palaeography, archives, dating of documents, diplomatic and law. Look for the *Oxford English Dictionary*, J. Wright's *Dialect Dictionary* and the revised guide to the Public Record Office published in 1963. Very useful too are the 'Discovering' pocket books issued by Shire Publications covering subjects such as wall paintings, canals, windmills and the Exeter Road.

The student enters the search room and immediately writes his name, address and purpose of visit in a register. He repeats this at every visit. On the first visit he reads the office rules carefully. The rules which follow are adopted in some archives. Use pencil for writing because ink may mark a document and biro leaves an indelible stain. Have clean hands. Never smoke, eat or drink in the search room. Place over any particularly fragile or important document a sheet of clear cellulose acetate with some yellow Kodagraph to keep manuscripts clean and to filter bright light. The first may be had from Monsanto Chemicals, the second from Kodak. Never talk loudly in the search room. Do not ever expect to borrow a document because all manuscripts are unique and priceless. Buy photocopies of important documents. Then choose from the list, index or calendar, the documents you require, asking for no more than three at a time. Fill in a requisition with the document number, your name and date. Part of this is left on the strongroom shelf from which your document is taken. It is reunited with the other portion on return of the document. This gives the archivist a perpetual record of the documents read by each student.

The archivist will always help choose a subject for study. He points out significant documents, deciphers difficult handwriting and translates from Latin or French. He welcomes everyone to the office, both county ratepayers and visitors from outside. But he cannot undertake to complete research for you except to answer specific questions and solve problems that crop up during work. Nor can he take the place of university professor or teacher and lecture on the background of your chosen subject. One young man intent on examining quarter sessions records with a view to writing the history of county administration prior to 1889, did not even know what quarter sessions meant. Recusancy, enclosure, manor and parish are similarly popular topics of research but few are the students that have read the essential background history before embarking on the perilous seas of documents relating to those subjects. Never ask the archivist for 'everything available' on your chosen topic unless it is a very limited field : 'the construction of the Trent and Mersey Canal in Little Leigh in 1775-6'. Once a talkative teacher having to prepare a local history lecture came and asked me for everything I could find on poor relief in the county.

'There are in the strongroom some 450 volumes of minutes of the poor-law unions from 1834; overseers' accounts for at least two hundred townships; and goodness knows how many petitions to quarter sessions', I answered. 'As it happens I am calendaring here six boxes of charity papers from the eighteenth century. These show the life histories of paupers. It would take you only six or seven weeks to study the collection.'

'Time is my problem', replied the student. 'I have just a couple of afternoons.'

'A couple of afternoons a week?'

'No, Thursday and Friday afternoons next week. I'm standing for the council, you know. Perhaps instead I'll have you photocopy that article you once mentioned to me by what's his name on medieval tournaments. That will be an amusing topic.'

The archivist usually arranges to copy documents in the record office collection probably employing the services of expert county council or police photographers. Although the materials used for this are very expensive, regardless of labour costs, the result is outstandingly clear and pleasing. Small documents can be enlarged, extensive documents reduced to suit the convenience of the student. Indeed the finished print occasionally appears sharper than the original document and if in matt finish may be sent for making a printer's block prior to publication of the photograph. It is possible to take slides of documents. When projected these are useful for lecture purposes and even serve for research projects in place of photographs. It is no trouble to sit in front of a projected coloured slide taking note of details, and a slide is certainly cheaper than a coloured print though overheating will have to be considered. Record offices nowadays generally reproduce documents by means of one or other of the machines manufactured for the purpose. Varying in the quality of the result and in cost per sheet, such methods as photocopying and contact reflex none the less provide satisfactory copies for most purposes, though fading and discolouring are worries in some cases. Of course machines take only small sections of large documents at each attempt and a few are useless for bulky documents or books because items to be copied are swallowed and regurgitated, single sheets alone being digestible. For duplicating large numbers of a given print, firms like Messrs Roneo and Messrs Gestetner produce an electronic duplicating stencil. The initial cost is high but dozens of copies can be cheaply run off thereafter.

But suppose you have the rules of your vestry meeting or manor court in secretary hand, dated 1597 and in Latin. Even the clearest police photograph is no use if you do not read Latin or secretary hand. What can be done? If your research project is genuine and worthwhile, if you have shown by your previous efforts that you yourself are dedicated and perfectly capable of using other documents—which are in English and more legible—to bring the project to fruition, the archivist is always more than willing to transcribe and translate for you. Of course the amount of work he can complete in the available time is limited but a ten-page document should not be too burdensome. He will generally provide you with a typescript. This helps the record office too because a copy goes in the files for future reference and for lecture purposes. It is not wise to consult professional records searchers unless these people have been recommended personally for the specific task by the county archivist.

PALAEOGRAPHY

Palaeography is a branch of the science of documentary criticism. It concerns reading and interpreting old documents, the influence of handwriting and illumination schools, rules of calligraphy and scribal conventions, dating and origin of literary and ecclesiastical texts, and distribution of styles. In this book it is necessary to deal only with the reading of manuscripts, a task that is time-consuming but informative, tantalising but within the average person's understanding. If you can read old handwriting you can tap the wealth of English archives.

There are obviously several ways of dealing with old writing. You can by dint of hard work learn by heart the shapes of all letters of the alphabet used every century. With a good memory and keen eye you will recognise, for example, a fifteenth-century *a*, a secretary *b* and a chancery *c* as a matter of course. The letters so interpreted soon form words and sentences. You could also learn the characteristics of various handwriting. Take the king's remembrancer's hand described by L. C. Hector in *The Handwriting of English Documents* (1958) thus: 'slight departures from the generally vertical towards right or left, together with a certain squatness in the minuscules, produce a sprawling appearance. There is no avoidance of links between letters or minims; indeed the wide angle at which the foot of descending *r* is carried up to join the following letter . . .' and so on. This precise description, studied with the aid of a sample of the handwriting, is nevertheless not a recommended means of learning palaeography.

It is essential to learn by regular practice with documents, at first under tuition, then by yourself. There are many advantages in beginning with the latest documents, say from the Victorian period, mastering these and working backwards in time. This certainly shows stage by stage how individual letters develop, while the various shapes become more comprehensible. But Victorian correspondence can prove an almost insuperable obstacle. Even expert archivists stumble over the slovenly style of some missives. It is not worth waiting till you can master all documents of one period before embarking on earlier scripts. The sixteenth-century italic is usually as simple to read as Victorian scrawl.

It is therefore advisable to adopt the following plan:

1. Take a clear photocopy of the document you would like to read. Make sure there is an accurate transcript with translation if need be. You may hold or even mark the photocopy and have it with you at home. A manuscript is too precious to treat like this.
2. Read letter by letter. Abandon without reservation your habit of taking in whole words or phrases at a glance and of guessing what is to come next. Take the first letter of your document and find it in one of the model alphabets printed in palaeographical works. There is a 'secretarie alphabete' of 1571 and various 'old Law Hands' of Tudor and Stuart times in H. E. P. Grieve's *Examples of English Handwriting 1150-1750* with transcripts and translations (1959). The classic works are C. Johnson and H. Jenkinson *English Court Hand, 1066-1500* (1915) and H. Jenkin-

son *The Later Court Hands in England* (1927). Consult also N. Denholm-Young, *Handwriting in England and Wales* (1954). Then write down each letter you have deciphered. Some will always be easier to recognise than others. Leave spaces where the reading is beyond your power.

3. Learn the most common letters like *a, e, r* as a start in reading documents of all centuries.

4. Fill in gaps as you learn more letters. Do not guess because at first this will produce errors. But intelligent deductions are allowed.

5. Complete three or four lines as far as you are able. Work these out from the first letter onwards some eight or nine times before taking the transcript to fill in missing letters. Now you will see that the letter which descends and curls so distinctively is an *h*. This you will not easily forget. That is another letter learned.

6. Now try to decipher three or four more lines. It will be surprisingly clear this time.

Languages

The knowledge of Latin and French is indispensable for the reading of many documents. You can learn the handwriting of manuscripts by practice but to read other languages needs formal training. If important documents are in medieval Latin or French you can either set about learning the languages or ask your county archivist for assistance.

Latin, the language of the church, was known to all clerks both in holy orders and in government service. It became the written language of business and administration, the sole language till about 1280 and still important when abandoned in 1733. Medieval Latin is not very different from classical Latin except that grammatical constructions of the former are less complicated.

Norman-French or Anglo-Norman, spoken by polite society since the conquest, became the language of law courts and of documents less ceremonious than charters or letters patent. It is most usually found between 1310 and 1390. In 1487 it ceased to be used as the language of parliamentary statutes, surviving only in a few phrases like *le roy le veult* meaning 'the king consents to the act'.

English never disappeared despite the use of Latin and French. Most people spoke it in medieval times, and in the fifteenth century people wrote English in correspondence, account books and business minutes. By 1500 English had supplanted Latin in many informal documents. In 1650 English became the sole language of government though Latin was restored for the period 1660-1733.

It is evident that many writers are finding Latin and French beyond their powers. As time goes by scribes either make up their own Latin words and endings or insert English phrases. There is a renowned mixture of three tongues describing a law case in 1631 when a prisoner 'ject un Brickbat a le dit Justice que narrowly mist, & pur ceo immediately fuit Indictment drawn . . . & son dexter manus ampute & fix al Gibbet'. The two most useful dictionaries are R. E. Latham's *Revised Medieval Latin Word-list* (1965) and R. Kelham, *Anglo-Norman Dictionary* (1779). See also E. A. Gooder, *Latin for Local History* (1961).

WRITING MATERIAL

Medieval scribes wrote on parchment, a material supposedly perfected at and deriving its name from Pergamum in Asia Minor. Skins of goats, sheep or calves are scraped free of hair and reduced in thickness, soaked, stretched, smoothed and dried. This produces at best a thin, smooth and white parchment, the flesh side being whiter and shinier than the hair side or dorse. Thus only notes or endorsements are written on the dark hair side. Fine vellum is strictly veal-parchment. Parchment began to lose ground to paper after 1500, though conservative government departments held on till Victorian times.

Paper was used in fourteenth-century England. Its manufacture in this country dates from only the seventeenth century. The watermark in paper is an excellent way to date documents very closely. Check the mark by holding the paper to the light and find its date of manufacture in C. M. Briquet, *Les Filigranes* (1907, facsimile edition 1966).

The quill pen governed writing styles until about 1850. Taking goose, swan or crow quills the scribe cut an oblique edge. By holding the pen at an unchanging angle to the surface he produced thick and thin strokes according to the angle the nib made with the surface. Quills needed constant attention. For later round hands the quill was cut to a fine point. Fine steel pens after 1830-1 were sufficiently flexible for swift neat writing but could produce thick strokes only when the pen was brought towards the scribe. Up-strokes are therefore always thin.

Good medieval ink contains iron salts and lasts for centuries. The recipe demands galls (oak-apples) produced on the oak tree by the parasitic gall-fly and therefore acidic; gum; and copperas (vitriol) or proto-sulphate of iron. Here is a fifteenth-century recipe :

> To make hynke take galles and coporos or vitrial (quod idem est) and gumme, of everyche a quartryn other helf quartryn, and a halfe quartryn of galles more; and breke the galles a ij other a iij and put ham togedere everyche on in a pot and stere hyt ofte; and wythinne ij wykys after ye mow wryte therwyth (PRO C47/34/1/3).

Other recipes called for blood, urine, even beer.

The mixing of acidic galls and iron salt produced a purplish-black liquid which grows black with age. This burns into parchment and paper to such an extent that even wetting does not remove the ink. Most ink-makers diluted their product with water. After about 1500 a suspension of carbon (usually lamp-black) in gum-water produces really black ink which however does not bite into the material and is not waterproof. When the gum rots the ink scrapes off. Writing that is faded can be made legible to some extent by using an ultra-violet lamp to cause a visible glow. Never under any circumstances use chemical reagents applied directly to the writing because eventually these give an ineradicable stain.

FORMAT

Formal documents like charters are written on the flesh side or recto only. Endorsements are on the hair side or dorse. A seal is attached by cords to the doubled-up foot of the parchment. When writing continues from sheet to sheet—and this applies also to exchequer and common law court records—the sheets are piled one on top of the other, flesh side uppermost and secured together by cord at the head. This pad or roll is easy to consult by leafing through the bundle.

Chancery sewed membranes of parchment together head to tail and rolled them like a cylinder, flesh side or face innermost. Both recto and dorse are written on. In references 'm.2' means membrane 2 face and 'm.2d' membrane 2 dorse. The whole roll must be unwound if you want to read the parchment in the centre.

DATING

During Saxon and Norman times the new year began on 25 December. From about 1190 to 1751 Lady Day, 25 March, started the year. Only from 1752 did England revert to the Roman date, 1 January. If your document is dated 1751 or earlier and relates to any day between 1 January and 24 March, take care. What we should call 29 January 1649 is by old style counting still 29 January 1648. People stayed in 1648 till 24 March. Modern historians often write this as 29 January 1648/9 to save confusion.

There is also the problem of the eleven days by which in 1752 England had fallen behind the calendars of some European countries. James II left England before Christmas in 1688 to land in France and find Christmas already over. This difference may explain some puzzling dates especially in English-European correspondence. You should not be without C. R. Cheney, *Handbook of Dates for Students of English History* (1961).

SEALS

The use of seals to authenticate or to secure documents was known to antiquity. The popes employed a seal in the early seventh century, and European kings followed suit. The practice spread to bishops and great nobles, cities and corporations, merchants and gentry by 1300 and to guilds in the following century. After the sixteenth century the signature replaced the seal as a means of authentication, though papers were still secured by a seal.

The stamp or matrix which produced the impression was usually of latten, silver or lead. This was pressed on wax which either lay on the face of the document or hung by parchment tag, twisted silk or cord from the bottom of the record. Many pendent seals had an impression on both sides to foil forgers. Thus the great seals of England showed the king in majesty on one side and his equestrian figure on the other. Most seals are circular though clergy and noblemen preferred the pointed oval.

Ecclesiastical seals showed a conventional view of a church and patron saint. Universities and colleges displayed the chancellor and masters in convocation while towns preferred a view of the guildhall, city gate or harbour. Equestrian figures suit knight's seals but merchants and landowners accepted flowers, beasts and trees. The lower clergy used a Virgin and Child. Many people adopted a legend round their seals if merely the simple *SIGILLUM HENRICI* meaning 'Henry's seal'. The script varied from Roman capitals prior to 1150 (and after 1500), Lombardic 1150-1370 and black letter 1370-1470.

King John adopted a privy seal, held by a clerk of the king's chamber, for work not requiring the great seal. The officer gradually acquired a department of state and as Lord Privy Seal still survives. Edward III began to use his signet ring to bypass privy seal but the king's secretary also assumed wide powers, foreshadowing the office of secretary of state. Read A. B. Wyon, *The Great Seals of England* (1887) and the PRO's *A Guide to Seals in the Public Record Office* (1954).

RESEARCH METHODS

Suppose now that a collection of documents is made available to you in a record office search room. You should head your notes in the following fashion :

SOURCE NOTE 22

1. Location of document(s) : North Riding County Record Office.
2. Owner : Guisborough Urban District Council.
3. Type of document(s) : civil parish records.
4. Dates : 1699-1927.
5. Subjects : rating, poor law, law and order.
6. Record office reference : PR/GU.

Then read the documents, writing in pencil such notes as seem relevant to the subject in hand. Some documents will be copied in full, and in these cases a photocopy is often the best means of solving the problem of time and accuracy. For most local histories a complete copy of the tithe map and schedule is essential. Other documents may have to be transcribed by copying in the original language whatever lies before you. Suppose that you find an important letter from the council in London to the local landowner concerning religious affairs in 1584. A photocopy of the letter would be of little use to those readers whose palaeographical skill does not include secretary hand. A printed version is therefore called for. The transcriber never alters a writer's spelling in any language and certainly not in English documents, never corrects a scribe's supposed mistakes, leaves capital letters and punctuation alone no matter how strange the results may appear in typescript but usually does extend abbreviations that are correctly employed, such as *par.* standing for parish. For examples of transcription look at G. E. Dawson and L. Kennedy-Skipton, *Elizabethan Handwriting 1500-1650* (1968).

Suppose that the publisher requires a transcript of part of the parish register as an appendix to the local history. In such a case the transcriber purchases special lined paper to ensure that entries are not subsequently confused by the typist. He works in pencil, writing on the first page of his notes the name of the parish, covering dates of the volume in question, condition and size of the register, type of binding and cover, whether pages are paper or parchment, details of missing or indecipherable pages. When entries are in Latin the date, occupations and Christian names may be translated if the interests of the reader are paramount. Should the publisher desire an exact copy then of course the original language and spelling is carefully transcribed. Surnames, if Latinised, had better always be left alone. Entries are never interpolated or guessed. The work is typed on quarto paper, using one side only of course and allowing a one and a half inch margin. Copies are produced for the owner of the register, the county record office and the Society of Genealogists.

When notes rather than transcriptions are in question it is allowable to use abbreviations with caution, provided that the researcher and any readers know what rules are agreed on. Thus *c* may mean baptism or christening when parish registers are being studied; it also means *circa* or 'about' before a doubtful date; *b* means burial; *m* marriage; *d* died; *bn* banns; *brn* born; *s* son; *dau* daughter. I usually take the first three letters of the names of months clearly writing Jan or Jun, Mar or May. Names of people and places should not be abbreviated nor spellings altered with the exception of common Christian names.

In the majority of cases your notes should be modelled on an archivist's calendar which aims to provide so much information from each document that few researchers need consult the original. A calendar exhibits full description of the document, full date, all personal and place-names with details of covenants and provisions. Here is an example of a calendar of a charter.

Gift: for a rent of six barbed arrows yearly paid on the feast of St John the Baptist: Humphrey lord of Bunbury to Robert son of Baldwin—one bovate in Bunbury which Geoffrey brother of Hugh the Bule held and a croft between Gorstanescroft and Bunbury which was held by David Futur—witnesses Richard the chaplain, Tomas Patric, Hugh of Masefen, and many others—seal pendent from blue-green-white lace, missing—n.d. *c.* 1170-1180.

(n.d. means no date; *c.* means *circa* or 'about')

Occasionally only a descriptive list, manuscript by manuscript, is necessary for research purposes.

Manor of Berry in White Waltham

1. Court book   1 vol. 1684-1875
2. Court book   1 vol. 1875-1932
3.4. Minute books   2 vols. 1865-77

And there could be so little of relevance in certain collections that only a short note embracing hundreds of documents becomes useful.

Holker estate correspondence 1664-1810

Bills and accounts 1790-1810

Documents will usually be marked with a record office reference, and this should always be noted. Thus when copying from the 1798 manuscript, setting out the Guisborough overseer's duties, your extracts should be headed by the document reference : PR/GU 1/4/1. This will appear in the footnotes of your book to lead researchers swiftly to the source of information.

As research into archives continues it is wise to card index the information by places, persons and subjects. For the period after about 1740 every inhabitant should be mentioned somewhere in documents if only as recipient of a pauper's funeral. Each man and woman fourteen years old or over is given one card. In addition a family unit card brings together man, wife and children showing dates of baptism or birth, burial or death.

```
JENKINSON
      James of Netherton, farmer, 1701-58
      Elizabeth 1696-1770
   William    c.  7 Feb 1719/20   died after 1780
   James      c.  2 Apr 1721      b. 14 Apr 1735
   Betty      c. 19 May 1723      m. 1748
   Philip     c. 18 Sep 1726      d. 7 Jul. 1741
   Matty      c. 28 Jul 1728      m. 1749
```

Such cards are essential tools of the local historian not merely for tracing family trees but to elucidate problems of population change, migration, spread of disease, family characteristics and other subjects. Take just one question : what was the population of Netherton in June 1741? Use the Jenkinson card as an instance. Both parents are alive in 1741 and probably in residence, so they are two people in the village.

1. James Jenkinson 1701-58.
2. Elizabeth Jenkinson 1696-1770.

The couple may have been temporarily absent in June perhaps visiting relations or in the workhouse but of this we have no evidence either way. This listing cannot therefore take the place of a census conducted on the spot but is accurate enough because if the couple were actually absent it is more than likely that two people from elsewhere were temporarily in Netherton unnoticed by our card index. Be this as it may, now move on to the children.

3. William 1720- post 1780.

But James had died in 1735.

4. Betty 1723 not married till 1748.

Philip did not die, according to the gravestone, till July 1741.

5. Philip 1726-41.
6. Matty 1728 not married till 1749.

Thus six members of the family are to be added to the list of residents in June 1741. The final figure is accurate if you have examined all records and made thorough notes, card indexed patiently and counted carefully. When I checked my own census figure from these cards against the national census return of 1801 I had found two more people in a population of over four hundred. Since historians do not consider the 1801 census to be particularly reliable my own computation might just be the more correct.

CHAPTER 9

Maps

MAPS and plans are perhaps the clearest and almost the most informative of all sources for local history. These should be studied before all other records. Photocopies of maps are carried during walks about the territory. Features that have changed over the years as well as the more permanent landmarks, parish church, castle hill and roads, ought to be particularly noted because alterations in shape and position may be significant. Maitland in *Domesday Book and Beyond* as early as 1897 considered 'two little fragments' of the one-inch Ordnance Survey map to be 'more eloquent than would be many paragraphs of written discourse'.

ORDNANCE SURVEY

Ordnance Survey maps are essential sources for many historical subjects and the scale is sufficiently large for the indication of most points of interest in a village. The Board of Ordnance began its survey in 1795 and the one-inch to the mile map of Kent appeared in 1801. This series continued with maps of the south-east of England and the west country, the midlands, Wales and the north so that by 1840 the whole country south of a line from Preston to Hull was surveyed. In the British Museum map room are manuscript surveyors' drawings from the one-inch survey of 1795-1873 showing more detail than the printed maps. But even the published maps set out place-names that have since disappeared and indicate archaeological features now lost under new buildings.

As a result of the public demand for maps on a scale larger than one-inch, the Board of Ordnance initiated a six-inch survey first in Ireland in 1824, then in Northern England (1840), finally in Scotland (1843). An even larger scale was adopted after much dispute in 1853 when surveyors began the twenty-five-inch to the mile plan of Durham. This survey had covered all except uncultivated land in England and Wales by 1893. One-inch maps of 1842-95 are reductions from the larger scales. A few one-inch surveys published after 1840 are revisions of early nineteenth-century sheets with railways added and built-up areas extended though the map confusedly still carries its original date, for instance 1825. Later revisions of the original twenty-five or six-inch plans took place between 1891 and 1914 and between 1904 and 1922. At the same time certain areas where change was most rapid were resurveyed. After 1922 revision tends to be confined to these expanding districts.

A town map of St Helens on a scale of five feet to one mile was published in 1843-4, and this successful project initiated a fifty-year programme during which many British towns were surveyed in great detail. Scales vary from five to ten feet to the mile. From Wick to Penzance, Aylesbury to York, towns with a population over 4,000 were accurately and beautifully mapped. The Board of Ordnance surveyed London in 1847-52 at five feet to one mile. The work was improved and completed in 1862-71 at about the time of the twenty-five-inch survey of Middlesex, Essex, Kent and Surrey. London's plans were revised in 1891-5 and again over a wider area in 1906-9.

Ordnance Survey maps are an essential starting point for village history because they provide a picture of the district at a number of dates from the beginning of the nineteenth century onwards. Even if you are studying Saxon or medieval topics, a map of 1840 can help to show what the place looked like before any sweeping Victorian changes. The pattern of open fields quite often survived until Ordnance Survey times. The twenty-five-inch maps especially show every detail of the landscape : every road, fence, field, stream, shed, house; names of many woods, lanes, dwellings and districts; the use of industrial and commercial premises. From 1855 to 1886 each piece of land is given a number so that it is possible to check in a reference book for area and land use. After 1886 the area appears on the map itself. Details such as bay windows, individual trees in hedgerows, paths, flower beds are surveyed and shown on maps of 1853-93, a remarkable achievement.

For a full guide to Ordnance Survey maps including a key to what is available for every area of Britain see *The Historian's Guide to Ordnance Survey Maps* by J. B. Harley and C. W. Phillips (1965). Older maps are usually held by the county record office, library or surveyor's department of the local county or borough council. Copies can be had from the Ordnance Survey Office in Southampton. The first edition one-inch is now published in facsimile. More recent editions, including an excellent survey on a scale of two and a half inches, should be purchased for use while investigating local history.

TITHE MAPS

Tithe maps are excellent parish and township surveys produced at the time when church tithes in kind (hay, pigs, eggs) were commuted into money payments, usually after 1836. The process of commutation demands a village meeting to agree on the value of tithes and the terms acceptable to all parties. Minute books of meetings may usefully survive in parish church collections or at solicitors. Then an award of rent charge is made which has to be shared among all proprietors. So there becomes necessary the accurate large-scale village or town map, known as the tithe map, to show every parcel of land, every road, path, house, shop, stream, every inch of ground in the township. The scale can be twenty-five inches to the mile and most maps are coloured. The tithe map is frequently the earliest township map, especially in northern England, though some places commuted tithes prior to 1836 and possess no plans.

The key to this map is the apportionment in which are named owners and occupiers of every parcel of land. Acreage and tithe payments appear against each parcel. Apportionment, award and map are sealed and then fixed together. The document provides a picture of many places about 1840 just before the great changes of Victorian days. It shows landownership, state of cultivation, names of occupiers of property, size of estates, routes of canals and railways, number of farms and houses, traces of old earthworks and medieval cultivation, names of woods, lanes, closes, commons and houses, in all an unrivalled survey of town and village. There are three copies of every tithe map and apportionment. One is at the Public Record Office, another at the diocesan registry (usually now the county record office), the third in the parish chest.

PRINTED MAPS

Most printed maps prior to 1810 are on too small a scale to be really useful. Printed county maps have been on sale since Elizabeth Tudor's reign. Only the one-inch maps can indicate an area in any detail but even the smallest occasionally show in one corner an enlarged plan of an important town. Some plans are the bird's eye view type so popular in Tudor and Stuart days. They do indicate layout of streets and fields, size of houses, place-names and some industries. A number of oblique and bird's eye views of British towns drawn about 1560-87 and 1611 appears in Braun and Hogenberg's *Civitates Orbis Terrarum* (facsimile edition, 1966). Only a few towns like London and Norwich boast of sixteenth-century printed town plans. But a landmark in cartography is the inclusion by John Speed in his *Theatre of the Empire of Great Britaine* (1611-12) of seventy-three town plans and views. Salisbury, Buckingham, Ipswich and Nottingham are all represented.

Eighteenth-century plans are accurate, large-scale and often colourful. Rocque's Exeter (1744), Perry's Liverpool (1769) and Jefferys's Yorkshire towns (1771-2) are examples of this indispensable source for street names, layout of building estates, industry and agricultural history. Map-makers continued to flourish into Victorian times producing maps for such purposes as gazetteers, commercial directories and the Municipal Corporation Boundaries Commission (1837). Bennison's Liverpool (1835) indicates proposed building schemes across the surviving town fields.

The availability of Ordnance Survey and tithe maps after 1840 effectively limited the use of privately printed maps. For a good introduction to maps and plans with a list of places surveyed by Speed and other map-makers see an important series of articles by J. B. Harley beginning in volume 7, number 6 (1967) of *Local Historian*. The articles deal with all types of maps needed by the local historian. Most libraries and record offices produce a varied selection of local maps. The British Museum owns an unrivalled collection, to which there is a printed index.

Maps Created by Inquiries

Many maps have been produced as a result of government curiosity or to help in a law case. Thus in the sixteenth century the Tudors ordered strategic towns to be surveyed in detail. Defences were clearly shown. These maps survive at the British Museum (Cottonian MSS) and Public Record Office (State Papers). There are lists of these sets of documents. Look also at the alphabetical descriptive list of *Maps and Plans in the Public Record Office relating to the British Isles c. 1410-1860* (1967). These maps were either used in court cases or preserved for the information of government departments.

Enclosure Maps

Enclosure of open fields, moorland or meadow, all at one time common land, has long been a feature of the English economy partly because landowners preferred to hold private enclosed parcels of land for the sake of sound administration and greater efficiency.

Enclosure merits a section of its own in any local history and references to the far-reaching effects of the process are found in many types of record. The map and award often produced at enclosure time provide a good survey of the township (showing fields, houses, family names, roads, land use and much else) and should be examined at this early stage of research.

Medieval enclosures were effected by brute force or by agreement and records exist in manorial or state papers. From Tudor times people appealed to the courts of chancery and exchequer, and documents concerning such enclosures remain in the Public Record Office. But unless you know names of parties and dates, relevant papers are almost impossible to extract. Later still, intending enclosers secured private acts of Parliament especially after 1750. Consult the parliamentary return of enclosure acts in *House of Commons Sessional Papers,* 1914, lxvii, to learn if your parish was affected. General acts have been passed since 1801 to facilitate enclosure. There is a printed alphabetical *Index of Local and Personal Acts 1801-1947*.

Documents which are likely to be of most use date from about 1740. Each enclosure document whether rolled or in book form consists of an award that sets out exactly the disposition of all affected common land. Not only farmers and freeholders but the poor and the parson obtain portions. There may also be available the minute book of the enclosure commissioners, with letters, agreements and sketches. If you are lucky a map will accompany the award to show where all the enclosures are situated. Some surveyors show a plan of the entire village, not merely the common, in order to mark the property in respect of which allotments are claimed. You know exactly from numbers on the map which land is taken by each inhabitant. What has happened to these allotments? Look especially for old versions of place-names, ancient lanes, new access roads, houses erected in the enclosures, signs of medieval farming, land given to charities, poor, parson and school. Try to work out which men were losing, which gaining from enclosure.

Where do you find enclosure maps and awards? To discover where pre-1801 documents were sent, consult the authorising acts themselves or a record office index. Some were deposited with the courts at Westminster and so are at the Public Record Office, some with the clerk of the peace (now at the county record office), yet others with the local parson or churchwardens and so lie at the church or with church solicitors. Awards dated between 1801 and 1845 were usually deposited with a court of record at Westminster or with the county clerk of the peace. Awards made after 1845 are in the Public Record Office. Copies were deposited with the clerk of the peace and with the churchwardens. Most record offices have lists of all documents since 1801 and there is a return of awards in *House of Commons Sessional Papers*, 1904, lxxviii. Some churches have handed awards to local district or county councils. It is worthwhile remembering that in Yorkshire and Middlesex enclosure awards have been enrolled in the county registries of deeds since the early eighteenth century.

CHAPTER 10

Estate papers

ESTATE papers consist of leases, rentals, maps, correspondence, deeds and other documents concerning the administration of property belonging to local squire, monastery, industrial company or modest freeholder from as early as Saxon times to the present. Relevant collections might still lie in the muniment room of the property owner, or at his solicitor's, but are frequently held on loan by county record offices. Books and documents reveal the names of estates and their proprietors from various centuries, and the county archivist may know the present location of relevant estate papers. Occasionally the documents of a family that died out five hundred years ago have survived in the hands of later owners of the property. The whereabouts of many archives are discussed in the reports of the Historical Manuscripts Commission, which was established in 1869 to list all manuscript collections in private hands. This organisation now has two subsidiaries, the National Register of Archives and the Manorial and Tithe Documents registers. Reports are available in reference libraries and there is an index of persons mentioned in volumes up to 1957 (HMSO, 1935-66). The secretary of the commission, Quality Court, Chancery Lane, London WC2, deals with further enquiries about estate papers. Townships divided among resident freeholders tend to develop differently from those owned by various non-residents such as monasteries or West India merchants, or by one landowner whether in residence or not. The pattern of landownership has some bearing on such diverse topics as local religious and political allegiance, opportunities for employment, vernacular architecture and industrial expansion.

Crown estate records (deeds, leases, rentals, maps and accounts) lie mostly either at the Public Record Office or at the Crown Estate Commissioners, 55 Whitehall, SW1. These documents concern all hereditary lands of the crown, together with property obtained by forfeiture or confiscation, and begin in the thirteenth century. The Duchy of Lancaster papers are also at the Public Record Office but Duchy of Cornwall records are at 10 Buckingham Gate, SW1. Monastic land confiscated after the dissolution became crown property though accompanying medieval manuscripts were often destroyed. The land itself was, however, carefully surveyed and accounted for in ministers' accounts. When portions of the property were disposed of, valuations and descriptions appear in particulars for grants and for leases that survive at the Public Record Office. These vital documents also deal with all crown land whether confiscated or not. Surveys of monastic granges about 1536-50 appear in court of augmentation records.

Estates of old landed families have generally been built up slowly by purchase, royal grant or marriage. Manors, farms, industries, village houses, market rights, all may come into the possession of one family. Documents concerning private and business matters of these units are all bundled together in one great muniment room. Alternatively collections may be split up and scattered when estates are sold. The local watermill may form part of a peer's estate in one century, even if he lived a hundred miles away, but part of a villager's small farm by 1743. To follow the mill's history from 1320 to 1912, when it fell down, you may have to consult a dozen family and estate archives. Nearly anything may turn up in these collections : this category overlaps all other types of record without exception. In one estate deed-box I found a parish register, the local borough charter, an electoral list and the town tithe map.

Estate Maps

Among the most useful of estate papers are maps and plans. These show the property of one landowner who had employed a surveyor to indicate the extent and important features of the estate. If the chosen area has been divided among many proprietors at one time or another, then you expect to find a number of maps showing sections of the township. Each record office usually produces a list of estate maps. Maps may be of all sizes, big rolls of parchment or small pieces of paper, be wonderfully coloured or merely etched in black and white. At times the surveyor draws a whole district or village but often leaves blank spaces where land does not belong to his employer. This is not waste land. Estate maps first appear in any number in the sixteenth century and continue to be produced until rendered obsolete by Ordnance Survey maps.

Maps of country estates may be bird's eye views or ordinary ground plans delineating houses, inns, barns, mills, gardens, fields, scenes of husbandry, churches, gallows. An accompanying schedule could indicate tenants' names, acreages and land use. Pictures of the church,

mill or inn may be sufficiently detailed for you to describe architectural features, even the inn sign. Individual trees in woodland and
field gates can be seen. This type of map is usually with the landowner's muniments at the hall, estate office or county record office.
A firm such as Imperial Chemical Industries is a landowner and
possesses many estate maps relating to ancient lands that have been
purchased.

Urban landowners also have produced maps especially since 1750.
Corporations like London and Liverpool, city guilds, railway companies, all have owned, perhaps still own, large areas of towns which
have been mapped. Some proprietors ordered surveys of their property
to see if rents could be raised, others prepared schemes of housing
development. Large areas of countryside were swallowed up by
houses in the period of industrial expansion after 1740, and maps
illustrate the previous state of the district.

SURVEYS

A survey is a word picture of an estate, dating from about 1540 to
1720, giving information in several forms :

John Swanne owns one close called Big Heye 0-2-31 adjoyneinge
Northe on the Common, northeaste on widow Bell's croft, south
and west on Westfield furlonge.

Term	Description	Tenant	Acreage
for 3			
lives	messuage	William Thompson	0 - 0 - 20

These documents set out many place-names that have now disappeared
and indicate the situation of forgotten windmills, woodland, cottages,
commons, moors and trackways. They show whether farmers employed the enclosed or open-field system of agriculture and how
much common land remained. The historian can calculate the pro-
portions of arable and pasture, the average size of fields and holdings,
the normal terms under which farms were held. Local development
often depends on how land is held, whether by one non-resident
proprietor, by an ambitious former merchant turned lord of the
manor, by dozens of equal freeholders, by long lease or for the
uncertain term of lives. It may be that the single landowner is able
at the stroke of his pen to convert the entire parish into a depopulated
sheep run or a large industrial community while freeholders find it

difficult to alter the habits of centuries, perhaps being content to establish modest shops in the high street as a contribution to the creation of a small market town. Surveys name local people and indicate their wealth or poverty. When studied along with earlier and later documents they enable the historian to say which families rose or fell economically speaking and to hazard reasons why this should be so.

RENTALS AND LEASES

Rentals and leases are complementary documents. I have traced one estate cottage and garden back to 1520 with no more than a good set of these records. I followed tenants' names in the rent books beginning at the latest date and working back. When one man disappeared, say in 1777, I looked at 1776 for another person who paid the same rent for a 'cottage and garden'. Then to make certain I examined leases for 1776-7 to find the authority by which one tenant replaced the other. Notice particularly the terms under which people hold property. Are they tenants at will, or by the year, or for term of years, or for lives? In a lease for lives the ages of family members are provided. At what dates do rents increase? Which fields attract wealthy tenants, which poor householders and why? What is the landlord's clear annual rental?

TITLE DEEDS

Without further ado try to see title deeds relating to each property in the township. Every piece of ground ought to be represented in someone's deeds. Some lands will be named with hundreds of other acres in the comprehensive deeds of a large landowner. Quite small gardens could have title deeds of their own stretching back some centuries. It may be possible to obtain full lists of owners and occupiers over the centuries, descriptions of different properties, place-names and family histories from a careful examination of deeds.

Deeds of title include any document that has been used to prove ownership to property. Most owners have kept deeds bundled together to ensure that none strays. These documents were drawn up to give legal evidence of Brown's disposal of property to Smith on such and such a day. They were not intended to provide a history of village estates and their rambling legal style may at first defy understanding. Lawyers retained Latin in some cases until 1733. On the other hand deeds when treated intelligently form a firm basis of research. For fuller guides to the use of title deeds see an excellent pamphlet obtainable from Birmingham University Extra-Mural Studies Department by Julian Cornwall, *How to Read Old Title Deeds XVI-XIX centuries* (1964) and also E. Legg, 'Title Deeds' in *Amateur Historian,* volume 7, number 3 (1966).

The normal medieval conveyance is concisely written on parchment and in Latin, names the parties, describes the property and notes conditions in the *habendum* clause. The deed is witnessed, authenticated by the donor's seal and, from about 1280, dated. An endorsement records the actual transfer of title by livery of seisin, that is the handing over of a piece of turf or twig from the estate prior to the writing of the document. After Parliament passed the Statute of Uses concerning beneficial interests and legal estates in 1536, lawyers conveyed property by bargain and sale, a contract to convey interests in realty following payment of an agreed price. This document is written in Latin or English in duplicate on one parchment which is divided with an indented cut and also enrolled with the clerk of the peace or with a court at Westminster. It names the parties, sets out the property and states the consideration or money paid. Its operative words are 'doth grant bargain and sell'. From 1536 to about 1640 people employed the bargain and sale followed by a feoffment recorded as an endorsement or as a separate deed with the operative words 'alien grant bargain sell enfeoff and confirm'. But on account of the publicity inherent in the use of the bargain and sale, legal men adopted the lease and release from about 1614, and this ousted the older deed by 1660. On one day the seller bargains and sells a lease for six or twelve months to the purchaser who normally pays only five shillings. On the following day the seller releases the freehold reversion to the purchaser who pays the full price for the property. The lease is generally folded inside the more substantial release whose operative words consist of 'hath granted bargained sold remised released quitclaimed and confirmed'. The dates of the two documents are given in the form 10/11 Jun. The lease and release was eventually replaced in 1841 by a simple release and in 1845 by a deed of grant.

Landowners have always tended to tie up property by legal means so that it should descend in certain ways and not otherwise, for instance to the heirs of the body by a particular wife or to heirs male, and to achieve this created the fee tail or entailed estate. This policy is advantageous when heirs are not to be trusted to administer family possessions responsibly though it hinders development or sale of the land, exploitation of minerals, building of housing projects and so on because such activity may not be possible under the terms of the entail. The modern settlement protected by chancery dates from the sixteenth century and regularly takes the form of a lease and release with a special *habendum* clause to limit uses and remainders. Very common is the marriage settlement dealing with the property of two families, usually of substantial means, united by marriage. Documents are complicated but are important in setting out the conditions on which land, money, industrial premises, trading ventures and other goods are settled on the parties, in naming family members, in reciting family history and in describing estates in very welcome detail. Marriage settlements sometimes explain why rival enterprises cease competition and form a strong united company or why a bankrupt estate gains a new lease of life. Until 1856 settled land could not be disposed of without an act of Parliament which should be sought in the House of Lords Record Office.

The historian frequently comes upon common recoveries which record the disentailing of property. Heirs have naturally always wished to hold their estates free of all restriction, perhaps to sell one portion in order to raise money for the development of the remainder. From Edward IV's reign if not earlier tenants in tail initiated in the court of common pleas a fictitious suit in which some friendly plaintiff was allowed to recover the whole entailed estate freed of all encumbrances according to the judgment of the court. The plaintiff (who wins through the default of the other side) eventually returns the estate to the former tenant in tail in fee simple, though wherever a sale is planned the plaintiff is often the purchaser. Recoveries were enrolled on court rolls in the public records and engrossed and sealed for the parties. Documents are in Latin till 1733 and in a difficult court hand but certain ones exhibit a royal portrait within their initial letter. Much of the wording is common form and of no interest to the local historian. Hugh Hunt, Richard Rowe and Edward Howse who appear in the documents are fictitious persons. Even the description of property is conventional, normally just round figures and far too large in acreage. The researcher merely seeks location of estate, date and the name of the tenant in tail who is recognised first in the grant of the life estate to the tenant to the praecipe and next in the recovery itself as one of the vouchees. Common recoveries were replaced by disentailing deeds in 1833. Whenever this type of action takes place

the historian inquires whether the case resulted in a major change
in estate administration, even a sale or the disintegration of the property, and if so, seeks the reasons for and effects of this upheaval.

The simplest kind of deed relates to one compact piece of property
which has long been freehold. One man sells and another buys the
whole, and so on through the centuries. It is worthwhile writing a
calendar or abstract of each deed or, more simply, extracting the
names of all parties to the document, their places of residence and
jobs, an exact description of all lands as well as the date. Conditions
of sale and price paid may be useful.

1. Miles Geldert of Carleton, yeoman, to
2. George Swann of Mellmerby, cordwainer
— all that Messuage or Dwelling House scituate and being in
Carleton aforesaid called or known by the name of St Thomas
Chappell — 4 May 1681.

In many deeds there is a whereas clause in which the lawyer quotes
back to previous conveyances partly to show that the seller's title
is good, and this practice is invaluable where older documents have
been lost. The historian of course finds much the same information in
an abstract of title prepared by a lawyer for his client whenever old
deeds were not going to be handed over. Thus a document dated
17 February 1838 relates to 'all that Messuage called Tylas with four
and one half acres of land adjoining the turnpike road'. This same
deed quotes previous records of 1587, 1646, 1712, 1722 and 1810.
The house appears as Tilehowse in 1587. In 1646 the road is the
'kinges highwaie'. In 1712 the land is 'all that Croft called Mossey-
crofte containing by admeasurement two Acres and thirty perches
together with Two appleorchards and the Gallowsmead'. Occasionally
after 1800 the researcher comes upon a detailed plan of the farm,
house, shop or estate which is drawn on the deed itself.

Deeds tell the history of all kinds of property. The date at which
a house or factory first appeared may therefore be proved as by the
mortgage of 19 July 1796 of 'all that plot of land formerly part
of the estate of the late William Peel together with the Mill waterwheel
Engine-house and other necessary buildings thereon lately erected
and used as a cotton Manufactory'. An old deed reveals changes in
land use : 'formerly part of Newton common landes'. Deeds to what
is now the bus station describe 'all those Messuages known as the
tanneries with the ropewalk storehouse and shop'.

Deeds may be brought to light by first courteously and carefully approaching various village property owners, preparing the ground by explaining the scope of the proposed history. Deeds will be in sideboards or under carpets, at the bank or with the solicitor. Some owners have deposited documents on loan with the county record office. If the property forms part of an estate, deeds will be among the landowner's muniments. At times deeds have been copied out in chartularies often before the destruction of the originals. I wrote an account of one farmhouse whose deeds were no older than 1910 but the family that had owned the place from about 1210 to 1680 possessed a comprehensive Stuart chartulary containing all deeds to the farm from 1483 to 1620. In Middlesex and the Ridings of Yorkshire there are four deeds registries where officers have copied out and indexed essential facts from every deed that concerns property in those counties from 1704-36 to the present. In quarter sessions records, usually now in the county record office, may be seen enrolments of deeds of bargain and sale from 1536 to the early eighteenth century. Papist conveyances are also enrolled. An act of 1715 required every Roman Catholic to register his name and real estate with the clerk of the peace. A second act in 1717 compelled papists to enroll their wills and conveyances of property.

NOTICES AND PARTICULARS OF SALE

Notices of sale of houses, land and personal goods were often inserted in local newspapers or nailed on walls prior to disposal of property. Conditions and particulars of sale with plans also appear at this stage though these were to be consulted at the local solicitor's, estate agent's or inn. Documents are boldly printed on paper and dozens of copies may survive. In one small collection I found notices dating from 1705 onwards advertising the sale of a farm, tolls of a turnpike road and the office of parish tithe farmer. (In return for a fixed rent to the rector he got what profit he could from collecting tithes in kind.) Most surviving notices are in family muniments at the solicitor's or county record office. Copies are of course in old newspapers.

ACCOUNTS

Many archives contain tradesmen's bills and family account books. The Elizabethan household kept a volume into which were entered details of expenditure and income for home, farm and business purposes. Great estates of Georgian days usually preserved the bills sent in by bricklayers, saddlers, tailors and others; vouchers recording payments out of the estate to workers and tradespeople; separate volumes for rents, mining royalties, sale of cattle or crops, wages and family needs. You will be able to picture how a family lived, how the estate was administered, state of wages and prices and standard of living by examining surviving accounts of as many families as possible. In *Tudor Food and Pastimes* (1964), F. G. Emmison drew on the household accounts of substantial families.

FAMILY MISCELLANEA

Every family has its bundles of miscellaneous material that might be junk or a treasure house for the historian : letters, diaries, journals, photographs, drawings, newspaper clippings, medical or recipe books, genealogical notes, samplers and the family Bible. Old diaries and letters, some dating from Elizabethan times, tell of village disputes, church rebuilding, royal visits, enclosure of waste, establishing the cotton mill. The Bible has often passed from eldest son to eldest son. It was for long a custom to write in the flyleaf all births, marriages and deaths as well as significant family happenings. Most diaries that have not been destroyed lie neglected in boxes of family papers in the muniment room or solicitor's attic. Fortunately diaries have been presented to archives centres and some are in print. There is a useful list of *British Diaries 1442-1942* (1950) compiled by W. Matthews showing the trade or profession of each diarist and his subject matter.

MANORIAL RECORDS

Manorial organisation dates from before the conquest when communities were already divided into estates of varying size. The lord of the manor held courts for his manorial people at regular, possibly fortnightly, intervals. Organisation evolved during medieval times and by Elizabeth I's reign the court leet and view of frankpledge elected such officers as hayward, aletaster and constable and dealt with misdemeanours and nuisances. The court baron concerned itself with tenancy changes, regulation of open fields, heaths or meadows and infringement of property rights. A locality may be a manor on its own or part of a large manor embracing several townships or divided between two or three manors. The manorial lord's influence need not always have been strong especially in urban areas. The most interesting documents date from the period 1270-1700 and may be held by anyone who has owned the manor or by their solicitors. Court rolls are protected by law and some owners have deposited in county record offices. The Public Record Office published a useful list of court rolls in its possession in 1896.

Often written on pieces of parchment which were then stitched together and rolled like pipes, usually in Latin, court rolls begin with place and date and continue with names of local jurors. These people present cases for the court's consideration and wrongdoers are punished, normally by fines. Any kind of village problem can come to court: administration of the open fields, scouring of ditches, stray cattle on cornfields, decisions about fallow land, labour services, witchcraft, assault, theft, water meadows, disputes about boundary stones, rents and the corn-mill. In one Whitby (Yorkshire) roll William Ward is fined 'for emptying his chamberpot into the common high-street to the detriment of the populace'.

Court records include extents of the manorial estate which describe in admirable detail the bounds and value of the lord's property, indicating tenants' names, rent and services as well as mills, cottages and new enclosures from the waste. Very useful also will be manor court surrenders of property on the death or departure of one tenant and the admittance of his successor. The tenants would hold copies of the roll to prove this change, which is fully described in the court book or roll in addition, the people therefore holding by copy of court roll or copyhold. I have traced one east Lancashire copyhold farm in these surrenders from 1910 back to 1582. Custumals set out the customs of the manor. Tenants' privileges and duties are laid down so that the manor might be administered efficiently. Here is seen the community's daily routine. In his *Open-Field Farming in Medieval England* (1972), W. O. Ault prints several hundred of these bye-laws beginning from 1270. 'No one shall put sheep in the field sown with wheat, barley and oats before the feast of the holy trinity (1534) . . . no man shall have his beasts in the stubble from the time the grain is beginning to be reaped until three weeks have passed (1369) . . . each one of them shall have suspect gaps and lanes near the fields repaired (1330) . . . no one shall gather peas, beans or vetches in the fields except on land that they have sown (1290) . . . no one shall have his own herdsman for his beasts but that they will be kept with the common herdsman (1354) . . . no one shall put anything filthy in the rivulet (1469).'

Historians studying rural communities and many towns between about 1220 and 1700 carefully read manorial records. Especially significant are documents from places where the vestry had not yet become an administrative body or from the period prior to the introduction of active quarter sessions. Since these rolls will be in Latin, the historian who does not read that language must rely on printed versions by the local record society or the help of the county archivist. Although amusing entries like the one quoted for Whitby can be noted when appropriate, the main reason for studying these documents is to gain an account of the social and economic organisation of the community. Obviously the records are not going to provide this information in any direct way so the student tries to understand the implications of each entry, bearing in mind the kind of questions he desires answered. To take an obvious example, when a court is held by the serjeant representing the priory of St Swithun's, Winchester, the student sets this manor in the class that had no resident lord to top the social tree and to direct local affairs with an intimate touch. He begins to consider the wider estate administration, the powerful and rich lord with his entourage, such paid officials as accountants, auditors and stewards, the wily legal experts advising on rights and duties of lordship. This might explain the intensive exploitation for the market of the demesne, the rents demanded from newly assarted lands (acreage taken in from the wilderness), the commutation of labour services for rents, the increase in sheep farming at the expense of arable, despite the disadvantages for local inhabitants.

The local historian establishes from manorial records which men ultimately decided how the manor would be run; how independent of external pressure the official on the spot could claim to be; who settled when crops should be planted, which squatters on the wastes were allowed to become legal rent payers, when minerals were exploited and custumals revised. He determines as far as possible how competent the decision-makers were and what effects their resolutions had on village affairs, why certain methods continued to be followed decade after decade, whether these were profitable to one section of the community or to all, or unprofitable but hallowed by tradition. The historian investigates types of crops, the use of horses or oxen as working beasts and the effect of this on speed of ploughing, drainage and marling or manuring of land, the extent at various dates of arable, pasture, meadow and wood, the increase of flocks, herds and harvests by good management, labour services, rent payment, the means of farming the lord's demesne or home farm, holdings of villeins and freeholders, enclosure, assarting, disease among plants and animals. The writer tries to show the position in society of such people as steward, parson, villein, freeholder, labourer and miller and to estimate what this means for community feeling. If a freeholder farms villein land that is subject to week-work while a villein owns freehold land, the traditional legal difference between the two men cannot have meant much in practice. There are many more questions to be asked and aspects of local life to be investigated. Indeed some medieval local histories must rely almost entirely on manorial records which necessarily may be endlessly squeezed by the conscientious student for significant information.

CHAPTER 11

Town books

THE township has been the basic administrative unit of English local government since Tudor times. It does not necessarily cover the same area as parish or manor, though manor court and parish vestry meeting had a hand in its governance. Thriving townships might contain several ecclesiastical parishes and, by obtaining a charter of rights and duties, become boroughs or cities. Northern townships within vast parishes ran their own affairs with a town meeting. In the lowlands parish and town may coincide : here the vestry governs each community. Victorian reforms created other local units like urban and rural districts, civil parishes and county boroughs. The term town books is here adopted for all local government records but includes only civil records such as overseers' accounts not parish registers or tithe maps. For a guide to village administration see W. E. Tate, *The Parish Chest* (third edition, 1969). The type of documents found in parish chests varies little whether the parish is in a rural area or part of a large borough.

Town books remain the property of the authority which first created them. Thus most village and town documents should be in the vestry safe. In large villages containing many townships each place might keep its own records and these have survived in the hands of the parish clerk or of descendants of former township officers. Boroughs have often built their own muniment room at the town hall or guildhall. Records of authorities, such as urban and rural district, county borough, parish council and so on, are in the relevant district council office. Of course all documents may have been deposited at the county record office. Conurbations of recent growth, such as Birmingham, possess records only from the date of borough incorporation. Prior to this each constituent township of the built-up area created its own administrative records. Documents could still be located in the old church of each village or even in private hands. But usually city librarians and archivists have collected records diligently into one central repository known as the city record office.

MINUTES

A meeting of parishioners in the vestry of the church or a town meeting, probably at the inn, governed most places. Incorporated towns normally had their mayor and council. In all cases minutes of meetings would usually be kept in volumes or on paper by a clerk who also dealt with petitions and correspondence. Documents may begin as early as the fourteenth century and concern sewers, town common, repair of town grammar school, apprentices, markets, smoking chimneys, rights of freemen and parliamentary representation, to name just a few subjects. Many decisions that altered the course of local history were taken at these vestry and borough council meetings, and the researcher learns the reasons for the local land-owner's influence, the clash of interests between freemen and outsiders, the unseemly rush to sell town property or the construction of industrial premises. The Weymouth and Melcombe Regis Borough Council met on 23 December 1631 and its minutes for that day have been printed in the minute book, 1625-60, by the Dorset Record Society. Members resolved to present to Sir Francis Ashley 'a Rundlett of the best wyne' holding 'eight or tenn gallons . . . for his Love and readinesse to pleasure this Corporation'. The historian wonders what Ashley had done and whom his action benefited, whether the town in general gained and how all this affected the course of local development. Minutes should resolve many such questions if studied along with whatever else survives of the council archive.

During the nineteenth century new councils dealt with problems of urban expansion. For the sake of efficiency many of these councils resolved themselves into committees to deal with pressing problems such as streets, housing and sanitation. People intending to erect or alter dwellings, to cut roads or drains, had to contact the council and deposit plans, and committee records deal in detail with such items as new windows and sanitation. The exact date at which houses were built during the last hundred years may be gained from these documents.

RATE AND ACCOUNT BOOKS

The administration of villages and towns demanded the collection of rates on property so that essential local services could be performed. The resulting records of money collected and spent by such officers as constable, overseer of the poor, surveyor of the highways and market overlooker provide a full and reliable history of town finances, possibly from the fourteenth century but usually from Tudor or Stuart times. Exeter's accounts run from 1339 to date. Most rate books are no older than 1744 when an act allowed residents to examine these records.

Not all documents are in book form but the presentation of information is very similar in all cases. The relevant officer makes a list of all sources of income mainly from lands and buildings. This quite often turns into an annual house-by-house town and parish directory because each property is listed in order especially after 1840. Owner, occupier, value and rates appear alongside. Names of estates, houses and streets may be inserted. Early vestry accounts are usually short and simple. Victorian records of rural, urban and borough councils are sufficiently detailed to pass the scrutiny of the most scrupulous auditor. Look at up-to-date rate books in the council offices to see who owns village property : these people may possess title deeds.

Then in account books the local officers explain all expenditure : 'for repaireing longbrigd £2 7s', 'dinner for burgesses £5 17s 6½d', '3s 6d per Weeke for Jane Cooke's Bastard'. Entries throw light on the economic conditions in the community, the social status of various families, poor relief, law and order, transport and roads, the cost of building, wages, the price and type of food and clothing in the locality, the political sympathies of villagers, education, farming, industries, church life, nearly every topic the student wishes to research into. By card indexing all persons named in my own town's accounts from 1733 to 1828 I have almost a complete list of local inhabitants.

Rate books enable the historian to work out the names of the successive occupants of a particular house or property as well as the various uses to which owners put the site. The best plan is to work backwards. The researcher cannot assume that there has never been a renumbering so he extracts details of the house he is interested in and particulars of three houses on each side also. If all residents and rateable values suddenly change (as they do in the example below in 1862-3) there has probably been a renumbering. Number 7 Smithy Houses is today occupied by the Gleave family and local directories show that great-grandfather Gleave died in that house in 1896, after paying his rates. The search in rate books can therefore begin in 1896 and end in 1770 when rate books for that town start.

Number 7 Smithy Houses

occupied by William Gleave 1896-1863 as 7 Smithy Houses
William Gleave 1862-1856 as 2 Smithy lane
Jane Troughton 1855-1836 as smithy fold
Overseer of poor 1835-1816 as poorhouse
Jas. Jackson 1815-1791 as warehouse late Thompsons
Jo. Thompson, smith 1790-1770 unnamed but by its
position between neighbours who continued
to live both sides of Jas. Jackson it is
obviously the same property as 'warehouse
late Thompsons'

The historian may also like to know in which house a certain person lived, perhaps because the man was a renowned local worthy or is named in an interesting probate inventory or left a bundle of title deeds to an as yet unidentified house. In this case the researcher works forwards from the last rate book in which his man's name appears to the present day. Once again three ratepayers are noted on each side of the required person to guard against changes of house numbering or even of street names. It is essential to follow names of ratepayers, not house numbers or street names. The following names were extracted from a rate list of 1798 in order to identify the present site of the house of John Birkenhead, then living at number 10 Low Row. The three names on each side of Birkenhead are in the position they occupy in the document.

Blue Boar	T. Swift
Warehouse	Cooke & Co.
Low row 9	Jane Holland
10	Jo. Birkenhed
11	Henry Hand
Market row	Will Smith
Red Lion	J. Smith

A town map of the same date shows that the above houses all adjoin, number 11 Low Row being a corner building. The historian follows these people's names through successive rate books and notes changes of occupancy until the present day. There is no doubt that the first five premises which all still stand are now in High Street, John Birkenhead's house being now number 57. Obviously all this work is most readily completed in a town where houses are arranged in rows and streets. London houses began to be numbered in 1767 but other towns followed suit generally only after the Towns Improvement Act of 1847. In villages the rate collector probably haphazardly wrote down the names of ratepayers as he visited each in turn. Most places are so small that it is not difficult to work out from a study of surviving records who lived where at any date after about 1600.

Rate and account books show how far the vestry or its equivalent authority obeyed an Elizabethan poor-law act that sought the establishment of a house in each community where poor, aged, infant or invalid people might work and live. Many villages built or rented a poorhouse for such folk : the workhouse was none too popular on account of the difficulty of providing profitable work. Do probate records reveal legacies to the poor and aged in your parish? Rate books are usually listed at the local record office. The majority begin no earlier than 1690. See for instance the published *London Rate Assessments and Inhabitants Lists in Guildhall Library and the Corporation of London Records Office* (second edition, 1968).

SETTLEMENT AND REMOVAL RECORDS

Parliament has since medieval times attempted to suppress the movement of rogues and vagabonds as a threat to law and order. Paupers, orphans, the aged and the infirm were all supposed to be looked after in their home towns. Then after the Civil War the law of settlement and removal was codified. Every person should have one place of legal settlement where alone poor relief would be granted. To this place would be compulsorily removed any person likely to be chargeable to the rates. Settlement might be gained by birth in a place, payment of rates on property assessed at £10, completing a year as hired servant or the full term as apprentice in the township.

Documents so created include the settlement certificate. When Jonadab Morten wanted to go and live in Manchester, his home town armed him with a certificate. If he became a burden on the rates in Manchester he would be accepted back home. This certificate was to be deposited by Jonadab with the churchwardens and overseers of Manchester. Towns frequently removed paupers without formality though some cases went to quarter sessions resulting usually in the magistrate's removal order. Settlement and removal records are found as separate papers in the parish chest and are often copied out in some special town memoranda book. There is an eighteenth-century alphabetical list of settlements in Northallerton (Yorkshire) with a note of previous place of residence in the parish records of that town. Some examinations prior to removal furnish place of birth and marriage; towns of residence and work over twenty or thirty years; age; and job as well as other personal details that the magistrate thought fit to ask for.

APPRENTICESHIP

Most local collections contain apprenticeship registers and deeds. Young people, especially paupers and orphans, were apprenticed perhaps as butchers or shoemakers for a period of years. The apprenticeship deed is written out twice, one copy for master, one for parish or parent. The single sheet of paper on which copies are inscribed head to head is cut with an indented line to separate the texts. This produces the indenture. Each deed will give the name, age and parentage of the child; his residence; name and job of his master; and the date. Such records provide a good idea of the type of work most easily available in the locality. Sometimes there appears to be a shortage of work because the parish apprentices a child many miles away. Was the vestry careful in setting children to worthwhile work and good masters?

CHARITIES

Many charities have been founded by private and public benefactors to provide comforts for old and young. Charities may well be administered by independent trusts, and records must be sought from officials of the charity itself. But benefactors also left money to parishes or towns. In such cases local officials generally dispose of the money for the use of the poor or for education. Records are in the parish chest, sometimes as separate bundles, sometimes as an integral part of the town accounts. Charity deeds should be enrolled in chancery and may therefore be consulted at the Public Record Office, though charity papers themselves survive only by chance. Histories of charities like schools, almshouses and donations of money or food are in the abstract of the returns concerning charitable donations, published 1816, and the relevant report of the commissioners for inquiring concerning charities in England and Wales dated between 1819 and 1837, all in *Commons Sessional Papers*. There is an index to the latter in *Sessional Papers* for 1840.

Court Books

Large boroughs established courts with judicial and administrative functions. These courts had varied names : mayor's court, pie-powder court, petty view and court of assembly. The magistrates heard cases of assault, illegal trading, insanitary habits and so on. Rules were made for the better governance of the town. Proceedings, minutes and orders are found on loose parchments as well as in hefty volumes. Occasionally records date from the thirteenth century. Borough archives sometimes contain manorial records also, perhaps in places where the lord had himself granted the borough charter but still retained a hold on the inhabitants. Boroughs acquired the right to hold their own quarter sessions courts independent of the county.

Estate Documents

All types of communities own property and so create estate records of value for the local historian. Deeds of title numbering millions lie in dozens of council strongrooms accompanied by leases, maps, accounts, surveys and correspondence. Professor W. G. Hoskins in his *Fieldwork in Local History* (1967) stresses the importance of corporation, town and village documents for all kinds of historical work. He takes one parcel of town land in Exeter that appears first as an open space in a 1564 corporation survey. City rentals reveal that a cottage was built on the site about 1575. This must have decayed because in 1661 a local man was empowered to rent the ground provided that he erect 'a decent and Convenient dwelling house' thereon. Leases continue the history up to 1815 when the property passed into private hands.

Improvement Commissioners' Records

Improvement commissioners were set up by private act of Parliament during the eighteenth and early nineteenth centuries to undertake some aspects of the government of metropolitan and provincial towns. By the time of the 1835 Municipal Corporations Act there were some one hundred such bodies in the London area and two hundred elsewhere dealing with paving, lighting, street cleaning, drains, sewers, police work and the abatement of nuisances. The commissioners included senior officers of the town government, magistrates and substantial inhabitants who were elected or co-opted for life and succeeded in their tasks in so far as they could rely on the co-operation of the majority of citizens. They had few powers of

coercion and were often opposed by the poorer ratepayers who felt
that improvements took place only in the more prosperous districts
of town. In Manchester the commissioners carried out fire service
and police work independent of the vestry and in 1817 erected a gas
works, though such activity aroused the bitter opposition of radicals
and devotees of *laissez faire*. The 1835 act allowed new municipal
corporations to take over the work of the improvement commissions
but few did so, and the older bodies survived in many cases until the
second half of the century. Records, which are usually with borough
or city archives today, throw light on the struggles of the first town
planners against wretched living conditions.

Guild Records

Tradesmen, merchants and craftsmen have since Norman times
formed within corporate towns an association known as the guild
merchant. To this any member of the burghal community could
belong regardless of occupation. Members were free of local tolls
and were given a monopoly of trading save in victuals. The guild
provided aid in times of sickness or adversity and granted money
for education and funerals. Documents of the guild deal with every
aspect of local economic affairs as will be evident from a study of
The Gild Merchant (1890) by Charles Gross. Original guild records
are usually with borough archives at the guildhall.

During the thirteenth century craft guilds grew up in large towns
to cater for individual trades like weaver, fishmonger and silversmith.
Often fiercely opposed to the policies of guild merchants and town
corporations, the craft companies retained their own records. What
has survived the centuries may still be in the hands of individual
companies, though sixty London livery companies have deposited
records at the Guildhall Library and Coventry guilds have placed
papers in the city record office. Guilds together with chantries that
have similar purposes are surveyed in returns of 1389 and in chantry
certificates of 1548, all in the Public Record Office with inquisitions
concerning the founding of these institutions.

Pollbooks

Pollbooks set out lists of men who actually voted in parliamentary
elections for borough and county seats. Dating from the year
1694 to 1872 the books record men's names, sometimes addresses, usually
professions, and indicate how each man voted. Until 1872 voting took

place in public ordinarily for two out of four candidates, and officers filled in a draft pollbook as each man cast his vote. The originals rarely survive but a commercial printer at the time often published the book, so that copies are now available in libraries and record offices. The local historian studies pollbooks partly to follow the voting pattern of his district over a century and a half; to learn if radical or conservative elements won and by what margin and to discover what such victories imply about town affairs and conditions, to ascertain how different areas of the borough, different professions and different religious groups voted. It is normally possible from church archives and the card index of persons to know a man's religious affiliation and so to divide the polling list into church groups. There is a model textbook about the use of these records in J. R. Vincent's *Pollbooks; How Victorians Voted* (1967). The student analyses the documents in some detail to uncover the action of pressure groups such as liquor merchants, textile manufacturers, gentry and trades union members; the influence of the wealthy and educated on reform candidates; the power of prosperous customers over shopkeepers and landowners over tenants. Pollbooks are sometimes useful as directories to enable the researcher to trace men and houses, perhaps to see when a person first appears in town, and are one basis of the table of a town's occupational structure discussed below.

OCCUPATIONAL STRUCTURE

The general occupational structure of each community may be studied by analysing the few types of documents that mention men's jobs prior to the census of 1841. Pollbooks, apprentice registers and lists of freemen, jurors or militiamen sometimes show occupations. The process of research is as follows. From each list individual jobs are noted and totals counted : in 1770 in one town butchers number 14, shoemakers 16, glovers 2. These totals are then placed in categories previously worked out. There is no agreement about how best to arrange jobs in categories and a few different ideas are discussed in Alan Rogers's *This was their World* (1972). Obviously general categories are acceptable and include crafts; processors of raw materials such as miners or farmers; retail shops; and gentry. But the division into more specific groups is difficult especially when one man has two very different jobs or describes himself by one occupation though working in another, for instance where the goldsmith is really the banker. The work can therefore be left to individual taste, and categories evolved by trial and error. The following partial and simplified list shows the total number of men in each work category and the figure as a percentage of the total listed work force. Documents from three years have fortunately been found to provide men's occupations. The table below indicates how men earned a living at

	1770		1800		1830	
	No.*	%†	No.*	%†	No.*	%†
Primary Producers	12	11	25	17	30	12
Timber	7	6	20	13	21	8
Crafts	22	20	38	25	70	28
Wood	2	2	10	7	8	3
Clothing	6	5	8	5	14	6
Leather	4	4	13	9	13	5
Retail	12	11	30	20	60	24
Food	1	1	4	3	6	2
Clothes	2	2	6	4	12	5
Beer	5	5	14	9	31	12
Farming	42	38	32	21	35	14
All others	22	20	25	17	55	22
Total	110	100	150	100	250	100

    * Number of people engaged in various categories of work.
    † Percentage of labour force in each category of work.

three dates and emphasises changes in the pattern of employment. As the industrial revolution continued, farming occupied a smaller percentage of the work force. The destruction of forests helped the timber trade to develop rapidly after 1770 and its labour force increased until 1830, though other craftsmen and primary producers had by this time reduced its importance in the economy. The tanning of leather was a dominant craft in the period 1770-1800 partly on account of the plentiful supply of hides and partly because oak trees in the district provided sufficient quantities of bark for tanning purposes. The leather and timber trades encouraged the town to grow, and as men from surrounding smaller market settlements changed their shopping habits local inns and shops prospered. Retailers quintupled in number between 1770 and 1830 and grew even more important as a percentage of the work force. It is not surprising then that shopkeepers and landlords of inns come to dominate the town corporation and parish church vestry meetings at this time. Craftsmen and farm labourers form the backbone of nonconformist societies in the town, workers in the declining weaving crafts making up the majority in the more radical religious groups. From this table of the occupational structure the historian interprets some features of local affairs, putting forward the facts of economic life as indications of what changes might be expected in politics, education, religion and so on. The table depends on the reliability of original documents and on intelligent categorising on the part of the researcher.

CHAPTER 12

Church archives

ARCHIVES of religious bodies yield so much information to the local historian that these documents cannot be overlooked even when religion as such will not figure in the survey. The church has for long touched every aspect of human affairs. Documents make this very clear.

RELIGIOUS HOUSES

The abbeys and priories of medieval England were influential in education, politics, finance, trade and agriculture. Possessing possibly one-third of the land and most of the scribes and lawyers, religious houses owned vast muniment rooms of charters, title deeds, leases, estate accounts, chronicles and court rolls. The dissolution of the monasteries in 1536-9 consigned many records to oblivion. The remainder went to the crown or to lay purchasers of the estates. Surviving documents are therefore in the Public Record Office, British Museum or other national repositories, or with the estate archives of families who have owned the monastic property since 1536.

CAPITULAR RECORDS

The dean and chapter administer a cathedral and its endowments. Some cathedrals own property over a wide area of the diocese, and capitular records therefore include title deeds, surveys, rentals, manor court rolls and correspondence from as early as the eleventh century onwards. Minutes of decisions of dean and chapter affecting cathedral estate matters and services are in chapter act books. The York book starts in 1290. Records usually remain in the possession of the dean and chapter or with diocesan solicitors.

DIOCESAN RECORDS

From medieval times the bishop as head of the diocese has created administrative and judicial records of great complexity. For most purposes records of the two archbishops and of the bishop's deputies known as archdeacons can be classed as diocesan. For episcopal estates there are the usual kinds of documents: title deeds, manorial court rolls, maps, leases, rentals. These are separate from capitular records and are held by the diocesan solicitor or county record office. Especially voluminous are the archives of Canterbury, York, Durham and Lincoln. Landed property of bishops and chapters has been administered by the Ecclesiastical (Church) Commissioners since 1836. This body owns a vast collection of documents in London, though since 1950 older records have been partly dispersed to their places of origin and deposited in county record offices. Before commencing research into these voluminous but rewarding documents consult J. S. Purvis, *Introduction to Ecclesiastical Records* (1953) and D. M. Owen, *The Records of the Established Church in England excluding Parochial Records* (1970).

BISHOP'S REGISTERS

Bishop's registers are the oldest diocesan records dating back to 1209 at Lincoln. Contents are various, including records of consecrations of churches, notes about probate of wills, institutions to benefices and cases of clerical misbehaviour. For your parish church story these documents are essential reading from the thirteenth to sixteenth centuries. Some registers are printed by the Canterbury and York Society. Others must be consulted in manuscript in diocesan archives usually at the cathedral itself and are in Latin and in a difficult court hand. After about 1490 records of institutions, ordinations and resignations as well as other series separate themselves from the general registers to form books or bulky files of their own. Documents concerning consecrations, petitions to build new churches, title deeds and similar records are numerous for the eighteenth and early nineteenth centuries. Most are in English and relate to new suburbs or industrial towns.

LICENCES

A faculty is a bishop's licence allowing the local church to alter buildings, reserve vaults, erect monuments and so on. It may date from as early as 1240, though most are no older than 1720. Licences are found granting schoolmasters, surgeons, midwives, curates and parish clerks the right to work. Incumbents are permitted to be non-resident and to hold several livings.

Sometimes a couple obtained a bishop's licence to wed when banns were not, for some reason, convenient. Prior to granting their licence diocesan authorities made enquiries and took statements or allegations concerning the two parties. Bonds and allegations, possibly dating from the sixteenth century, usually show the couple's abode, age (often merely 'over 21') and occupation. The place of intended marriage and names of sureties also appear. Marriage bonds are in the county record office where some indexes are available. Their use for the local historian is partly genealogical, partly an indication of the age when people married and the type of work that was available in the district.

TERRIERS

A terrier is a list of all the landed possessions of a church. Generally the document begins with a description of the church itself, its fabric and furnishings and of the churchyard. Then parsonage and garden are sufficiently surveyed to enable the researcher to picture the place clearly. Any other outbuildings and cottages belonging to the church are mentioned in this way : 'a mere cottage built with clay walls and covered with thatch containing 3 rooms' (1604). Terriers rarely date from before the seventeenth century. Some are written in Latin, some in English. Documents vary in size and clarity according to clerk or incumbent and survive both in the parish chest and in the bishop's own records at the diocesan registry.

RETURNS

The privy council sent to all the bishops in 1563 queries concerning the state of the dioceses. These included requests for the number of households in each parish. The surviving returns are in the British Museum Harleian Manuscripts, though extracts sometimes survive locally. Bishop Compton's return of 1676 concerns much of the midlands, Wales and south. The information includes an estimate of population as well as numbers of Anglicans, papists and dissenters in each parish. The William Salt Library, Stafford, possesses a good copy of the return while other extracts are found in diocesan and parish records, also at Lambeth Palace and the Bodleian, Oxford.

BISHOP'S TRANSCRIPTS

After the church injunction of 1597 each parish clerk was to send to the bishop a transcript of the entries in the parish register of baptisms, marriages and burials. These documents, usually of parchment, are signed by the incumbent and churchwardens. Their value lies in being a substitute for missing, illegible or damaged parish registers. Most transcripts date from 1598 to 1837. They are usually now in the county record office.

VISITATION RECORDS

A bishop was supposed to travel round his diocese at not too infrequent intervals. Prior to the visit articles of inquiry were sent out to determine the state of each parish. Most were duly answered by incumbents or clerks and filed in the diocesan registry. Surviving documents mostly come from the period 1660-1860 and are usually in the county record office. The bishop naturally wanted to know whether the incumbent was resident or not, the value and age of the church plate and the date of the registers. Such facts give a good picture of church organisation. But other queries concerned Methodist Sunday schools; the main opportunities for employment in the district; charities; the extent and a description of farms and fields owned by the church authorities. Records of the visitation court itself survive and, where reform had not been effected prior to the visit, reveal some of the sins and wrongdoings of church officials. Very interesting are examinations of recusants and schoolmasters especially in Elizabethan times. Why did one village schoolmaster not attend church? What people played football on a Sunday? Why did the vicar bitterly vilify local nonconformists?

EPISCOPAL COURTS

The bishop has since medieval times and until 1860 dealt with a variety of offences committed by clerics and laymen. Flagrant cases of clerical immorality or problems concerning high society were reserved for the bishop's own court and recorded in the general registers. Minor courts heard the majority of cases concerning, for instance, matrimony, wills, parish bounds, trading on feast days, tithes, slander, and much else. Act books set out the date and place of the hearing; the name, residence and fault of the accused; and court proceedings. Individual documents brought to court by people involved are most valuable because of the detail afforded about local places, persons and customs. These documents are often labelled *responsa personalia*, articles or *materia*, allegations and depositions. Court records are, sadly, still largely not calendared or transcribed so the researcher has to face an abbreviated Latin (or Latin-English mixture) and very difficult handwriting. Because records are generally now with the county archivist he may be willing to help the student.

PROBATE RECORDS

Ecclesiastical authorities began proving wills in medieval times and continued to do so until 1858. Hence pre-1858 wills needed in your survey should be sought in diocesan record offices or in courts of peculiars (a district exempt from jurisdiction of the bishop in whose diocese it lies). Both registries have by now usually handed records over to the county record office. Most inhabitants prove wills in the court of the local bishop. People owning property over a wide area of England and Wales might go to the courts at York or Canterbury. The locating of probate copies of wills is in any case not difficult if you know in what district a person died or owned property. To learn where the will is likely to be deposited nowadays consult A. J. Camp's *Wills and their Whereabouts* (1963). Should the local history require wills later than 1858 these are obtained from the relevant local probate registry or from Somerset House, Principal Registry of the Family Division.

Historians examine probate records for various reasons.

1. The testator usually mentions relatives, friends and neighbours. This is useful in proving relationships within a community, and intermarriage usually explains otherwise puzzling features of local affairs. Men try to build up businesses and estates through marrying themselves or their children to the right people. It is interesting when the dead man leaves a fortune to unlikely folk such as 'Jane Bousfield my servant'.

2. Wills serve as family settlements tying up property and interests for generations.

3. Wills are often title deeds. I found in one bundle of deeds to a cottage that the two earliest documents did not seem to be connected. The first dated 1620 showed James Fogg selling a house of two bays to William Grey. The second told me that a lady called Betty Fuller sold a substantial farmhouse to a city merchant. Since the deeds were now relating to a petrol station occupying the site of a demolished farm, I was interested to know if the cottage was in any way a predecessor of the larger house of 1690. I therefore looked through will indexes to find William Grey's will. This was no difficult task and I was soon able to hold in my hands Grey's original signed will

dated 1658 and proved in the bishop's court in 1664. Grey mentioned that his sons were already dead so that his property falls to his daughter Elizabeth, wife of Oliver Fuller. He described his house as 'all that my messuage or dwellinghouse in which I now dwell lately rebuilt and consisting of five bays of building'. The probate copy of this will would at one time have been placed with the bundle of title deeds but for some reason had been lost, perhaps extracted by the daughter Elizabeth when she sold the house to a stranger. Most probate copies have in fact disappeared because families are not very careful keepers of records. It is therefore fortunate that the original wills signed by the testators have been in the main safely kept in diocesan registries.

4. A charity or school is often founded by will: 'to the church-wardens for erecting four almshouses and donating every year at Christmastime six loaves of bread to poor widows . . . to the parish for building a school and master's dwelling'.

5. Wills describe property in useful terms: 'my Messuage or Dwellinghouse with my new Stable and the Rooms over the same now used as a dwellinghouse and occupied by . . . all that my meadow called Salthousemead . . . my landes in west-feilde called loonts cockshuttes and foureselyons . . . house called factors house'.

6. Commercial, farming and industrial interests are sometimes described in wills: 'my Cotton-mill . . . land and house held of William Johnson together with the machines engines and materials of trade . . . my counting house in Bristol'. Business partners, debtors, creditors and customers are named. Heirs may be instructed on the correct means of running the business.

7. The diocesan copy of a will is marked with the approximate value of the deceased's personalty.

Until about 1740 inventories of the deceased's goods accompanied his will. Appraisers walked through the house, workshop, farmyard, barn and storehouse writing down every item of property and estimating the value of everything. This enabled the diocesan officials to work out how much the man was worth and how much to charge for probate. It allows the historian to gain a glimpse into ordinary town homes from about 1550 to 1740. Appraisers name each room in the house. Ground plans and elevations follow certain patterns so the student of vernacular architecture can be reasonably sure of reconstructing houses described in inventories. Using only inventories an architect has drawn pictures of early Stuart houses that have long since disappeared in J. West's *Village Records* (1962). M. W. Barley read inventories from all over the country in order to work out house types for his studies on *The English Farmhouse and Cottage* (1961). The local historian could use the drawings in that book to help him reconstruct his own village houses. The appraisers name all the furniture, utensils and clothing. Their work enables the student to estimate the comforts of local homes and the standard of living; to study the price of most items needed at home from cresset, broche and posnett to jerkins, drawers and stays; to write a study of local fashion or at least of clothing. Inventories of tradesmen mention goods from all over Europe and indicate what the housewife might find on the market stall. Craftsmen's tools and raw material are surprisingly varied and their sums of money about the house sometimes substantial. Creditors and debtors are named, providing at least the framework for a discussion on local financial institutions before the period when solicitor and bank can be recognised. From farmers' inventories it is possible to work out what crops are grown locally, what animals are kept, where the produce is sold, what implements are available and their relative values and the survival of strips in the open field. Inventories enable the historian to compare local tools, clothing, furnishing and wealth with goods, money and implements possessed by people in other places. Similarly he contrasts the goods found in local homes and shops in 1600 and in 1700. He may even estimate whether household and craft utensils altered and improved over the years or remained more or less the same and what effect the situation had on the local economy. Differences of wealth from trade to trade and class to class are usually quite marked, and reasons should be sought for this. It is pleasurable nowadays to wander round museums to study reconstructed Victorian shops or to visit country houses to look at rooms preserved from past centuries. Inventories provide the same authentic evidence, and the historian can mentally refurnish a home or restock a shop item by item as he deciphers these documents. Museums and country houses are sometimes set up from descriptions in reference books or from possibly unrepresentative objects that have fortuitously survived from the past, so the resulting exhibition may be nowhere near as accurate as a restocking or restoration from information in inventories recording real houses on specific days.

Inventories may be useful in providing indications of the differing wealth of craftsmen, shopkeepers, farmers and others at various dates between about 1550 and 1750. For my own village, as well as others that I have studied, the sample of inventories is not sufficiently wide to yield a worthwhile tabulation but the situation is better elsewhere. To achieve accuracy every local inventory will have to be discovered and the following information extracted.

Name of deceased	Occupation	Personalty	Date
John Smith	tanner	£240	1720

If there are many inventories then it is possible to compare these decade by decade, but it is just as satisfactory if all for 1550-1600 are compared with all for 1600-50, 1650-1700 and 1700-50. When all inventories are summarised in the manner above, each is placed into a category depending on the occupation of the deceased. Thus all the tanners' inventories are put together for each period, whether a decade or fifty years. A sum total of all the tanners' wealth is calculated for the period. This can be set out eventually as a percentage of the total wealth of all the local men. It can then be shown what proportion of wealth was held by tanners, in each decade or longer period, whether tanners gained or lost comparatively over the centuries and what significance this had for the community.

When a person left no will his heirs might take out an administration bond prior to dealing with the estate. Bonds show names of relatives and of husband or wife; date of death; and value of personalty. If the will is lost, the diocesan act book, the daily record of work undertaken at the registry, exhibits the essential details of probate records. Canterbury archdiocese acts date from 1526. Most act books will have to be consulted in the original.

Almost all collections of wills are in the county record office. But wills proved in the prerogative courts of Canterbury and of York are at the Public Record Office and at the Borthwick Institute, York, respectively. Wills proved during the Commonwealth period, 1653-60, are at the PRO.

Many indexes are in print. The British Record Society's *Index Library* lists wills proved at Canterbury and other courts in alphabetical order of testators. Canterbury indexes begin in 1383. For wills after 1858 consult the Principal Registry, Family Division, Somerset House, or the local probate registry.

PARISH RECORDS

Anglican parish registers, minutes and related documents may lie in the church safe or chest, at the diocesan registry or on loan with the county record office. The oldest records are likely to be vestry minutes and accounts setting out the decisions of the incumbent, churchwardens and local worthies who administered church affairs. Documents sometimes begin in the fourteenth century. The historian can read about charities, disputes over church rates, discussions on altering and rebuilding church property, fabric repairs, building of extensions, purchase of plate or vestments and the administration of church lands. The vestry also governed the parish as a civil unit, and documents in this case have been discussed on pages 149-54.

Parish registers of baptism, marriage and burial were first produced under the provisions of Thomas Cromwell's mandate of 1538. Each vestry was to acquire a chest with locks and keys where a register could be safely stored. The parish clerk entered details from notes or memory fairly regularly but his early records, usually on paper and unbound, have not always survived and it was not till 1597 that a church injunction forced incumbents to use parchments bound in book form and to send a fair copy of entries yearly to the diocesan registry. From 1754 marriage entries are in a separate book on printed forms, while baptism and burial entries are standardised after 1813.

Because banns and licences cost time and money people contracted clandestine marriages from about 1660 till Lord Hardwicke's marriage act of 1753. Ceremonies performed in certain London churches, Fleet Prison liberties and some rural centres run into hundreds of thousands, and registers at the Public Record Office cover the period from 1667 to as late as 1777.

Some vestry minutes and many parish registers are in print. There is an index to manuscript registers by A. M. Burke, *Key to the Ancient Parish Registers of England and Wales* (1908) which lists parishes alphabetically and shows the date of the earliest register entry. By far the most authoritative work on church archives is the *National Index of Parish Registers* (Society of Genealogists, in course of publication). This is to provide a guide on all surviving records. The first two volumes introduce sources of births, marriages and deaths before 1837. Later volumes deal with Anglican and other denominations' records in each parish of England and Wales. The articles and the comprehensive bibliography should assist most researchers.

PARISH LISTS

Lists of parish inhabitants are found in parish chests. These may well be names of householders for the purpose of rate collection or of men eligible to serve as parish officers, on the county grand jury, in the militia or the army of reserve. It is not impossible to work out approximate population figures from parish lists, though it must be kept in mind that paupers, large numbers of servants, most females and children, itinerant families and evaders of military service will not appear in these lists. Multiplication by five or six may be necessary. What purport to be full lists of inhabitants generally date from the eighteenth century onwards, though Ealing, Middlesex, has a census dated 1599, Stafford 1622 and Cogenhoe, Northampton-shire, from 1618 to 1628. April 1676 is the month of the Compton census and a few lists date from this time. Later lists may be drafts for the censuses of 1801, 1811, 1821 and 1831 since only totals not names had to be sent to London.

In 1694 Parliament laid a tax on births, marriages, burials, bachelors over 25 and childless widowers. The impost survived till 1706. Each parish was supposed to exhibit a complete list of all inhabitants by households. Parents, children, servants and lodgers are named. Some lists provide details of jobs, addresses and the approximate value of real and personal estate because the tax was graduated according to social and economic status. Thus these documents may be the earliest of census returns. Only a few documents now remain, mainly in local record offices. The index of names for London in 1695 is printed in the London Record Society's second volume, *London Inhabitants within the Walls 1695* (1966). From these lists you can work out population, economic condition of inhabitants, family pedigrees and the social class of local people.

HISTORICAL DEMOGRAPHY

English historical demography means the study of the population of English communities mainly from the late sixteenth century onwards when parish records, the raw material of this science, become readily available. The numerical study for each parish when finished need never be re-done. Once a majority of parishes are completed informa-tion could be computerised and the results printed in quite a small volume. The standard English textbook on this subject is edited by E. A. Wrigley, *An Introduction to English Historical Demography*

(1966). See also T. H. Hollingsworth's *Historical Demography* (1969); *Population in History* (1965) edited by D. V. Glass and D. E. C. Eversley; and the journal *Population Studies*. Figures are collected to yield information about the family, industrial men and village society that is essential to our understanding of the past. Demography seeks to ascertain statistically why and how the change took place both by an aggregative analysis of registers and by family reconstitution. There is a most fascinating and balanced view of Stuart village society based on a demographic approach in Peter Laslett's *The World We Have Lost* (1965).

Aggregative analysis of parish registers seeks to produce from a mass of individual figures significant totals that help the historian to know more fully what English communities were like over the past four centuries. It is of course essential to choose first a register that is reasonably complete over at least fifty years and then to devise a simple form for recording numbers of christenings, marriages and burials. Excellent forms are exhibited in *An Introduction to English Historical Demography*. Such forms are reasonably swiftly filled out especially if two people work together. The exploitation of information consumes much more time. It is of course relatively simple if unreliable to subtract all burials over ten years from all christenings to produce an indication of natural increase, or to multiply by thirty an averaged annual number of baptisms to learn the population; to divide all christenings by all marriages over a period to show the number of children per marriage; to divide infant burials by all burials to indicate infant mortality at various dates. Other calculations are more intricate, involving in not a few cases knowledge of approximate population figures, for example, by using the seventeenth-century hearth tax records, later parish census lists or your card index of all inhabitants. Wherever proof has been available, demographers have found that the average country household held from 4·1 to 4·6 persons in the seventeenth and eighteenth centuries, the average town household from 5·5 to 6·5; so multiplication by 4·5 and by 6 should yield approximate population figures for the community. The card index of persons ought to provide an accurate figure too for any date chosen. It is equally acceptable to plot on a graph census figures that are known, perhaps from the Compton census of 1676, a parish rate list of 1735 and the national census of 1801. The line joining the three points shows an approximate population in any intermediate year ignoring temporary disasters such as plague. Armed with population statistics and an aggregative analysis of parish registers the researcher works out crude baptism, marriage and burial rates by referring five-year averages of register figures to population at those dates. Such figures do not have much value except to indicate an expanding or declining town, a place with large families or one where death was an ever-present menace.

The second main section of a demographer's work is family reconstitution whereby all references in parish records to each family are drawn together in such a way that significant characteristics more readily appear. This is done for the whole community over a stated period and is little different essentially from tracing a family tree save that in the latter case the genealogist deals with one interrelated group over an unstated period. Reconstitution cannot begin before 1538 when registers commence, demands registers with long complete runs of at least one century and asks for sufficient detail to identify individuals and families. It is almost impossible in large towns on account of continued migrations and the necessity of examining so many registers from different parishes.

The detailed work on card indexing family information has already been discussed in the section on research methods. The technique of family reconstitution, first developed in France but recently adapted for application to English parish registers, places each member of the family in the limelight. A separate slip is written out for each family baptism and burial; one slip also for each partner in a marriage. A family reconstitution form, FRF for short, is produced to show all the information from registers. Individual families can then be grouped by parishes, occupations, size, by the century in which each flourished, by the terms on which they held land and so on. This comparative and cumulative work will continually clarify the demography of England from Elizabethan times till 1837. FRF may be obtained from the Cambridge Group for the History of Population and Social Structure, 20 Silver Street, Cambridge.

The FRF enables the researcher to calculate the age at marriage of every inhabitant and to work out an average marriage age for each decade of a century. To deduce this age and the age when couples conceive children is a most important calculation because a change in people's habits probably greatly affected population movement in the period 1650-1870, and population increase probably ties in with economic growth. Did people in the first half of the eighteenth century really marry at an average age of twenty-nine?

Were wives generally a little older than their husbands in Stuart times? How many children might such a couple expect to produce before one partner died or the wife reached the end of her child-bearing years? Family reconstitution relates the total number of women in each five-year age group (say 20-4, 25-9 and so on) to the total number of legitimate children born to this group indicating fertility, and a comparison of female fertility decade by decade is essential in any demographic study. Information emerges about the average length of marriages, the interval between the death of a spouse and subsequent remarriage and the proportion of families that lost a parent before the end of their child-bearing life. Probably about one-third of people in Stuart times had been married more than once mainly because death had snatched away a breadwinner or helpmeet, and village life must have been affected by the presence of step-mothers and step-children in so many homes. Researchers generally discover a high number of births and children's deaths, half the population under the age of twenty-one and half the people getting married only because the loss of one or both parents released a home, job and land for the younger generation. Few grandparents lived with their children. Two-thirds of Stuart households seem to hold the modern nuclear family of parents and children perhaps with a servant or two. But the pre-industrial and Victorian communities had at least one factor in common, a young population, energetic, quarrelsome, noisy, arrogant and impatient, a force (one might think) for radical change.

Family reconstitution follows the career of each individual and therefore enables the historian to trace people's movements into and away from the settlement. Whenever it has been possible to study the question of mobility in pre-industrial decades the answer has emerged that folk were always on the move despite economic and legal barriers. The population of townships altered from decade to decade by four means. Firstly births and deaths changed family composition. Then servants shifted jobs not only within the community but from village to village. Most servants were unmarried young people working as personal domestics, agricultural labourers, apprentices and industrial helpers, composing some fifteen per cent of the population. Thirdly other individuals and fourthly whole families migrated. A five per cent annual turnover of population seems to be nothing remarkable in the period 1600-1780. This the card index of persons will prove as the historian follows each departing individual to the graveyard and parish boundary or visits newcomers in their homes. Half the people of a town might possibly disappear in ten years during an age when, according to some writers, folk rarely moved from their own hearths.

Reconstitution reveals the life span of individuals. Parish registers have until 1813 been somewhat reticent about people's ages so the card index of christenings and burials alone proves age at death by a process of subtraction. It should not be hard to trace the effects of disasters such as famine, wretched weather, war and plague. A sharply rising death rate followed by a fall to normality usually indicates some calamity, and this parish register information might be supplemented with evidence from overseers' accounts, diaries and correspondence as well as from secondary sources such as the *Gentleman's Magazine* and Lord Ernle's *English Farming Past and Present* (sixth edition, 1961) where there are references to harvests and weather ('great heat of 1757'). Parish records which purport to provide information about causes of death are seldom found before 1813. Most earlier references cannot be used for specific evidence because they are too gossipy : 'died of plague', 'senile decay', 'fell on a pitchfork which penetrated his fundament'. Even Victorians could not always recognise causes of death. Consumption is very popular with them and the term lunatic might conceal a tumour on the brain. Reconstitution does enable the historian to recognise periods of calamity and to calculate where the burden fell heaviest.

RECORDS KEPT BY NON-ESTABLISHED CHURCHES

Many English communities have gained a special character by the presence of people who refused to attend the Anglican services. The *Amateur Historian,* volume 3, has articles on dissenting records. See also A. G. Matthews's *Calamy Revised* (1934), a new edition of Edmund Calamy's *Account of the Ministers and Others Ejected and Silenced 1660-2*. The 1851 census of religious worship covers all places of worship almost without exception, giving the size of congregations on a certain Sunday, the number of available sittings and the date when the church or chapel was erected (Public Record Office, HO 129).

Roman Catholic documents contain registers of baptism, marriage and burial; records of itinerant priests; financial statements; school log books and progress reports; diaries and accounts of the local congregation. Most documents are no older than 1778 when the first

Catholic Relief Bill became law and so made record-keeping less dangerous. Documents are usually at the Catholic presbytery though some record offices are places of deposit. Registers, journals and lists of communicants are published by the Catholic Record Society.

Methodist collections may begin as early as 1760. There are registers of baptism and burial from about 1800; minutes of society meetings; preaching plans; Sunday school log books; day school accounts and logs and correspondence. Minutes of society meetings help with social history in detailing poor relief expenditure, proposals for education and donors to society budgets. Look on circuit plans and in minutes of local preachers' meetings to see if the community supported a Methodist society possibly prior to the building of the first chapel. Trust deeds of chapels describe the land purchased and show names, jobs and the residence of trustees. The *Methodist Magazine,* starting in Wesley's time, has a good index and should be consulted for village and family histories. Records are usually in the central safe of each Methodist circuit rather than in the local church.

Quaker documents are superb. The Friends are among the best record-keepers and have been since 1650. Monthly meetings preserve original registers of births, marryings and deaths; minutes of meetings; accounts of sufferings; financial statements; title deeds; correspondence and charity papers. Quaker documents are wonderfully informative about local affairs. The tyrannical behaviour of squire, parson and local farmer is described in detail. A number of Quakers became important figures in the industrialisation of the country and their origins are as a result all the more fascinating. Quarterly meetings often still hold on to records and the name of the relevant clerk of each meeting can be obtained from Friends House, London. Some collections are being deposited in county record offices where calendars and lists are available.

SCHOOL RECORDS

Education has for long been a church affair. Records of some grammar and village schools still lie in the parish chest. Many schools and masters appear by name in diocesan and parish documents, almost yearly from 1547 to about 1840, and occasionally till 1902, and disheartening situations frequently come to light. Thus three un-licensed 'infirm sailors' were discovered by the bishop to be teaching school at Northam in 1724. The foundation charter or title deed of a school should be sought first, perhaps among school records but possibly at the county record office. Original deeds of charity schools are enrolled on close rolls in the Public Record Office. Daily summaries of school life appear in log books, masters' diaries and in correspondence.

Quarter sessions records contain references to schools. The people of Swarkeston built a village school about 1639 but when the schoolmaster left during the Civil War, a prosperous outsider came and settled in the schoolhouse but did not teach. Therefore the villagers petitioned that 'hee may be cast out'.

The Society for Promoting Christian Knowledge founded village schools from 1699 onwards. Documents are held by the society at Holy Trinity Church, Marylebone Road, London, and include letter books, minutes, circulars and reports. The British (1808) and National (1811) Schools Societies between them erected hundreds of schools during the nineteenth century and the latter's archive is at its London office.

For the most reliable information the historian consults various parliamentary papers. R. B. Pugh describes some of the most significant documents in 'Sources for the History of English Primary Schools', *British Journal of Educational Studies*, i (Nov. 1952). A few House of Commons papers are listed below. During the sessions 1816-18 two Commons select committees discussed the education of the lower orders in the metropolis and provinces. The digest of parochial returns is published in 1819 and 1820. Every parish is surveyed in the abstract of education returns to queries sent out in 1833, *Commons Sessional Papers*, 1835, xli-xliii. Schools in manufacturing towns are dealt with by the committee on the education of the poorer classes, 1837-8, vii. The return of parliamentary grants for education during the years 1834-7 appears in *Commons Sessional Papers*, 1837-8, xxxviii, to show which parochial schools benefited from government subsidy.

To learn about buildings, teachers, equipment and grants in Victorian days consult the *Minutes and Reports of the Committee of the Privy Council on Education 1839-99*. School building grant plans have recently been transferred to county archives. The Schools Inquiry Royal Commission (Taunton Commission) is a useful survey of endowed schools, published in 1867-8, and possibly the most complete sociological study on education ever produced in this country. In 1870 the government set up school boards over districts, and records such as minute books survive in county archives or local council offices. Also very useful are two returns dealing with elementary education, in *Commons Sessional Papers,* 1871, lv, and 1875, lix. Returns of endowed grammar schools are in *Commons Sessional Papers* for 1865, xliii. Schemes for the reorganisation of these ancient institutions are printed by the Commons in various years from 1871 to 1899.

The printed report on the education census of 1851 indicates for each district the number of private fee-supported schools, the ones financed by local or general taxation, by religious groups, by endowments, by poor-law authorities, those operating as factory, blind, ragged, deaf or dumb establishments or as Sunday schools. In each class is noted the number of male or female scholars in attendance on census Sunday or Monday. Enumeration schedules for each school survive only by chance and some it seems were never even filled in.

The local historian is probably now aware that the history of a school must ordinarily be written from evidence not in fact created or held by the institution itself. Especially does this apply to lowly village schools, even those once called grammar schools, and to those that moved or rebuilt premises several times in the past. Educational history and facilities are thus surveyed more adequately in such documents as chantry certificates of 1545-8 (in the public records) or bishop's visitation books and probate papers left by donors of land and capital (in the county records) than in the school archive itself. Moreover a school is just one of numerous local features to which this statement applies. The researcher therefore bears in mind that a history need not be abandoned because the relevant organisation no longer seems to possess its own documents. Material, if in existence, might well regularly be located in repositories such as manor house, vestry or attorney's office. Even when discovered muniments do not always prove as detailed, satisfactory or indeed truthful as letters and reports prepared by such comparatively independent bodies as bishop and magistrate.

CHAPTER 13

Quarter sessions

THE Tudor dynasty first seriously considered employing magistrates in quarter and petty sessions not only as judges in criminal and civil cases but also as administrators and record keepers. Sessions documents in most counties are so voluminous that a local history cannot be completed unless a year or more is spent examining these documents. Records have always lain in the charge of the clerk of the peace who has usually handed these over to the county or borough archivist.

COURT IN SESSION

Law cases at the sessions concern many offences that were not settled in the villages or in royal courts : assault, theft, riot, bastardy, witchcraft, breaches of the peace. Lawbreakers were brought to court after arrest by constables, depositions by local inhabitants, presentments or indictments by justices or juries or the granting of a magistrate's warrant. One example of form is shown in this 1599 Essex sessions document : 'We presente that Thomas Whistock . . . with nyne other of his fellowes the xxvth day of february . . . beinge the sabaothe day did play at an unlawfull game called the fote bale.' The wording means that football was illegal on Sunday rather than a game that should not be played at all.

The poor occupied much of the court's time. Petitions from paupers asking for relief, from villages demanding money to erect a workhouse, from sailors needing help to return to their ships, from orphans, wounded soldiers, mothers heavy with child, idiots and other types of unfortunates, all are found. Magistrates ordered the removal of families to their place of legal settlement, and the order names family members, gives ages and occupations and shows the two townships involved. Appeals by towns and families against these orders are interesting in the range of excuses stated.

The main documents collected by the court in session are indictments, various bonds or recognisances to appear at court or keep the peace, presentments, depositions, jury lists, calendars of prisoners and petitions. All these parchments and papers were put into court, dealt with and then threaded on a single file for permanent preservation. This is the sessions bundle or file. The clerk of the peace kept a minute book of proceedings. When the court came to a decision the result might be scrawled by the clerk on the papers before him. It is certainly formally entered into the order book. Sentences include imprisonment, fines, whipping and transportation. In bastardy cases the man is usually forced to provide a weekly pension for the mother and child. Administrative decisions concerning such matters as the repair of bridges also appear in these books. The information in sessions bundles is presented in no set form and, with the possible exception of minute and order books, is not usually indexed. Thus you must wade through original bundles or rolls containing the various loose papers and parchments put into court. The writing is clear and in English from about 1650, aiding research. Some record offices have listed records so that you can swiftly look through typescripts. Other counties such as Buckingham and Hertford have published detailed calendars.

Calendars of prisoners awaiting trial at the sessions and the assizes are found from about 1750 onwards, usually in printed form. This is a typical kind of entry :

1848 Surrey Quarter Sessions.

Prisoner	Henry Binham (aged 16, can neither read nor write)
Committed	on 8th of February charged with felonously stealing at Newington one leg of pork.
Sentence	14 days solitary confinement and privately whipped.

Some calendars, especially those printed afterwards in newspapers, contain details of the sentence.

Transportation of prisoners to America, the West Indies and Australia was a well-organised business. Orders, correspondence, accounts and convict lists are usually filed in a separate section. Most documents date from 1790 to 1867. But the researcher may also find lists of emigrants, mainly indentured servants, who went to America as early as 1630. These people, not usually convicts, may well be paupers, unmarried mothers or spendthrift sons.

ACCOUNTS

Annual rates were imposed on counties from the seventeenth century, and there gradually emerged a county stock and county treasurer. After 1739 proper accounts were submitted to the magistrates. Expenditure is detailed in vouchers, account books and quarterly returns. Salaries of officials, repair of bridges and gaols, transportation of felons, relief of vagrants and militiamen's families, cattle disease, all appear in the sessions accounts.

ADMINISTRATIVE RECORDS

The justices in sessions acted as administrators before the formation of county councils in 1889. Parliament continually placed heavier burdens on these unpaid local officials in the shape of legislation concerning poor relief, vagabondage, road repair, armed forces, wage rates, weights and measures, lunatics, bridges, diseases of animals, county buildings, elections and so on. Documents reflect these duties and relate to every village in the county without exception.

REGISTERED AND DEPOSITED RECORDS

The sessions became a place for the deposit or registration of many types of record. Rules and accounts of savings banks from 1817 and friendly societies from 1793 are deposited. The latter institution might be set up as a burial club, an educational charity or a sickness insurance policy. All boats on navigable rivers and canals were registered from 1795 to 1871. The magistrates also registered charities from 1786, gamekeepers from 1710 and printing presses, 1799-1869. By an act of 1795 people who used hair powder took out a one guinea certificate annually. Registers of duty-payers name local gentry and their servants together with those aspiring to genteel status, such as the parson. Accounts of road, gas and water companies date from after 1815. Details of bankrupts' estates are useful for histories of property, houses and commercial interests.

The supervision of inns and alehouses by magistrates started in Edward VI's reign but records are seldom earlier than 1640 and usually no earlier than 1780. For a series of alehouse documents turn to recognisances, 1640-1830, and to licensed victuallers' registers, 1753-1828. In a recognisance an alehouse-keeper finds sureties and promises to maintain a good house. Up to about 1780 books or parchments list the names of licensed keepers and their sureties, the place of and possibly name of the alehouse. Check the wills of these people for further clues about their alehouses. Then from 1780 to 1830 original forms survive so that you can read in full all the conditions of a licence, indicating by the way just what kind of places the worst houses might be : no bear-baiting, no gaming with cards on the part of common people (the squire and parson were presumably excepted), no harbouring of women of 'notoriously bad fame'. You can trace year by year the names of all inns and occupants.

Under standing orders of the Commons, first made in 1792, whenever an authority planned public works, canals, railways, harbours or turnpiked roads, the project had to be properly surveyed and a plan presented both to Parliament and to the clerk of the peace. Such plans show the whole project, with ground plans, elevations and sections. Each parcel of land adjoining is numbered and a schedule accompanying the plan gives owner, occupier and acreage. You can thus follow the development of local projects as well as gaining a plan of houses, fields and farms in the vicinity. If the project actually got Parliament's approval, check the relevant act for more details. The county archivist compiles a list of all projects for which he holds plans.

Road diversion records since 1697 and plans since 1773 have at times been deposited with the clerk of the peace. There is usually a plan of the old and new roads delineating the adjoining property whether affected or not. Accompanying the plan are landowners' depositions and magistrates' orders about the project. If there seems to be anything out of the ordinary in the route of roads in the village check for diversions. During bouts of rebuilding and the landscaping of halls and parks between 1700 and 1914, landowners sometimes moved ancient roads further from their front doors.

The Test Act of 1673 forced all civil and military officials to deposit at the sessions certificates of their having received the Anglican sacraments. These sacrament certificates dating from 1673 to 1829 may yield significant personal information. Various other oaths and declarations were required by acts passed as late as 1812. Parliament's distrust of dissenters from the Anglican church led to the registration of nonconformist meetings. From the Toleration Act of 1689 to 1852 the clerk of the peace kept a register of buildings licensed as places of worship. You will find names of owners or occupiers, possibly names of members, denomination and addresses in the register. In addition original returns from townships for a parliamentary inquiry of 1829 into nonconformist strength should be sought.

Under an act of 1696 township constables were obliged to return every year to quarter sessions lists of men who were qualified to serve as jurors. These lists are in effect registers of local freeholders and therefore of electors in parliamentary elections. The constables might enter men's ages, occupations and places of abode. Lists of free-holders as such may survive for 1788-9, lists of jurors for 1696-1832. In 1832 printed electoral lists begin. These yearly documents name all men qualified to vote for members of Parliament. These lists are very useful in providing a voter's address and the address of the property in respect of which he claimed a vote. The history of a house, land and a family may be sought in these lists. By chance you come across poll lists from the early eighteenth century to 1868 to tell how people actually voted at various general elections.

Land tax returns, if used with diligence, may provide an excellent history of landownership from as early as 1692 to 1831. Parliament granted the new king William III a tax on such property as houses, land, tithes and public offices to enable him to make war. Valuers surveyed all property and the king got a varying proportion of the total annual value each year. The tax came more and more from landed property as years passed. It became perpetual in 1798 when the tax might be redeemed for a fixed sum. Every spring, returns were made to local magistrates who were responsible for sending abstracts and money to London. Some justices preserved original tax lists in their own family muniments until 1780. But between 1780 and 1831 returns were supposed to be sent to the clerk of the peace to satisfy electoral registration regulations. Documents are simple in form.

Land Tax 1828

OWNER	OCCUPIER	PROPERTY	TAX PAID	TAX REDEEMED
William Leigh	Mary Guest	Cottage and garden	0-0-9½	0-0-9½
John & Matthew Ledward	Themselves	Smithy & house	0-1-6¾	- - -

Your first impression of land taxes may be : 'interesting but nothing special'. Yet if you can spare some weeks to examine lists year by year these documents are among the most useful for many purposes. I have copied all land taxes for my village from 1731 to 1831, put results side by side and so have a perfect chart of owners, occupiers, changes in property ownership, new houses built and old dwellings demolished. Apart from the card index of persons, places and subjects this twelve-feet long list is my most valuable aid during research.

The process needs some explaining, and you should read David Iredale's *This Old House* (Shire, 1968) for the only guide to this. But in short follow this plan :

1. Begin with the latest list available, say 1831.
2. Write down each entry in turn on long narrow cards and arrange these under one another.
3. Compare the names on land taxes with tithe or estate maps to plot the location of each property.
4. Now take the next year, 1830. Write down the estates on cards as before. Place these alongside the 1831 cards estate to estate. If an 1831 estate has been formed through the joining of several 1830 estates there will be more cards in 1830 than in 1831. The 1831 cards can be moved apart to allow for this difference. The process also works the other way if an 1830 estate is divided.
5. Now take 1829 and repeat the process. Work back as far as you can. A land tax every five years may be sufficient. Remember that in general total tax for the village is always the same and the rate is usually 4s. in the £.

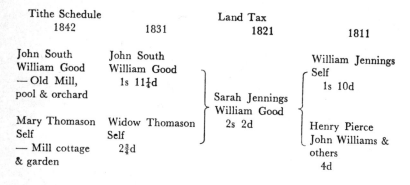

Tithe Schedule 1842	1831	Land Tax 1821	1811
John South William Good — Old Mill, pool & orchard	John South William Good 1s 11¼d	Sarah Jennings William Good 2s 2d	William Jennings Self 1s 10d
Mary Thomason Self — Mill cottage & garden	Widow Thomason Self 2¾d		Henry Pierce John Williams & others 4d

Henry Pierce's row of cottages had appeared on land taxes since 1762. The row was purchased by Sarah Jennings in 1815, according to land taxes of that year, and presumably demolished about 1820 because the present house on the site is no older. Land taxes indicate that Sarah Jennings sold the newly built cottage to Mary Thomason in 1822. The corn-mill was worked by William Good from the death of William Jennings in 1814 till about 1835 when the premises were converted by the owner into a dwelling house.

CHAPTER 14

Business records

BUSINESS records are created or accumulated by craftsmen, shop-keepers or industrialists in the course of their work. More often than not local businesses such as the mill and smithy, especially in the period before about 1850, are on so small a scale that no records were created, the only information about their activities now being derived from manor court rolls, overseer's accounts, vestry minutes and similar documents. Thus the medieval corn-mill may be mentioned in manorial accounts and court rolls but will almost certainly have left no documents of its own. Most businesses too experienced only an ephemeral existence, perhaps three generations in the hands of one family; and on the family's disappearance records also were destroyed. Business records are usually found today by the researcher browsing through the calendars of county and borough record offices; in the attics of old-established solicitors who sometimes allow historians access; in the ruinous cellars or offices of derelict factories; or in the possession of the present owners of the site where the business once flourished. Whenever an old enterprise still functions, records could be available if the proprietor is courteously approached. Nineteenth-century businesses will be listed in local directories; possibly one in ten survive and one in a hundred will have preserved records. Earlier businesses include the corn-miller, shoemaker, blacksmith and carpenter but almost nothing in the way of archives can be expected. For some guide on how to tackle this type of historical research consult the Historical Association's pamphlet number 59 on *Business History*; the journal *Business History* (1958 to date); publications of the Business Archives Council; and histories of specific industries, firms or regions.

PUBLIC UNDERTAKINGS

Canals, rivers, railways and roads can normally be expected to hold large archives, including plans, accounts, title deeds and leases dating from the time of the first discussions about improvement and building until cessation of operation. One river navigation in Cheshire has accumulated documents in large amounts for two centuries and more. Maps and plans begin in 1730 and show the surrounding property in some detail. The standard survey of Great Western Railway property is on a scale of two chains to one inch. Archives of many railways and other transport undertakings are held at the British Transport Historical Records Office. In some cases the company has itself retained old records, and occasionally collections turn up in the hands of firms of solicitors whose partners were once clerks or treasurers to the companies. Archives centres hold thousands of documents; for instance, the Brunel records are kept at the University of Bristol library.

TRADESMEN AND INDUSTRY

Tradesmen, such as shoemakers and carpenters, probably kept some kind of records especially in the period after 1850 but their accounts and bills rarely survive unless the enterprise prospered and expanded. Most local industries rise and decay fairly swiftly and their records disappear too. Their history will be learned only from township records and estate papers. Records of these firms may even have been stored in the manager's head, so to speak, in order to save clerical work, competitors' piracy and government snooping. Documents have generally been destroyed whenever a business has ceased operation partly because until very recently there has been no record office to take over archival material. Only a few collections from each town survive in the hands of local solicitors. Even such a firm as Pilkington Brothers of St Helens, the glass manufacturers, possesses merely a small number of documents relating to its own works for the period prior to the First World War. Business history must be learned from material not created by the firm, parliamentary reports, probate records or estate surveys.

On the other hand the business documents that do still exist tell the researcher much about the enterprise itself and many aspects of local affairs. The large chemical firm of ICI preserves title deeds and plans of houses and farms purchased as investment or for industrial development. The share registers of one of ICI's predecessors reveal the names of early shareholders, people whom the historian might have considered poor, certainly not prosperous enough to invest surprisingly big sums of money. The older records of Samuel Courtauld & Company, textile manufacturers, held in Essex Record Office, tell much about wages, working conditions, business prospects and local politics.

FIRE INSURANCE RECORDS

Premises have been insured against fire since the second half of the seventeenth century. Original policies are found in some private collections and describe the property in detail. People also fixed to their walls a numbered and distinctive plaque called a fire-mark which occasionally remains in place. The researcher notes the symbol on the plaque as well as the number because this indicates the company responsible for the insurance and the exact place in the registers where details of the transaction are recorded. The Sun Fire company employed the symbol of the sun, and its registers, now at the Guildhall Library, begin in 1710. The registers give the names of insurers and a description of the property over the years. It is possible to learn that the house was first insured, say, in 1772 when 'newly erected'. Or the place could be 'one ancient dwelling house now rebuilt in brick and slate and used as an academy for the daughters of gentlefolk'. Since most registers are not indexed it is difficult to locate premises by street or owner's name. Insurance companies usually hold their own archives at their London headquarters, though some of the earliest fire offices have deposited records at Guildhall Library.

TRADE CATALOGUES

Firms often issue catalogues of products or services in order to attract customers. Textiles, tools, steam pumps, bridges and food-stuffs are included in these documents that range in size from one page to a stout volume. The most accurate and informative catalogues begin to appear about 1820 and may be illustrated with a picture of the works and various products or even a short history of the firm. Such documents are found by chance in company or private hands.

CONTRACTS

Drawings, specification, submission of tenders, a bill of quantities and conditions of contract have for a century or more accompanied the establishment of factories or the undertaking of construction projects. These documents, usually among company records, enable the historian to build up in his mind many a vanished industrial feature, though it is as well to recall that contractors may modify or even abandon entirely original plans as time elapses.

SOLICITORS' ACCUMULATIONS

Solicitors or attorneys have for centuries held estate, business, official, manorial and parochial documents on behalf of the various owners. Landowners, waterways and industries employed solicitors as clerks or estate agents. Documents were created in and preserved at the solicitor's office where they have remained unless sent to the county archives. Every kind of record might be discovered at the solicitor's: wills, land taxes, correspondence, surveys, deeds, maps, to mention half a dozen types. In one office I came upon several allegedly pre-conquest charters, in another the minute books of an early nineteenth-century association of manufacturers to fix prices. It is not usually easy to find out which firm of solicitors at present possess documents relating to a specified area, partly because these busy men rarely know themselves the extent of their holdings. My investigations combine clues from directories and law lists, requests to the county archivist and enquiries in the neighbourhood itself. When consulting documents I look at the signatures of clerks and attorneys as a clue to which firms were operating in the past and then I follow successive partners in directories till I track down their present whereabouts. The law business itself will preserve its own old records, especially correspondence, accounts, diaries and drafts of deeds and legal cases. These reveal the widespread influence of attorneys in the financial, commercial, landed and business fields as, for example, they arrange loans for businesses and farms, value property, discuss the political situation and suggest industrial projects.

CHAPTER 15

Government records

THE government in London has for nine centuries extended its authority over most parts of England. Some areas like Durham and Cheshire remained for long very independent with their own palatinate administration and records (now in the Public Record Office). At certain periods, notably from 1689 to 1834, provincial affairs were left very much in local hands. None the less government documents will be valuable in any local study. Most central government records are in the Public Record Office where lists and calendars are prepared to help the researcher. Many volumes of calendars have been published (detailed in sectional list 24 published by HMSO) and should be available in local libraries. The List and Index Society reproduces without editing typescript lists of documents that will not appear in printed calendar form for years yet. For a general idea of what national records are available consult the *Guide to the Contents of the Public Record Office* (1963-8). The local historian may well obtain much information from the printed calendars if his period of study coincides with the years for which calendars are available. He can also send for microfilms or photocopies of documents that he sees mentioned in the guide to the Public Record Office. He will probably find it essential to visit London personally to consult documents that are not calendared but mingled within a series too vast for Record Office staff yet to sort through. A reader's ticket will first have to be obtained by providing name, address and subject of research on the appropriate form. Then a number of days at least should be set aside for research into any unlisted series of records. Handwriting of documents will prove a hindrance until about 1700 unless the historian is in practice. Latin is employed for some purposes up to 1733.

The exchequer was the department where the king's debtors were called to account. It took its name from the chequered tablecloth on which officials performed their calculations prior to the introduction of Arabic numerals. Pipe rolls beginning in 1129 and similar records of account are only of slight use to local historians being too general. But the Domesday survey should be examined in translation because it is by far the earliest documentary record of most English settlements. During 1086 royal commissioners questioned the lords and tenants of English manors about the ownership and extent of their properties. Unfortunately the four northern counties are not surveyed, and Yorkshire and Lancashire are very hastily recorded. The west country and East Anglia appear in great detail.

Domesday is primarily a personal enquiry into those holding land in chief of the king together with a full picture of each of their manors at the end of five hundred years of English settlement. The unit is the manor, possibly embracing several communities, perhaps containing just part of a village. Who owned the manor prior to 1066? What changes had there been? Were these detrimental to the king's interests? To learn the extent of possible losses the commissioners asked : how many plough-teams in the manor; how many villeins, cottars, freeholders; how much wood, meadow, pasture; how many mills and fisheries? But the record tells incidentally whether the town and church existed in 1086; whether a market was thriving; what farmsteads lay in the countryside. It gives an authentic version of the original place-name. Domesday Book is available in facsimile (by the Ordnance Survey, 1861-4) and in translation in your *Victoria County History*. Domesday statements are not easy to understand without guidance. V. H. Galbraith in *The Making of Domesday Book* (1961) shows why and how the survey was compiled, interpreting many puzzling Domesday practices. E. C. Darby with others has published since 1952 a series of regional books on the Domesday geography of England.

Subsidies from clerics and laymen date from the late thirteenth century until 1689. Documents record money raised from individuals or parishes. The earliest actually name villagers and state each person's contribution thus providing an indication of personal wealth. This attempt was abandoned in 1334 and village totals alone remain. Even this allows the historian to compare his own and adjoining places and to estimate local prosperity or depression. The poll tax of 1377 sought a fixed sum of money from individuals again. Then assessors tried to grade the tax of 1379 according to wealth but they failed. Hence the tax of 1381 reverted to a fixed payment from each person. This caused opposition and widespread evasion. Records of 1377 and 1379 are therefore most accurate as a source of local wealth and population : servants are named; and people's occupations are occasionally given. The 1428 parish tax exempted places with fewer than ten households. Such places are named and sometimes the actual number of households is written down. In 1524-5 a comprehensive subsidy was levied by Henry VIII's government which records taxpayers and individual payments. Although subsidies are written in Latin it is not difficult to learn the simple formula such as 'de Gulielmo molendinario vs.' (from William the miller 5s.). A few returns of the 1660 poll tax survive.

Householders paid a tax on each of their hearths during the late seventeenth century. A township officer compiled a list of all houses in his village, naming occupiers and noting the number of fireplaces. He divided people into two categories: taxpayers and paupers. In theory every house should appear, enabling the researcher to work out approximate population figures (say four and a half persons per house). Check occupiers' names and see if these people left wills in the diocesan registry. Do wills describe the cottages? How many hearths went undeclared? Township returns survive in county records or in the muniments of a local landowner. The Public Record Office can provide copies of hearth taxes between 1662 and 1674.

Certificates of musters name adult males liable to serve in local defence forces. The earliest date from 1522 when Cardinal Wolsey ordered an inquiry into military preparedness and, incidentally, a true valuation of property. Most sixteenth-century lists are in State Papers Domestic or in exchequer records. Later documents are usually with lieutenancy collections in the county record office accompanying surveys of the local food supply, weapons, carts, watermills or windmills.

Other exchequer records include those concerned with church revenues after the break with Rome such as *Valor Ecclesiasticus* of 1535 (printed by the Record Commissioners). Monastic muniments, leases of monastic property, documents dealing with schools, colleges and dissolved chantries as well as particulars for grants of crown property to lay owners may also be studied. Surveys of feudal services mentioning estates and knights of the twelfth and thirteenth centuries are mostly available in the printed *Red Book of the Exchequer* and the *Book of Fees* of 1198-1293.

The chancellor acted as king's private secretary, adviser on home and foreign affairs, keeper of the great seal that authenticated documents and organiser of the civil service. He established a law department which extended its jurisdiction over all cases for which the common law offered no remedy. Chancery records include copies of all letters despatched since 1202 and originals of those received. Letters patent (public) and close (private) concern grants of land or offices; castles and bridges; taxation; town charters; church affairs and much else of local interest. On the back of the close rolls are copies of such documents as title deeds, wills, deeds of papists and trust deeds of charity, school and chapel property. Medieval close and patent rolls are calendared, together with charter rolls from 1199 to 1516.

Special commissions and inquisitions of chancery date from medieval times. Miscellaneous inquisitions of chancery start in 1219. Inquiries deal with manors, churches, parks, bridges, commons, estates and towns. Disputes led to the detailed surveying of boundaries, manorial wealth and houses. A windmill is 'worth nothing because the post is broken'. 'Small buildings built in the market-place' add to the rents of another estate. Calendars are available from 1219. Perambulations of medieval forests are scattered among chancery and exchequer records and date from the thirteenth to the nineteenth centuries. Documents mention boundaries, customs and settlements within the forests which covered wide areas of the country in medieval times and included arable land, villages and heath.

Inquisitions *ad quod damnum* were taken in medieval times when any grant of market or fair or similar privilege might threaten someone's rights. There is a published calendar of these records. Commissioners inquired into abuses of charitable donations from the end of Elizabeth I's reign until George III's reign. Other commissions dealt with colleges and chantries; forests; sea-banks; and sewers, a term embracing cleansing of rivers, streams and ditches whose records run from 1600 to 1871.

Inquisitions *post mortem* were taken by the crown after the death of tenants in chief. These documents are estate surveys and valuations to determine death duties. They usually give a summary of family history and tell the name, age and relationship of the deceased's heirs. Inquisitions date from the thirteenth century until the Civil War period, and are useful in documenting the descent of landowning families; the extent of royal forests or parks; the existence of water-mills, industries and trade; types of service by which property is held; land values; size of estates. Proofs of age accompany inquisitions to ensure that the heirs are old enough to inherit. Otherwise the king temporarily enjoys the fruits of the estate. Most inquisitions are listed by county record societies and some are calendared in full. The original documents are in Latin.

One useful commission dealt with the enclosing of arable land for hunting parks and sheep pasture in the generation prior to 1517. With the aid of a local jury, royal officers tried to discover what lands had been enclosed, what settlements destroyed, by whom, where, when and how. Answers reveal a changing landscape and altering farming practices in many places especially in the midlands and south. Many returns are printed in Latin by I. S. Leadam *The Domesday of Inclosures* (1897). It is vital also to study the chancery petitions of enclosing landowners. These men point out that enclosure means efficient productive agriculture, higher living standards for peasants, good new houses, higher rents for lords and king. One Warwickshire man whose land had been enclosed since the autumn of 1498 claimed about 1522 to have built himself 'a manor place where was none before but a sorry thatched house to his great cost and charge wherein he now dwelleth with little lack of sixty persons'. Proceedings against enclosing landlords can best be followed in great detail in exchequer records at the Public Record Office. Cases continue to be heard until about 1568 under later anti-enclosure legislation. The government also conducted inquiries into enclosure in 1548, 1565 and 1607. It is as well to remember that hundreds of lost villages are unmentioned in these records because they were enclosed prior to 1488, the limit of legal memory in these cases.

Among special collections at the record office are the hundred rolls, the records of Edward I's fiscal enquiry of 1274-5 in thirty-two counties where men had neglected duties, appropriated valuable services and usurped liberties. Along with this are returns to inquests of 1255 and 1279-80 on similar subjects. Most documents were published by the Record Commission. Action on the returns of 1255 and 1279-80 is to be sought in chancery and exchequer records, on the returns of 1274-5 in crown pleas on the roll of the next eyre court for the relevant district.

As a law court, chancery heard cases. Records date from 1386 to 1875. Evidence is often very detailed, recalling histories of persons and places back for two or three generations. Some records are listed, as in the Record Commission's *Calendar of Proceedings in Chancery in the Reign of Elizabeth, with Earlier Examples* (1827-32). Chancery procedure, terminology, script and legal Latin ensure that the study of uncalendared original records is very difficult for the local historian.

The royal law courts at Westminster dealt with every problem of justice and administration. During the thirteenth century this *curia regis* divided into three courts of record: common pleas, exchequer and king's bench. Records of the common pleas date from 1182 to 1875. Judges also went round the country and held assize courts. Royal justices have always dealt with the most serious offences, theft, fraud and murder that affected the peace of the countryside. As a result court documents are usually very informative. Early records are in Latin but there are available some indexes, calendars and transcripts. These calendars will indicate village name, details of property in the case, parties to the suit and date. In common-pleas court rolls are recorded title deeds, estate surveys, family pedigrees, common recoveries and final concords. Concords, often called fines, are enrolled from 1182 to 1834 and deal with land titles. A calendar entry of a fine for a place called Tylas farm looks like this:

Plaintiff : Oswald Metecalff
Deforceant : Christopher and Ann Metecalff
Messuage called Tylehowse graunge with lands in Tylehowse in the parish of Oldbyland
                    Michaelmas Sessions 1562

On account of the early date of the fine the house is obviously a genuine monastic grange used for the storage of grain. And did not a medieval chronicler mention that monks had abandoned the original site of their abbey and now made use of the buildings only as a tile manufactory? Nothing more is gained by reading the original fine. This is a good example of a calendar entry in practice replacing the original document.

The principal secretary or secretary of state became the king's principal adviser on home and foreign affairs during the sixteenth century. His departmental records concerning home affairs are called State Papers Domestic in the early days but, after 1782, Home Office records. Because English is used throughout and detailed published calendars exist for the Tudor and Stuart period, the local historian finds much material here. Abstracts of crown land grants, reports from magistrates or informers on local conditions, details of manufactures, strikes, riots, enclosures, crops, crime and punishment are among the subjects dealt with. Commonwealth committees for compounding with delinquents and the sequestration of delinquents' estates, 1643-60, contain personal details and surveys of estates of people out of sympathy with the parliamentary cause. Royalist and church property surveys about 1647-53 are held also in Lambeth Palace, family muniments and local record offices. The ecclesiastical returns of 1851 name each place of worship in the country with endowments, sittings and attendances.

Census returns in the Public Record Office provide a complete list of inhabitants of every village and town in the land for 1841, 1851, 1861 and 1871. The first census was taken in 1801 but this return and the subsequent ones of 1811, 1821 and 1831 show numbers of people and houses but no names. Of course these early documents are invaluable in providing the first reliable indication of local population. The 1831 census contains a breakdown of the numbers of men in the main fields of occupation : farming, trade, handicrafts, factories, mines, domestic service. But this classification is very dependent on the interpretation of the local census officer, and results have to be treated with care. These returns of 1801-31 are printed and available in most libraries. The returns of 1841-71 are handwritten on printed forms arranged by counties, parishes and townships. In each township all houses generally appear in street order sometimes with an address. Then all inhabitants are listed by name. Ages, jobs and birthplaces are detailed. The 1851-71 returns enable you to tell exactly when and where people were born. From returns it is possible to work out the occupational and age structure of the locality, family relationships, density of house population and position of houses that have disappeared. Some libraries and county record offices possess microfilms of county returns. Microfilms or photocopies may be purchased by anyone.

PARLIAMENTARY PAPERS

Parliamentary papers include records of the Lords and Commons and those published by command of the monarch. Each document is issued separately for sale, and at the conclusion of the session all papers are bound in volumes. These volumes, reprints or microcard copies are nowadays in public libraries. House of Commons sessional papers are divided into bills; reports of Commons committees; reports of royal commissioners; and accounts and papers. House of Lords documents follow a similar pattern. See W. R. Powell, *Local History from Blue Books: a Select List of the Sessional Papers of the House of Commons* (Historical Association, 1962). Papers nearly always contain evidence of witnesses in full with indexes of names and subjects.

Parliamentary papers deal with every conceivable subject : trade, village greens, factories, agriculture, public health, landed estates, justice, canals, enclosure of commons, poor law, crime and punishment. For town histories the nineteenth-century reports on sanitary conditions, municipal corporations, children's employment, factory and mining conditions, lighting and watching, harbours, houses and schools should be read carefully. Most towns are mentioned by name and local witnesses present evidence amounting to thousands of words. A whole report may relate to one fraudulent parliamentary election in one borough. Village overseers provide evidence for poor-law commissioners in 1834 about specific parishes. Individual charities, schools, mills and mines are named. There are several good indexes including the reprint of *Hansard's Catalogue and Breviate of Parliamentary Papers 1696-1834* (1953) and P. and G. Ford's *Select List of British Parliamentary Papers 1833-1899* (1953).

The printed sessional papers of the Lords contain little that is not in the Commons' papers. But the Lords have, since 1497, amassed a great manuscript collection that has never been printed. Since 1603 there is a large file for every week of the session. Original papers are supplemented by committee books, evidence books, plans and so on dealing with such various topics as estates, dioceses, naturalisation, waterways and industry. Look especially at the protestation returns of 1642 naming all men over eighteen who signed or refused to sign the oath to maintain 'the true Reformed Protestant Religion'. Here is a parochial census and an indication of the division of opinion at the opening of the Civil War. Returns are listed in the appendix to the fifth report of the Historical Manuscripts Commission and in the calendar of Lords' records. The Lords' records also contain one of Britain's most extensive collections for transport history : acts, plans, correspondence, estimates and so on. Original documents of Lords and Commons are in the House of Lords Record Office. There is a published calendar of Lords' records (1497-1714).

STATUTORY AUTHORITIES

Turnpike trusts took over the maintenance of main roads when villages proved incapable. Composed of landowners and merchants the trusts were established by Parliament, from 1663 until the coming of the railways to collect tolls at turnpike gates for the improvement of highways. For the history of roads between about 1710 and 1870 look for the turnpike act of Parliament, the plan of the project in quarter sessions records and the trust's own minutes, accounts, letters and plans. Some trusts employed great surveyors and engineers, Telford, Metcalfe and McAdam. Records of the trusts may still be held by the solicitor whose predecessors served as clerks. Luckily many are in county archives.

Documents referring to roads are found in the Post Office records at St Martins-le-Grand, London. District surveyors sent in all kinds of sketch maps and reports on road conditions along mail coach routes especially in the period 1790-1840. Post Office records of course cover a much wider field and period of time, being very useful for histories of the main post towns since Charles II's reign. In 1790 begin the secretary's reports on all aspects of local Post Office affairs.

Boards of guardians were set up under the 1834 Poor Law Amendment Act to administer poor relief. Already in the eighteenth century several groups of towns had joined together to build workhouses where able-bodied poor might work. But from 1834 the government compelled parishes to form unions with appointed officials and elected guardians of the poor to supplant parochial relief methods. All people needing relief—aged, impotent, vagabonds, children—were sent to a central workhouse. Records dating from 1834 to 1930 include minutes of guardians' meetings, accounts, lists of paupers, registers of births and deaths, health reports and detailed township rate books. Documents describe eloquently the social and economic condition of the locality year by year. Union records are sometimes with the firm of solicitors that served as clerks to the guardians, at the workhouse or local district council office or with the county archivist.

Local boards of health were set up in most towns (but not boroughs unless they chose) after 1848 but were superseded by urban district councils in 1894. Minutes and letters relate to disease, sanitation and epidemics, extremely important topics for Victorian studies. Records may be with the local council or at the record office. Highway boards covering several parishes may have been set up locally between 1862 and 1894. Minutes, accounts and letter-books deal with road maintenance in the face of railway dominance. Documents are with the council or county record office. School boards were established in 1870 after much local preparation and some wrangling, details of which are in newspapers and among the records of the local board itself. Minutes, accounts, correspondence and reports of the boards sometimes survive locally perhaps in solicitors' accumulations and are vital reading for the educational historian. Alternative sources of this information are the annual reports of the boards sent to and summarised in the records of the committee of council on education. Unpublished files on each grant-aided school lie in the Public Record Office. Records of the Local Government Board set up in 1871 are also essential reading and include annual reports, many returns such as workhouse building and improvement plans as well as reports by local inspectors on sewage farms, drainage, hospitals and lunatic asylums. Most documents that are not available in printed form can be studied at the Public Record Office.

Government records are advantageously studied at this late stage partly because London and to some extent Edinburgh or Aberystwyth repositories prove somewhat inaccessible to the average local historian holding down a full-time occupation. Collections are moreover so voluminous and yet so vital for local studies that just to mention them is not to say: 'finish research with a day trip to London'. Rather is this swift survey a means of whetting the appetite and initiating a period of research that might continue for years. In one of the most recent works on sources for English local history Dr W. B. Stephens chooses about half his examples of representative documents from manuscript and printed records originating in national repositories, thus emphasising that the serious student dare not neglect this fountainhead.

I myself once investigated the reasons for the desertion and decay of a tenant farmer's homestead at the time of agricultural prosperity about 1805. I employed documents locally available, seemingly suited to so modest a topic. A neighbourly and skilled archaeologist granted me a sight of his report on excavation at the ruin. This surprisingly revealed medieval iron, Tudor brick and several layers of settlement. The delightful combination of a litter of rusting nails and the field name Colepitte led me to a charcoal ironmaster's will, thence to the attics of a country solicitor's office and to the muniment room of a man whose ancestors last exercised manorial authority in Elizabethan times. Research showed I must travel to London in order to view chancery law court cases concerning enclosure about 1705, held at Chancery Lane, unpublished petitions in the House of Lords Record Office, ecclesiastical surveys at Lambeth Palace and finally medieval deeds in the British Museum. The modest brick cottage gradually but undoubtedly altered into a timbered manorial hall. I should like to be able to end my local history happily ever after by reporting that I discovered the place mentioned in Domesday but I expect such a stroke of good fortune only in a fairy tale.

Appendix I

SOME USEFUL ADDRESSES FOR FIELDWORKERS

Further details of these and similar addresses may be found in such handbooks as *Whitaker's Almanac*; *Scientific and Learned Societies of Great Britain*; *Industrial Archaeologists' Guide*; *Museums and Galleries in Great Britain and Ireland*.

LONDON
Aerofilms Ltd., 4 Albemarle Street, W1.
Air Photography, Curator of, Fortress House, 23 Savile Row, W1 (formerly Air Ministry; National Buildings Record, Ministry of Housing and Local Government; now part of Department of the Environment).
Council for British Archaeology, 8 St Andrew's Place, NW1.
Department of the Environment, Ancient Monuments and Historic Buildings Division, Fortress House, 23 Savile Row, W1.
Deserted Medieval Village Research Group, 67 Gloucester Crescent, NW1.
National Coal Board, Hobart House, Grosvenor Place, SW1.
National Maritime Museum, Romney Road, Greenwich, SE10.
National Monuments Record (incorporating National Buildings Record), Fortress House, 23 Savile Row, W1.
Newcomen Society for the Study of the History of Engineering and Technology, Science Museum, South Kensington, SW7.
Royal Commission on Historical Monuments (England), Fortress House, 23 Savile Row, W1.
Science Museum, South Kensington, SW7.
Society for the Protection of Ancient Buildings (with Wind and Water Mill section), 55 Great Ormond Street, WC1.
Standing Conference for Local History, 26 Bedford Square, WC1.
Victoria and Albert Museum, South Kensington, SW7 (arts and crafts).

PROVINCIAL
BATH. National Record of Industrial Monuments, Centre for the Study of the History of Technology, University of Technology, Bath, Somerset.
BEAMISH. North of England Open Air Museum, Beamish Hall, Stanley, co. Durham (industry of the north-east).
BIRMINGHAM. Museum of Science and Technology, Newhall Street and Sarehole Mill (water corn-mill from the eighteenth century).
BLACKBURN. Lewis Textile Museum, Exchange Street.
BUCKLAND ABBEY, near Yelverton, Devon (maritime, agriculture, building).
CAMBRIDGE. Curator in Aerial Photography, Sidgwick Avenue.

COLCHESTER. Colchester & Essex Museum, The Castle (local history, Romano-British objects).

DONCASTER. South Yorkshire Industrial Museum, Cusworth Hall.

HALIFAX. Folk Museum of West Yorkshire, Shibden Hall, Shibden (transport, craft, agriculture).

LEICESTER. Newarke Houses Museum, The Newarke (social life, hosiery, costume).

LEICESTER. University, Department of Transport History.

LIVERPOOL. City Museums, William Brown Street (industry, transport).

MANCHESTER. Museum of Science and Technology, 97 Grosvenor Street.

NEWCASTLE UPON TYNE. Museum of Science and Engineering, Exhibition Park, Great North Road.

University, Museum of Antiquities, The Quadrangles (Roman, Anglo-Saxon).

NORWICH. Bridewell Museum of Local Industries and Rural Crafts, Bridewell Alley, St Andrew's Street.

OXFORD. Ashmolean Museum (archaeology).

READING. University Museum of English Rural Life (exhibits and archives).

ST HELENS. Pilkington Glass Museum, Prescot Road.

SHEFFIELD. Abbeydale Industrial Hamlet (eighteenth-century scythe works; iron and steel; Huntsman crucible; forge).

SOUTHAMPTON. Ordnance Survey Office, Romsey Road, Maybush.

STOKE BRUERNE. The Waterways Museum, near Towcester, Northants.

SWINDON. Great Western Railway Museum, Faringdon Road, Swindon, Wiltshire.

TELFORD. Blists Hill Open Air Museum (canal, inclined plane, blast furnace, pithead gear).

Coalbrookdale Museum (iron smelting and casting, Darby furnace).

Ironbridge Gorge Museum, Southside, Church Hill, Ironbridge (tiles, pottery, iron, coal, fireclay).

YORK. Castle Museum (social life; water corn-mill),

National Railway Museum, Queen Street (reopening late 1975).

WALES

ABERYSTWYTH. National Monuments Record for Wales and Royal Commission on Ancient and Historical Monuments in Wales and Monmouthshire, Edleston House, Queens Road.

CARDIFF. National Museum of Wales, Cathays Park (industry).

Welsh Folk Museum, St Fagans (craft and industry, reconstructed buildings such as woollen mill and tannery).

SCOTLAND

EDINBURGH. National Monuments Record for Scotland and Royal Commission on the Ancient and Historical Monuments of Scotland, 52-4 Melville Street.

National Museum of Antiquities of Scotland, Queen Street (agriculture, social life, technology).

GLASGOW. Museum of Transport, 25 Albert Drive.

Old Glasgow Museum, People's Palace (visual record of town's growth).

IRELAND
ARMAGH. County Museum, The Mall (local history).
BELFAST. Ulster Museum, Stranmillis Road (engineering, local history, technology).
DUBLIN. Guinness Museum, Watling Street (brewing).
    National Museum of Ireland, Kildare Street.

Appendix 2

SOME RECORD REPOSITORIES IN BRITAIN

The following list is based on a handbook prepared by a joint committee of the Historical Manuscripts Commission and the British Records Association (fourth edition, HMSO 1971). By no means all local record offices are included below.

LONDON
    There are at least one hundred repositories in London whose documents may be of interest. These include government, religious, banking and borough archives, records of national institutions like the railways, of city livery companies, of societies and colleges and of religious foundations. Only a selection is listed here. Consult the Greater London Record Office for detailed help.

Public Record Office, Chancery Lane, WC2.
Church Commissioners, 1 Millbank, SW1.
Duchy of Cornwall Office, 10 Buckingham Gate, SW1.
House of Lords Record Office, House of Lords, SW1.
Principal Registry of the Family Division, Somerset House, Strand, WC2.
Department of Manuscripts, British Museum, WC1.
Lambeth Palace Library, SE1 (Canterbury Archdiocese records).
Methodist Archives and Research Centre, Epworth House, 25-35 City Road, EC1.
Society of Friends' Library, Friends House, Euston Road, NW1.
Westminster Abbey Muniment Room and Library, The Cloisters, Westminster Abbey, SW1.
British Transport Historical Records Office, 66 Porchester Road, W2.
Corporation of London Records Office, Guildhall, EC2.
Guildhall Library, Basinghall Street, EC2.
Greater London Record Office (London Records), County Hall, SE1.
Greater London Record Office (Middlesex Records), 1 Queen Anne's Gate Buildings, Dartmouth Street, SW1.
Corporation Muniment Room, Guildhall, Kingston upon Thames.

Southwark Diocesan Records and Lewisham Archives Department, The Manor House, Old Road, Lee, SE13.
College of Arms, Queen Victoria Street, EC4.
Society of Genealogists, 37 Harrington Gardens, SW7.
Customs and Excise, Mark Lane, EC3.
Dr Williams's Library, 14 Gordon Square, WC1 (nonconformist).
Westminster Public Libraries, Buckingham Palace Road, SW1 (Westminster parishes).
AVON Bristol Archives Office, Council House, Bristol 1.
BEDFORDSHIRE County Record Office, County Hall, Bedford.
BERKSHIRE County Record Office, Shire Hall, Reading.
BUCKINGHAMSHIRE County Record Office, County Offices, Aylesbury.
    Buckinghamshire Archaeological Society, County Museum, Aylesbury.
CAMBRIDGESHIRE County Record Office, Shire Hall, Castle Hill, Cambridge.
    County Record Office, County Offices, Huntingdon.
    University Library, Cambridge.
    University Archives, Old Schools, Cambridge.
CHESHIRE County Record Office, The Castle, Chester.
    City Record Office, Town Hall, Chester.
    Public Library, Museum Street, Warrington.
CORNWALL County Record Office, County Hall, Truro.
    Royal Institution of Cornwall, River Street, Truro.
CUMBRIA Cumberland, Westmorland and Carlisle Record Office, The Castle, Carlisle, and County Hall, Kendal.
    Public Library, Ramsden Square, Barrow-in-Furness.
DERBYSHIRE County Record Office, County Offices, Matlock.
DEVON County Record Office, Concord House, South Street, Exeter.
    City Library, Castle Street, Exeter.
    Cathedral Library, The Bishop's Palace, Exeter.
DORSET County Record Office, County Hall, Dorchester.
DURHAM County Record Office, County Hall, Durham.
    Palatinate, Capitular and Bishopric records, The Prior's Kitchen, The College, Durham.
EAST SUSSEX East Sussex Record Office, Pelham House, Lewes.
ESSEX County Record Office, County Hall, Chelmsford.
GLOUCESTERSHIRE County Records Office, Shire Hall, Gloucester.
GREATER MANCHESTER Central Library, St. Peter's Square, Manchester 2.
    Chetham's Library, Manchester 3.
    John Rylands Library, Deansgate, Manchester 3.
    Local History and Archives Department, Central Library, Wigan.
HAMPSHIRE County Record Office, 20 Southgate Street, Winchester.
    City Record Office, Guildhall, Portsmouth.
    Civic Record Office, Civic Centre, Southampton.
    City Record Office, Guildhall, Winchester.
    Cathedral Library, The Cathedral, Winchester.
HEREFORD AND WORCESTER County Record Office, The Old Barracks, Harold Street, Hereford.
    County Record Office, Shire Hall, Worcester.

HERTFORDSHIRE County Record Office, County Hall, Hertford.

HUMBERSIDE County Record Office, County Hall, Beverley.
 Registry of Deeds, Beverley.

ISLE OF WIGHT County Record Office, 26 Hillside, Newport.

KENT Archives Office, County Hall, Maidstone.
 Cathedral Library and City Record Office, The Precincts, Canterbury.
 Diocesan Registry and Cathedral Library, c/o Messrs Arnold, Tuff and Grimwade, The Precincts, Rochester.

LANCASHIRE County Record Office, Sessions House, Lancaster Road, Preston.

LEICESTERSHIRE County Record Office, 57 New Walk, Leicester.
 City Record Office, Museum and Art Gallery, Leicester.

LINCOLNSHIRE County Archives Office, The Castle, Lincoln.
 Gentlemen's Society, Spalding.

MERSEYSIDE City Record Office, Central Library, Liverpool 3.

MIDDLESEX See under LONDON.

NORFOLK Norfolk and Norwich Record Office, Central Library, Norwich.

NORTHAMPTONSHIRE County Record Office, Delapré Abbey, Northampton.

NORTHUMBERLAND County Record Office, Melton Park, North Gosforth, Newcastle upon Tyne 3.

NORTH YORKSHIRE County Record Office, County Hall, Northallerton.
 Registry of Deeds, Northallerton.
 York Diocesan Records, Borthwick Institute of Historical Research, St Anthony's Hall, York.
 City Library, Museum Street, York.

NOTTINGHAMSHIRE County Records Office, County House, High Pavement, Nottingham.
 Southwell Diocesan Registry, Church House, Park Row, Nottingham.

OXFORDSHIRE County Record Office, County Hall, New Road, Oxford.
 Archdeaconries of Oxford and Berkshire and Oxford Diocesan Registry, Bodleian Library, Oxford.
 University Archives, Bodleian Library, Oxford.

SALOP County Record Office, New Shirehall, Abbey Foregate, Shrewsbury.
 Borough Archives, Guildhall, Shrewsbury.

SOMERSET County Record Office, Obridge Road, Taunton.

SOUTH YORKSHIRE West Riding Archives and Diocesan Records, Archives Department, Central Library, Sheffield 1.

STAFFORDSHIRE County Record Office, County Buildings, Eastgate Street, Stafford.
 In association with
 Joint Record Office and Lichfield Diocesan Registry, Bird Street, Lichfield.
 Also in association with
 William Salt Library, 19 Eastgate Street, Stafford.

SUFFOLK County Record Office, County Hall, Ipswich.
 Bury St Edmunds branch, 8 Angel Hill, Bury St Edmunds.

SURREY County Record Office, County Hall, Kingston upon Thames.
  Museum and Muniment Room, Castle Arch, Guildford.
TYNE AND WEAR City Archives Office, 7 Saville Place, Newcastle upon Tyne 1.
WARWICKSHIRE County Record Office, Shire Hall, Warwick.
  Borough Archives, Shakespeare's Birthplace Trust Library, Henley Street,
  Stratford upon Avon.
WEST MIDLANDS City Library, Ratcliff Place, Birmingham 1.
  City Record Office, 9 Hay Lane, Coventry.
WEST SUSSEX West Sussex Record Office, Wren House, West Street,
  Chichester.
WEST YORKSHIRE West Riding Archives and Diocesan Records, Archives
  Department, Sheepscar Branch Library, Leeds 7.
  Brotherton Library, University of Leeds, Leeds 2.
  Yorkshire Archaeological Society, Claremont, Clarendon Road, Leeds 2.
  County Record Office and Registry of Deeds, County Hall, Wakefield.
WILTSHIRE County Record Office, County Hall, Trowbridge.
  Diocesan Record Office, The Wren Hall, 56c The Close, Salisbury.

WALES

National Library of Wales, Aberystwyth.
CLWYD County Record Office, The Old Rectory, Hawarden, Deeside.
DYFED County Record Office, County Hall, Carmarthen.
  County Record Office, The Castle, Haverfordwest.
GWENT County Record Office, County Hall, Newport.
GWYNEDD County Record Office, Shire Hall, Llangefni.
  County Record Office, County Offices, Caernarvon.
  County Record Office, County Offices, Dolgellau.
SOUTH GLAMORGAN County Record Office, County Hall, Cathays Park,
  Cardiff.

SCOTLAND

Documents are kept by towns rather than by counties. The Scottish Record
Office is the most important centre for research.
  Scottish Record Office, HM General Register House, Edinburgh.
  National Library of Scotland, George IV Bridge, Edinburgh.
  Office of Lord Lyon King of Arms, HM Register House, Edinburgh.
  Scots Ancestry Research Council, North Saint David Street, Edinburgh.
  City Archives, City Chambers, Edinburgh.
  Registrar General's Office, New Register House, Edinburgh.
  Commissary Office, Sheriff Court House, Edinburgh (probate).
  City Archives Office, City Chambers, Glasgow C1.

NORTHERN IRELAND

  Public Record Office of Northern Ireland, Balmoral Avenue, Belfast.
  Registrar General, Ormeau Avenue, Belfast 2.

BIBLIOGRAPHY

The date which follows the title is generally that of the edition consulted by the author. By no means all books quoted in the text are listed here in order to leave space to mention books that have not yet been recommended.

ARCHIVE ADMINISTRATION

FOWLER, G. H. *The Care of County Muniments,* 1923.
JENKINSON, C. Hilary. *A Manual of Archive Administration,* second revised edn with introduction and bibliography by R. H. Ellis, reissued 1965.
REDSTONE, L. and STEER, F. W. *Local Records: their Nature and Care,* 1953.

ATLASES

ORDNANCE SURVEY. Maps and plans, 1801 to date.
SPEED, John. *Theatre of the Empire of Great Britaine,* 1611-12 (facsimile edn relating to England 1953; facsimile edn of the 1676 edn relating to Wales 1970).

BIBLIOGRAPHIES

The following reference works provide lists of books and periodicals that may prove of use in researches.

BESTERMANN, Theodore. *World Bibliography of Bibliographies.*
EMMISON, F. G. and KUHLICKE, F. W. *The English Local History Handlist: a Short Bibliography,* 1965.
GROSS, Charles. *A Bibliography of British Municipal History,* second edn, 1966.
LIBRARY ASSOCIATION County Libraries Group (Readers' Guides). *Sources of Local History,* fourth edn, 1971.
MULLINS, E. L. C. *Guide to Historical and Archaeological Publications of Societies in England and Wales, 1901-1933,* 1968.
MULLINS, E. L. C. *Texts and Calendars: an Analytical Guide to Serial Publications,* 1958.
SOMERVILLE, Robert. *Handlist of Record Publications,* 1951.
WHITEMORE, J. B. *A Genealogical Guide,* 1953.

CHRONOLOGY

CHENEY, C. R. *Handbook of Dates for Students of English History,* 1961.
POOLE, R. L. *Medieval Reckonings of Time,* 1918.
POWICKE, F. M. and FRYDE, E. B. *Handbook of British Chronology,* second edn, 1961.

DICTIONARIES

Dictionaries and related works that will be invaluable for the study of documents. Languages, surnames, watermarks, seals and place-names are represented.

BARDSLEY, C. W. *Dictionary of English and Welsh Surnames,* 1901, reprinted 1967.
BRIQUET, C. M. *Les Filigranes: Dictionnaire Historique des Marques du Papier,* 1907, facsimile edn, 1966.
CAPPELLI, Adriano, *Dizionario di Abbreviature Latine ed Italiane,* second revised edn, Milan, 1912.
EKWALL, Eilert. *Concise Oxford Dictionary of English Place-Names,* fourth edn, 1960.
GLOVER, R. F. and HARRIS, R. W. *Latin for Historians,* third edn, 1963.
GOODER, E. A. *Latin for Local History,* 1961 (with useful formulary of some common documents).
KELHAM, R. *A Dictionary of the Norman or Old French Language,* 1779.
LATHAM, R. E. *Revised Medieval Latin Word-list,* 1965.
MARTIN, C. T. *The Record Interpreter: a Collection of Abbreviations, Latin Words and Names used in English Historical Manuscripts and Records,* second edn, 1910.
WRIGHT, Joseph. *The English Dialect Dictionary; the English Dialect Grammar,* 1898-1905.
WYON, A. B. *The Great Seals of England,* 1887.

PALAEOGRAPHY

One's ability to read the handwriting of documents depends mainly on perseverance. Practise therefore on documents themselves or of course on clear photocopies. Study the following books which usually provide transcripts, translations and photocopies of original documents as well as descriptions of various types of hand.

DAWSON, G. E. and KENNEDY-SKIPTON, L. *Elizabethan Handwriting 1500-1650*, 1968.

DENHOLM-YOUNG, N. *Handwriting in England and Wales*, 1954.

EMMISON, F. G. *How to Read Local Archives 1550-1700*, 1967.

GRIEVE, H. E. P. *Examples of English Handwriting 1150-1750*, second edn, 1959.

HECTOR, L. C. *The Handwriting of English Documents*, 1958.

JENKINSON, C. Hilary. *The Later Court Hands in England*, 1927.

JENKINSON, C. Hilary and JOHNSON, C. *English Court Hand, A.D. 1066 to 1500*, 1915 (volume 1 is a treatise on the handwriting of medieval administrative documents and contains the text of documents reproduced in facsimile in volume 2).

JUDGE, C. B. *Specimens of Sixteenth-Century English Handwriting*, 1935.

WRIGHT, Andrew. *Court Hand Restored*, 1776.

FIELDWORK

ALLCROFT, A. H. *Earthwork of England*, 1908.

ANDERSON, M. D. *History and Imagery in British Churches*, 1971.

ASHBEE, P. *The Bronze Age Round Barrow in Britain*, 1960.

BARLEY, M. W. *The English Farmhouse and Cottage*, 1961.

BARLEY, M. W. *The House and Home*, 1963.

BAXTER, B. *Stone Blocks and Iron Rails*, 1966.

BERESFORD, M. W. *History on the Ground*, 1957.

BERESFORD, M. W. *The Lost Villages of England*, 1954.

BERESFORD, M. W. *New Towns of the Middle Ages*, 1967.

BERESFORD, M. W. and HURST J. G. eds. *Deserted Medieval Villages*, 1971.

BERESFORD, M. W. and ST. JOSEPH, J. K. S., *Medieval England: an Aerial Survey*, 1958.

BOUCHER, C. T. G. *James Brindley, Engineer, 1716-1772*, 1968.

BRACEGIRDLE, B. *The Archaeology of the Industrial Revolution*, 1973.

BRUNSKILL, R. W. *Illustrated Handbook of Vernacular Architecture*, 1971.

BUCHANAN, R. A. *Industrial Archaeology in Britain*, 1972.

CHALONER, W. H. and MUSSON, A. E. *Industry and Technology*, 1963.

CLIFTON-TAYLOR, A. *The Pattern of English Building*, revised edn, 1972.

CLOUGH, R. T. *The Lead Smelting Mills of the Yorkshire Dales*, 1962.

COLES, J. *Field Archaeology in Britain*, 1972.

COLVIN, H. M. *History of the King's Works*, 1963-.

COOKSON, M. B. *Photography for Archaeologists*, 1954.

CRAWFORD, O. G. S. *Archaeology in the Field*, 1953

DARBY, H. C. *Domesday Geography of England* series.

FINBERG, H. P. R., general ed. *The Agrarian History of England and Wales*, 1967-.

FINBERG, J. *Exploring Villages,* 1958.

GRINSELL, L. V., WARHURST, A. and RAHTZ, P. *The Preparation of Archaeological Reports,* 1966.

HADFIELD, C., ed. *The Canals of the British Isles* series.

HAWKES, J. *Guide to the Prehistoric and Roman Monuments in England and Wales,* 1951.

HOOPER, M. *et al. Hedges and Local History,* 1971.

HOSKINS, W. G. *English Landscapes,* 1973.

HOSKINS, W. G. *Fieldwork in Local History,* 1967.

HOSKINS, W. G. *The Making of the English Landscape,* 1955.

HOSKINS, W. G. *Provincial England,* 1963.

HOSKINS, W. G. and STAMP, L. D. *The Common Lands of England and Wales,* 1963.

HUDSON, K. *Handbook for Industrial Archaeologists,* 1967.

HUDSON, K. *Industrial Archaeology,* 1963.

KLINGENDER, F. D. *Art and the Industrial Revolution,* 1947, revised by Sir A. Elton, 1968.

LEWIS, M. J. T. *Early Wooden Railways,* 1970.

MARGARY, I. D. *Roman Roads in Britain,* 1955-7.

ORDNANCE SURVEY. *Field Archaeology: some Notes for Beginners,* fourth edn, 1963.

ORWIN, C. S. and C. S. *The Open Fields,* third edn, 1967.

PANNELL, J. P. M. *The Techniques of Industrial Archaeology,* 1966.

PEATE, I. C. *The Welsh House,* second edn, 1944.

PEVSNER, N. *The Buildings of England* series.

RAISTRICK, A. *Industrial Archaeology; an Historical Survey,* 1972.

REES, D. Morgan. *Mines, Mills and Furnaces. An Introduction to Industrial Archaeology in Wales,* 1969.

REYNOLDS, J. *Windmills and Watermills,* 1970.

RICHARDS, J. M. *The Functional Tradition in Early Industrial Buildings,* 1958.

ROLT, L. T. C. *Tools for the Job,* 1965.

ROLT, L. T. C., ed. *Longmans' Industrial Archaeology* series.

SALZMAN, L. F. *Building in England down to 1540,* 1952.

SHIRLEY, E. *Some Account of English Deer Parks,* 1867.

SIMMONS, J. *The Railways of Britain,* second edn, 1968.

SINGER, C., ed. *A History of Technology,* 1954-8.

TATE, W. E. *The English Village Community and the Enclosure Movements,* 1967.

THOMPSON, F. *Lark Rise to Candleford,* 1945.

WOOD, E. S. *Field Guide to Archaeology,* 1963.

LISTS, GUIDES, CALENDARS, DIPLOMATIC

This section concentrates on documents themselves. A number of books deal with diplomatic, that is, the varying forms that documents take for different purposes century by century. Some documents or collections of manuscripts are published in full by photocopy, transcript or translation. Others are calendared, catalogued or merely listed. The literature in this section is extensive and the following books are listed merely as examples. Thus the chronicle of Richard of Devizes is not the only chronicle in print and not necessarily the most interesting.

APPLEBY, J. T., ed. *Cronicon Richardi Devisensis de tempore regis Richardi Primi. The Chronicle of Richard of Devizes of the Time of King Richard the First,* 1963.

BALLARD, A. *et al.,* eds. *British Borough Charters, 1042-1660,* 1913-43.

BICKLEY, F. B. and ELLIS, H. J., eds. *Index to the Charters and Rolls in the Department of Manuscripts,* 1900 (British Museum).

BIRCH, W. de G., ed. *Cartularium Saxonicum,* 1885-99.

BOND, M. F. *Guide to the Records of Parliament,* 1971.

BOND, M. F. *The Records of Parliament,* 1964 (pamphlet).

BORN, L. K., comp. *British Manuscripts Project: a Checklist of the Microfilms prepared in England and Wales for the American Council of Learned Societies 1941-1945,* 1955.

BRITISH MUSEUM, London. *A Guide to the British Museum,* 1968.

BUCKINGHAMSHIRE COUNTY COUNCIL and Buckinghamshire Quarter Sessions Joint Committee *Calendar of Quarter Sessions Records,* ed. by W. Le Hardy, in progress, 1933-.

BURKE, A. M. *Key to the Ancient Parish Registers of England and Wales,* 1908.

CAMP, A. J. *Wills and their Whereabouts,* 1963.

CHAPLAIS, Pierre. *English Royal Documents: King John-Henry VI, 1199-1461,* 1971.

COCKERELL, Sydney, ed. *The Gorleston Psalter: a Manuscript of the Beginning of the Fourteenth Century in the Library of C. W. D. Perrins, described in Relation to other East Anglian Books of the Period,* 1907.

CORNWALL, Julian. 'An Elizabethan census' in *Records of Buckinghamshire,* volume xvi, part 4, 1959.

CRANFIELD, G. A. *A Handlist of English Provincial Newspapers and Periodicals 1700-1760,* 1961.

DAVIES, J. C. and LEWIS, E. A. *Records of the Court of Augmentations relating to Wales and Monmouthshire,* 1954.

EMMISON, F. G. *Archives and Local History,* 1966 (with photographs and transcripts of manuscripts).

EMMISON, F. G. *Guide to the Essex Record Office,* second edn revised to 1968, 1969.

EMMISON, F. G. and GRAY, IRVINE, *County Records,* reprinted 1967.

FINBERG, H. P. R. *Early Charters of the West Midlands*, 1961 (calendar and introduction).

FINBERG, H. P. R. *Early Charters of Wessex*, 1964 (calendar with introduction).

FORD, P. and G. *Select List of British Parliamentary Papers 1833-1899*, 1953.

FRANCE, R. S. *Guide to the Lancashire Record Office*, second edn, 1962.

GALBRAITH, V. H. *An Introduction to the Use of the Public Records*, 1934.

GOSS, C. W. F. *The London Directories 1677-1855*, 1932.

GUILDHALL LIBRARY. *London Rate Assessments and Inhabitants Lists in Guildhall Library and the Corporation of London Records Office*, second edn, 1968.

HALL, Hubert. *Formula Book of English Official Historical Documents*, 1908-9 (diplomatic).

HANSARD, J. and L. G. *Hansard's Catalogue and Breviate of Parliamentary Papers 1696-1834*, 1953.

HARLEY, J. B. *Maps for the Local Historian*, 1972.

HARLEY, J. B. and PHILLIPS, C. W. *The Historian's Guide to Ordnance Survey Maps*, published for the Standing Conference for Local History by the National Council of Social Service, 1965.

HASSALL, W. O., ed. *Wheatley Records 956-1956*, 1956.

HEPWORTH, Philip. *Archives and Manuscripts in Libraries*, second edn, 1964.

HISTORICAL MANUSCRIPTS COMMISSION. *Calendar of the Manuscripts of the Marquis of Bath, preserved at Longleat, Wiltshire*, 1904-8.

HOSKINS, W. G., ed. *Exeter Militia List 1803*, 1972.

HOUSE OF LORDS and HISTORICAL MANUSCRIPTS COMMISSION. *Calendar of the Manuscripts of the House of Lords*, 1870-94 (HMC); 1900 to date (HL).

JONES, P. E. and SMITH, Raymond. *A Guide to the Records in the Corporation of London Records Office and the Guildhall Library Muniment Room*, 1951.

KEMBLE, J. M. *Codex diplomaticus aevi Saxonici*, 1839-48.

LEADAM, I. S., ed. *The Domesday of Inclosures 1517-1518*, 1897.

LEESON, F. *A Guide to the Records of the British State Tontines and Life Annuities of the Seventeenth and Eighteenth Centuries*, 1968.

LE HARDY, William, ed. *Guide to the Hertfordshire Record Office*, volume 1, 1961.

LONDON RECORD SOCIETY. *London Inhabitants within the Walls 1695*, 1966 (an index prepared for use in the Corporation of London Records Office, with introduction by D. V. Glass).

LOYD, L. C. and STENTON, D. M., eds. *Sir Christopher Hatton's Book of Seals*, 1950.

MAITLAND, F. W., ed. *Select Pleas in Manorial and other Seignorial Courts*, volume 1: reigns of Henry III and Edward I, 1889.

MAJOR, Kathleen. *A Handlist of the Records of the Bishop of Lincoln and of the Archdeacons of Lincoln and Stow*, 1953.

MARTIN, G. H., ed. *The Royal Charters of Grantham, 1463-1688*, 1963.

MILLAR, E. G. *The Luttrell Psalter*, 1932.

MUNBY, L. M., ed. *Short Guides to Records* series reprinted from the journal *History*.

NATIONAL LIBRARY OF WALES. *Handlist of Manuscripts in the National Library of Wales*, in progress, 1940-.

NATIONAL REGISTER OF ARCHIVES. *List of Accessions to Repositories* (HMSO, annual).

NORTON, J. E. *Guide to the National and Provincial Directories of England and Wales, excluding London, published before 1856*, 1950.

OWEN, D. M. *The Records of the Established Church in England excluding Parochial Records*, 1970.

POWELL, W. R. *Local History from Blue Books: a Select List of the Sessional Papers of the House of Commons*, 1962.

PUBLIC RECORD OFFICE. *A Guide to Seals in the Public Record Office*, ed. by Hilary Jenkinson, 1954.

PUBLIC RECORD OFFICE. *Guide to the Contents of the Public Record Office*, 1963-8.

PUBLIC RECORD OFFICE. *Maps and Plans in the Public Record Office*, 1. *British Isles c 1410-1860*, 1967.

PUGH, R. B., ed. *Calendar of Antrobus Deeds before 1625*, 1947.

PURVIS, J. S. *Introduction to Ecclesiastical Records*, 1953.

RANGER, F. 'The National Register of Archives, 1945-1969' in *Journal of the Society of Archivists*, volume iii, pages 452-62.

RECORD COMMISSIONERS. *Calendars of the Proceedings in Chancery in the Reign of Queen Elizabeth*, 1827-32.

RECORD COMMISSIONERS. *Rotuli hundredorum*, 1812-18.

RECORD COMMISSIONERS. *The Statutes of the Realm*, 1810-28.

RECORD COMMISSIONERS. *Taxatio ecclesiastica Angliae et Walliae auctoritate P. Nicholai IV, circa A.D. 1291*, 1802.

RECORD COMMISSIONERS. *Valor ecclesiasticus temp. Henr. VIII*, 1810-34.

ROSS, C. D., ed. *The Cartulary of Cirencester Abbey, Gloucestershire*, 1964.

ROYAL HISTORICAL SOCIETY. *Anglo-Saxon Charters: an Annotated List and Bibliography*, ed. by P. H. Sawyer, 1968.

SALTER, H. E., ed. *Facsimiles of Early Charters in Oxford Muniment Rooms*, 1929 (quoted sometimes as *Oxford Charters*, contains charters prior to 1170).

STEEL, D. J. and A. E. F. *et al.*, comps. *National Index of Parish Registers*, in progress, 1966- (published by Society of Genealogists; volumes 1-2 contain introductory matter).

STEER, F. W., ed. *The Lavington Estate Archives: a Catalogue*, 1965.

STENTON, F. M. *Facsimiles of Early Charters from Northamptonshire Collections*, 1930.

STEPHENSON, Mill. *A List of Monumental Brasses in the British Isles*, 1926 reprinted 1964.

THE TIMES, London. *Tercentenary Handlist of English and Welsh Newspapers 1620-1920*, 1920.

TURNER, G. L. Original Records of Nonconformity, 1911-14.

WAGNER, A. R. *The Records and Collections of the College of Arms*, 1952.

WARNER, G. F., ed. *The Stowe Missal*, 1906.

WEST, John. *Village Records*, 1962.

DOCUMENTS AT WORK

The following books show how historians have used documents. Some of the books are guides on the writing of histories.

ASHTON, T. S. *An Eighteenth-century Industrialist, Peter Stubs of Warrington, 1756-1806,* 1939.
ASHTON, T. S. *The Industrial Revolution, 1760-1830,* 1948.
BAGLEY, J. J. *Historical Interpretation,* 1972.
BAKER, W. P. *Parish Registers and Illiteracy in East Yorkshire,* 1961.
BARKER, T. C. *Pilkington Brothers and the Glass Industry,* 1960.
BARKER, T. C. and HARRIS, J. R. *A Merseyside Town in the Industrial Revolution:* St. Helens 1750-1900, 1954.
BERESFORD, M. W. *Lay Subsidies (1290-1334; after 1334) and Poll Taxes (1377, 1379 and 1381),* 1963.
BERESFORD, M. W. *The Unprinted Census Returns of 1841, 1851, 1861 for England and Wales,* 1966 (bound with R. L. Storey *Wills*).
BEVERIDGE, William (later Lord). *Prices and Wages in England from the Twelfth to the Nineteenth Century,* 1939.
BLOCH, Marc. *The Historian's Craft,* 1954.
BRACEGIRDLE, B. *Photography for Books and Reports,* 1970.
BULLOUGH, D. A. and STOREY, R. L. *The Study of Medieval Records,* 1971.
BYTHELL, D. *Handloom Weavers: a Study in the English Cotton Industry during the Industrial Revolution,* 1969.
CAM, Helen. *The Hundred and the Hundred Rolls: an Outline of Local Government in Medieval England,* 1930.
CARR, E. H. *What is History?* 1961.
CELORIA, F. *Teach Yourself Local History,* 1958.
CHAMBERS, J. D. *The Vale of Trent, 1670-1800,* supplement 3 to the *Economic History Review,* 1957.
CLAPHAM, J. H. *A Concise Economic History of Britain from the Earliest Times to 1750,* 1949.
CLARK, G. Kitson. *Guide for Research Students working on Historical Subjects,* 1958.
COLEMAN, D. C. *The British Paper Industry 1495-1860,* 1958.
COLEMAN, D. C. *Courtaulds; an Economic and Social History,* 1969.
COLLINGWOOD, R. G. *The Idea of History,* 1946.
CORNWALL, Julian. *How to read Old Title Deeds XVI-XIX Centuries,* Birmingham University Extra-Mural Studies Department, 1964.
COURT, W. H. B. *A Concise Economic History of Britain from 1750 to Recent Times,* 1954.
COURT, W. H. B. *Rise of the Midland Industries, 1600-1838,* 1938.
COX, J. C. *How to Write the History of a Parish,* fifth edn, 1909.
CROMBIE, J. *Her Majesty's Customs and Excise,* 1962.
DICKSON, P. G. M. *The Sun Insurance Office, 1710-1960,* 1960.
DOUCH, R. *Local History and the Teacher,* 1967.

DOWELL, Stephen. *A History of Taxation and Taxes in England*, third edn, 1965.

EDWARDS, Kathleen. *The English Secular Cathedrals in the Middle Ages*, 1967.

EMMISON, F. G. 'The Relief of the Poor at Eaton Socon, 1706-1834' in *Bedfordshire Historical Record Society*, volume 15, 1933.

EMMISON, F. G. and HUMPHREYS, D. W. *Local History for Students*, 1966.

ERNLE, Rowland E. Prothero (1st Baron). *English Farming Past and Present*, sixth edn, with introduction by G. E. Fussell and O. R. McGregor, 1961.

EVERITT, Alan. *New Avenues in English Local History*, 1970.

EVERITT, Alan. *Ways and Means in Local History*, 1971.

EVERSLEY, D. E. C. and GLASS, D. V., eds, *Population in History*, 1965.

FINBERG, H. P. R. *The Local Historian and his Theme*, 1952 (printed also in the author's *Local History*).

FINBERG, H. P. R. and SKIPP, V. H. T. *Local History: Objective and Pursuit*, 1967 (an essential and exhilarating book for the local historian)

FINBERG, H. P. R. *West Country Historical Studies*, 1969.

FITTON, R. S. and WADSWORTH, A. P. *The Strutts and the Arkwrights*, 1958.

FLEURY, M. and HENRY, L. *Nouveau manuel de dépouillement et d'exploitation de l'Etat Civil Ancien*, 1965 (demography).

GALBRAITH, V. H. *The Historian at Work*, 1962.

GALBRAITH, V. H. *The Making of Domesday Book*, 1961.

GALBRAITH, V. H. *Studies in the Public Records*, 1948.

GARDNER, D. E., HARLAND, D. and SMITH, F. *Basic Course in Genealogy*, 1958.

GARDNER, D. E. and SMITH, Frank. *Genealogical Research in England and Wales*, 1956-64.

GROSS, Charles. *The Gild Merchant: a Contribution to British Municipal History*, 1890.

HAMMOND, J. L. and B. *The Town Labourer, 1760-1832*, new edn, 1966.

HAMMOND, J. L. and B. *The Village Labourer*, fourth edn, 1966.

HATFIELD WORKERS' EDUCATIONAL ASSOCIATION. *Hatfield and its People*, twelve pamphlet volumes, 1961-4.

HODGKISS, A. G. *Maps for Books and Theses*, 1970.

HOLDSWORTH, W. S. *A History of English Law*, 1903-66 (volumes 13-16, ed. by A. L. Goodhart and H. G. Hanbury).

HOLLAENDER, A. E. J., ed. *Essays in Memory of Sir Hilary Jenkinson*, 1962 (seals, palaeography, archives, Public Record Office)

HOLLINGSWORTH, T. H. *Historical Demography*, 1969.

HOSKINS, W. G. *English Local History; the Past and the Future*, 1966.

HOSKINS, W. G. *Local History in England*, 1959.

INSTITUTE OF HERALDIC AND GENEALOGICAL STUDIES, Canterbury. *Parish Register searching in England and Wales*, 1967.

JACKMAN, W. T. *The Development of Transportation in Modern England*, second edn, revised with introduction by W. H. Chaloner, 1962.

JORDAN, W. K. *The Charities of Rural England 1480-1660*, 1961.

LASLETT, Peter. *The World we have Lost*, 1965.

McKINLEY, R. A. *Norfolk Surnames in the Sixteenth Century*, 1969.

MAITLAND, F. W. *Domesday Book and Beyond*, 1897.

NEWTON, K. C. *The Manor of Writtle*, 1970.

PROTHERO, R. E. *See* Ernle, 1st Baron.

PUGH, R. B. *How to Write a Parish History*, 1954.

READE, A. L. *The Reades of Blackwood Hill*, 1906.

ROGERS, A. *This was their World*, 1972.

RUSSELL, J. C. *British Medieval Population*, 1948.

STEER, F. W., ed. *Farm and Cottage Inventories of Mid-Essex 1635-1749*, 1950.

STEPHENS, W. B. *Sources for English Local History*, 1973.

STOREY, R. L. *A Short Introduction to Wills*, 1966 (bound with M. W. Beresford *Census Returns*).

STOREY, R. L. and BULLOUGH, D. A. *The Study of Medieval Records*, 1971.

TATE, W. E. *The Parish Chest*, third edn, 1969.

THOMAS, D. St J. *Non-Fiction: a Guide to Writing and Publishing*, 1970.

VINCENT, J. R. *Pollbooks; how Victorians Voted*, 1967.

WALNE, Peter. *English Wills; Probate Records in England and Wales, with a Brief Note on Scottish and Irish Wills*, 1964.

WARD, W. R. *The Administration of the Window and Assessed Taxes (1696-1798)*, 1963.

WARD, W. R. *The English Land Tax in the Eighteenth Century*, 1953.

WEBB, S. and B. *History of English Local Government*, 1903-29 (1. *The Parish and the County;* 2-3. *The Manor and the Borough;* 4. *Statutory Authorities for Special Purposes;* 5. *The Story of the King's Highway;* 6. *English Prisons under Local Government;* 7-9. *English Poor Law History;* 10. *English Poor Law Policy;* 11. *The History of Liquor Licensing in England*).

WRIGLEY, E. A., ed. *An Introduction to English Historical Demography*, 1966.

PERIODICALS

Agricultural History Review.
Archives.
Business Archives.
Business History.
Economic History Review.
The Genealogists' Magazine.
Geography.
History.
History Today.
Industrial Archaeology.
Journal of Economic History.
Journal of the Society of Archivists.
Journal of Transport History (Leicester University Press).
Local Historian (Amateur Historian).
Local Population Studies.
Population Studies.
Textile History.
Transactions of the Ancient Monuments Society.
Transactions of the Newcomen Society.
Transport History (published by David & Charles).

INDEX

Charity 19, 22, 45, 120, 135, 153, 154, 163, 165, 168, 174, 175, 179, 190, 194
Charter 5, 33, 52, 62, 65, 71, 115, 125, 128-9, 149, 155, 160, 174, 186
Chartulary 144
Chemicals 107-8
Cheney, C. R. 126
Cheshire 54, 59, 106, 108, 115, 183-4, 187, plate 13
Child birth and death 171-2
Child employment 194
Chimney 88, 90-3, 99, 101-2, 150
Christian: influence 73-6, 77, 86; Knowledge Society (SPCK) 175; name 128
Chronology 8-9, 31, 126, 204
Church 45, 47-8, 51-2, 63, 65, 73-6, 86, 188, 189; archive 157, 160-9, 173-4; building 5, 74-6, 145, 173; census 162, 169, 173, 193; commissioner 25, 161; injunction 162, 168; life 151, 163, 168, 190; place-name 71, 73; property 135, 162, 193; warden 135, 153; yard 64, 77, 162
Cistercian 63, 70
Civitates 133
Clapham, Sir J. 95
Clergy 52, 123, 161, 163, 188-9
Clerk of peace 115, 135, 141, 177-81
Close roll 52, 175, 190
Clough, R. T. 40, 97, 106
Coal 15, 18, 63, 66, 101, 103-4, 106-8, 197-8, plate 11
Coalbrookdale 104, 110, 198
Cogenhoe 169
Coin 77-8
Coker, West 41
Collison, R. L. 39
Colvin, H. M. 79
Common land 56, 61, 66, 133, 134-5, 139, 144, 150, 190, 194, plate 2
Commons, House of 135, 136, 175-6, 193-4
Communicant 162, 174
Communication, *see* road, river, etc.
Community organisation 3, 4, 69, 70, 71, 146, 148, 157-9
Company, *see* business
Compton census 162, 169, 170
Congleton 40
Constable, J. 48

Constable 18, 20, 150-1, 180-1
Context 9-10
Continuity 87
Conveyance (deed) 140-4
Copper 67, 105, 106
Cordingley, R. A. 93
Corn-mill 62, 81-2, 100, 103, 146, 182, 183, 197-8, plates 2, 4
Cornwall 67-8, 137
Correspondence 54, 145, 186, 189-90, 195
Cort, H. 104
Costume 46, 58, 77, 100, 102, 151, 166, 198
Cotswolds 67, 69, 75, 102
Cotton 8-9, 9-10, 102-3, 143, 145, 165
Cottonian MSS. 43, 134
County 5, 178, 179; archivist 41-2, 115, 116-21, 147, 149; map 133-4, 203
Court 155, 177-81, 191; church 163-4; common law 142-3, 191-2, 192; manor 21, 145-6, 183
Court hand 122-3, 142
Courtauld & Co. 184
Craft 14-15, 88, 156, 158, 159, 166. *See also* industry
Crane 108-10
Crawford, O. G. S. 67
Crime 17, 20-1, 49, 77, 192, 194
Crop 69, 84, 114, 145, 146-7, 147, 166, 192. *See also* farming *and* grain
Cross 65, 74, 80
Crown estate 137-8
Cruck 89
Cumberland 115
Customs, *see* social customs
Customs and Excise 25
Cyclopaedia of Useful Arts 96
Cyclopedia of Agriculture 114

Danish influence 8, 79, 84
Darby, Abraham (I) 104; (III) 110, 198
Dating 97, 125-6, 143-4
David & Charles 41, 42, 96, 109
Death 49, 77, 145, 167, 168, 170, 172-3, 174, 190, 195; rate 13-14, 171, 173. *See also* burial
Deed (title) 52, 140-4, 151, 155, 160, 161, 164-5, 174, 183, 184, 186, 190, 192

Repair 117
Report (government) 175, 193-6
Research method 25-8, 39, 44, 50-1, 56, 67, 132, 147-8; archaeology 99-100; archive 119-21, 127-30; questions 11-12, 12-23, 56
Richards, J. M. 100
Ridge and furrow 69
Ridge way 62
Riot 49, 177, 192
River 55, 56, 63, 81, 86, 96, 108-9, 183-4, 186, 190, 194
Road 1, 16, 61, 63, 80-1, 96, 132, 133, 135, 139, 150-1, 179, 180, 183; enclosure 70; packhorse 80, 81; Roman 60, 62, 68, 71, 80, 86. *See also* turnpike
Rocque, J. 134
Rogers, A. 13, 34, 157
Rolt, L. T. C. 96, 107
Roman Catholic 7, 144, 162, 173-4, 190
Roman remain 60, 62, 68, 71, 73, 78-9, 80, 83, 86
Romney 81
Roof 88, 90-4

'Saint' (church dedication) 74
St Helens 58, 132, 198, plate 12
St Ives 65
St Joseph, J. K. S. 49, 63
St Thomas chapel 143
Sale 144-5, 189
Salisbury 60, 68, 75, 86, 134
Salt 54, 59, 60, 80, 85, 106, 108, 165
Saltaire 85
Sand 56, 60, 112
Sanitation 60, 66, 94, 150, 155, 194, 195. *See also* privy
Saxon settlement 55, 61-2, 68, 71, 76, 78, 79, 83-6
School 21-2, 48, 52, 150, 154, 165, 189, 190, 194-6; master 21, 22, 161, 163; record 174-6
Scotland 53, 131, 198, 202
Seal 53, 125-7, 141, 189
Sequestration 192
Service (feudal) 146-8, 189-91
Sessional Papers 135, 136, 193-4
Settlement (estate) 142, 164
Settlement (removal) 11-12, 153-4, 177
Settlement pattern 48-9, 56-7, 60-2, 67-70, 71, 87, 190, 191
Sewer 150, 155, 190, 196

Shaft 103-5
Shardlow 109, 110
Sheep 63, 69, 139, 146-8, 191 190, 195, 197-8
Shirley, E. 70
Shoemaking 14-15, 154, 183, 184
Shop 53, 64, 65-6, 109
Shrewsbury 113
Shropshire 47, 111
Silk 102-3
Site survey (technique) 54-7, 59, 96-101, 103, 105, 106, 108-14
Sketch of site, 33, 55, 97, 98, 105, 110
Slate 90, 93, 111
Slum 46, 66
Smeaton, J. 100
Smelting 104, 105-6
Smithy 109, 151-2, 183
Social customs and welfare 5, 6, 17, 53, 58, 96, 111, 147, 148, 163, 171, 190, 195
Social status 151, 169, 179
Soil 49, 56, 57, 60, 67-9
Solicitor 54, 183, 184, 186, 195
Source note 26-7, 44, 50-1, 59, 127-9
Southampton 63
Speed, J. 134
Spelling 127-8, 128
Spinning 58, 102, 103
Squatter 61, 64, 147
Stafford 26, 78, 169
Standard of living 7, 21, 88, 94, 145, 166, 191
State Papers 52, 134, 189, 192-4
Statutory authority 194-6
Steam 82, 101-3, 105, 107, 111, 114, 185
Steel 104-5, 113, 198
Stencil 39, 121
Stephens, W. B. 196
Stockade 61, 67, 79
Stockbridge 78
Stoke Mandeville 84
Stone 60, 63, 72-3, 75, 92, 93, 101, 112; age 67-8, 72-3; boundary 59, 62, 73
Stourport 109, 110
Street 58, 61, 63, 85, 86, 134, 150, 151. *See also* lane, road, track
Strip (open field) 69, 84, 165-6, plate 2
Structure (community) 6-8, 13, 17-18, 34, 157-9, 193
Style (architecture) 75, 89